D0264616

A Practical Guide to

Managing
Web Projects

by Breandán Knowlton

A Practical Guide to Managing Web Projects
by Breandán Knowlton

Published in 2012 by Five Simple Steps
Studio Two, The Coach House
Stanwell Road
Penarth
CF64 3EU
United Kingdom

On the web: *www.fivesimplesteps.com*
and: *breandan.org*
Please send errors to *errata@fivesimplesteps.com*

Publisher: Five Simple Steps
Editor: Emily Robertson
Copy Editor: Owen Gregory
Production Manager: Jo Brewer
Art Director: Nick Boulton
Design: Nick Boulton, Colin Kersley

ISBN: 978-1-907828-07-2

A catalogue record of this book is available from the British Library.

INTRODUCTION

Web project managers come in all shapes and sizes. Some have project manager written on their business cards. Many don't. In fact, many don't have business cards at all. Most people managing web projects today didn't study project management at university. Nonetheless, project management sounds like a daunting task. Many people think of project management as an annoying overhead cost. In fact, I think there might be a few project budgets out there that label all of their project management time as 'annoying overhead'. And while time spent managing is not time spent designing, coding or deploying websites, it is not time wasted either. Good project management is all about making sure that you and your team have a better time doing something that you love.

If you are a football player, your coach is not an annoying overhead to the discipline of playing football. The coach helps you train, strategise and execute winning plays. It's the same with a good project manager. The person doing the project manager's job is making sure that you are at the top of your game, meeting your goals and conserving your resources for those crucial plays in the second half.

So what are my core principles, as a project manager?

First of all, I try not to break what's already working. I've seen some odd management fads come and go, but a creative and disciplined team can get a huge amount of work done just by respecting each other and keeping lines of communications open. Mess with working teams at your peril.

Second (and on the flip side), I'm not afraid to question why we're doing something and try to find a better way. It may be that you have a particular process because your predecessor did, because one of your clients read about it in a self-help book, or because it came to your former boss in a dream. It may or may not actually make any sense for you or for your team, today, with your current technologies and working environment.

So here's my third principle: stop, breathe, and think about how you're getting things done. If you've done something in exactly the same way many times, you must be in one of two states. Either you've found the very best way to perform a task through a technique so perfect and magical that it doesn't matter if the platforms, teams and technologies have changed; or maybe you haven't yet been able to draw breath long enough to learn about what worked and what didn't work in your last few projects. Don't be afraid to make some changes.

What you can expect from this book

This book walks through a typical web development project. It's told from the point of view of a small web agency, but the processes and steps along the way will be roughly the same for anyone who makes websites. Internal web teams or design shops, freelancers and large digital agencies all follow more or less this process, though the length of time and documentation required will vary depending on the environment.

The five sections (steps) of this book are:

1. Beginning a project
2. Analysing requirements
3. Design and prototype
4. Construction and testing
5. Deployment and evaluation

I describe what I call a typical twelve-week development cycle; a few months may or may not seem like a lot of time, depending on the projects that you've worked on. The team I describe analyse and consider the requirements for a good website, look clearly at content and audience, do some design, and think carefully about integration and deployment of the finished product. One way or another, you'll go through something like these phases on the next project you work on.

A note for internal web teams

A lot of this book may seem a little odd to you, with all the talk of clients and a clear separation between the delivery team and the people approving the work. If you're all part of the same organisation, this might be a jarring way to think about the relationship – you're not sending in invoices, you're not getting paid based on your delivery and, frankly, you may have a hard time separating your time on the project from the rest of what you do every day.

I have found, though, that it's helpful to think of the web team as a fairly autonomous entity, even within a larger organisation, or when people have things to do other than work on web projects. Thinking of yourself as an independent delivery team is useful for the following reasons:

- You can better celebrate your successes as a team, and better take pride in the work that you do. Making things together builds morale and gives your team some of the social support that you need.
- You will probably be able to make more accurate schedules and estimates if you can consider honestly the time that will be put into the project. Even if there is other work going on, thinking of the web team as a unit will help you to see what roles you have covered and where you need more help.
- You're more likely to finish. This can be a harsh lesson, but by some measures most technology projects fail. Setting a hard deadline for your team and thinking through the project schedule independently of your normal organisational schedule will help you get to done. And remember: perfect is sometimes the enemy of done.

OK, time to get going!

About Breandán Knowlton

Breandán (Ó Nualltáin) Knowlton is currently programme manager at the Europeana Foundation, an organisation bringing together the digitised cultural heritage of Europe. He has been a manager of some description at BearingPoint, Happy Cog, Comhaltas Ceoltóirí Éireann and quite a few other large and small organisations over the past two decades. He has worked for multinational businesses and IT consultancies as well as a couple of start-up technology firms and design studios, mostly as a technical architect. Thanks to some great teams, mentors and a little common sense, his projects have generally finished on time and on budget.

At university, Breandán studied music composition and philosophy, and earned an MA in ethnomusicology. He has lived in more than ten cities around the world, and now makes The Hague, Netherlands his home. He likes playing traditional Irish music with friends, and has worn geeky glasses since the age of two.

About this book

Are you:

- Someone who makes or commissions websites?
- Hoping to start or grow your web design agency or department?
- Starting or working on a project with a significant web component?

All of the above?

Then this book is for you. It won't talk about the specifics of constructing websites, but you'll find a few tips sprinkled throughout the book. And it will tell you quite a lot about how to have a better time during the building process, because unless you are extraordinarily lucky, chances are your last web project was a bit of a stressful experience.

You might have had a great time at the beginning, only to find out later that things weren't going as well as you thought. Or maybe you had trouble getting paid, even well after the end of the project. Perhaps the whole project was successful, but it just took more time and effort than you thought it would. If you've had a few bad experiences trying to build websites for money, you needn't be ashamed. You're not alone! The secret to the difference between a lousy web project experience and a really rewarding one is often project management.

Here's the thing about project management, and web project management in particular: there is not now, and never will be, a single way to do something – a practical sequence of techniques and processes that will get you out of every jam, manage every client and make any website. The best project management guide I can give you is a set of rules of thumb, checklists and some guidelines for each phase of work in a typical web project. And it's all right here, cleverly disguised as a book. These are ideas that have worked for me and for web teams that I have worked with. They've helped me when I was commissioning web work from outside agencies, and they've helped me to deliver web sites for internal and external owners. I hope that these guidelines, however familiar or strange, will help to make your next web project even better.

FOREWORD

Dan Mall

Emily and I got engaged in Dublin, Ireland.

At the time, I worked for a web design studio called Happy Cog, and we traveled to Dublin to help train the team at Comhaltas Ceoltóirí Éireann on managing the new website we built for them. Breandán Knowlton – the author of this book – was one of the small handful of people we celebrated with just minutes after popping the question during a horse and carriage ride around the city. That night is one of the fondest memories I have.

This book is a pragmatic, hands-on guide to the process of making websites. Like many books about web project management, it describes the myriad of steps that can be combined to conceptualise, create and launch a successful website.

However, unlike other books, Breandán has somehow managed to capture and articulate the seemingly intangible magic that separates good projects from great ones. Successful projects are a unique blend of the right people, clients, and processes. Those mixes are often difficult to replicate, and a great project manager can balance the need to be flexible and efficient, traditional and innovative, in order to establish a winning track record. This book goes into great depth about a plethora of techniques that are necessary to truly achieve excellence on a web project.

I didn't propose on our first date. When we got engaged, Emily and I had been dating for four years and had been friends for eleven years. Web projects are similar to relationships, in that they require time and trust to grow into something beautiful. Breandán has written about some fantastic ways to foster relationships with the teams you work with, both internal and external. Once you've read through, I have no doubt that you'll have the right tools to build that trust and watch it turn into something wonderful.

Happy reading!

Contents

PART 1

Beginning a Project

So you're going to do a web project? It's time to consider your goals, your project management process and to sketch out the trajectory of the project's phases. In this section, I'll examine established project management methodologies, the best ways of running meetings and the tricks to selling web work and presenting bids. Creating strong briefs and proposals, and estimating the scale of a potential project are also here. Once the bid is won and your team is geared up, this section will also give you tips for planning an effective kick-off, workshops and project communications.

1 Getting going

"The way to get things done is not to mind who gets the credit of doing them."
– **Father Strickland**[1]

What's here: Understanding your goals; considering structured methods; some project management certifications; and how to get into the flow.

Your goals

Whether you are in a website-making organisation, like a digital agency, or in a website-commissioning organisation, like a marketing department, you can agree on a few goals:

- You want a website that reflects the values of the organisation.
- You want a site that will create measurable business value.
- You want to get the project done on time and within budget.

These are great goals to have. But there are also subgoals that vary a bit depending on exactly where you are in the business of making websites.

Your goals within an agency

When working for a creative agency, or for the web-making group in a larger organisation, your job is to do work that you can be proud of and that fulfils clients' requests. But, unlike the marketing department that commissions your work, you'll probably be aware of a few other types of goals:

- You want the website to use current technologies, and to be supportable in future.
- You want to be able to reuse the strategies and technologies that you bring to bear.

---

[1] Quoted in several forms since an 1863 diary entry of Sir Mountstuart E Grant Duff. President Ronald Reagan had a plaque on his desk with a variant of this quotation.

- You want to be paid for the work you do, and not to do more work than you're being paid to do.
- You want to create a website that is beautiful, useful and accessible, a showcase for the talents of your design team.

As a website maker, you're not really as concerned with the time that a project takes, so long as you are paid for all of the time put into the project. This is where the fixed-price estimates that are the standard for web work can be tricky – you want to take all of the time available, but you don't want to spend any more time than that. Estimating, therefore, is something that you have to do really well.

You care a lot about the quality of the final product, in part because you'll include this work in your portfolio. You'll want the site to present you and your fellow website makers well, so you keep your skills current, knowing both the tricks and also the long-lasting best practices that will make a great site.

Given economic constraints, your main task is to keep the site design and build as efficient as possible. You need to make sure that every bit of work you do contributes to a deployable website that meets the requirements of your project. You need to keep every person on your team focused on how much time they put in, and how much is still to go, because that's how your organisation or unit is going to succeed.

The same goes, of course, whether you're a lone freelancer, a small to mid-size agency, or the IT department within a larger company – you'll be evaluated on your efficiency at delivering quality work without wasting time along the way. That will show up in your profit margin, if you're an agency, and in your budget item profit/loss score if you're a unit within a larger company. Either way, efficiency is going to direct much of your action during the project.

Your goals as a client

If you're commissioning a website, you probably don't worry as much about the nuts and bolts, and even the underlying technology platform won't have much to do with the way you perceive the bottom line of the project (unless you're making decisions in the context of larger standards in your organisation, in which case you'll be looking for some efficiencies of scale, staff capability and so forth).

You get to take a strategic view of the project, which can be a mixed blessing. You don't have to worry as much about the tiny details perhaps, but as the web person you might well be evaluated on how well the site performs for your organisation. And that can be a bit scary to think about.

You think about the website as something that will:

• Make money for your organisation (and yes, that's a goal for non-profits, too, though it works a bit differently).
• Expand the market share for your products, services or ideas.
• Save you time (and therefore money) by automating a process, reducing customer service staff, or reaching more people with a smaller outlay.

You may be worried about the elapsed time for the project: you might have other marketing or communications activities with which you need to tie in; you might have major events sponsored by your organisation coming up; you might need to think about how your brand values are being expressed in relation to those of your competitors, and in a competitive situation there may well be a first-mover advantage. Maybe you're waiting for a new or refreshed website to deliver a new service to your audience or customers, a service or path unique to the web that simply can't exist by other means.

Notice that none of your goals is to increase the number of page views that your organisation's website gets. While some of the other goals might be well-served by more site traffic, page views by themselves don't necessarily bring you any closer to your organisation's real goals for the site.

Not all management teams realise exactly how crucial the web
is to their business, or how much the internet has increased the
value of information processing and information dissemination
within their field. But they will. And when they come to realise
how important the website is to their strategic plan, they'll ask
you to make it happen. It might be a good time to look at your
organisation's goals, and to think carefully about the role that your
website will play[2].

So while your website builders are worried about efficiency,
you're primarily concerned with effectiveness. The actual
efficiency of how time is spent matters less to you than whether
the work being done will directly support the larger goals of your
organisation. The agency will certainly know those goals (or at
least it should), but it will be your job to keep the project focused
on delivery. You'll need to put yourself into the shoes of your
audience and customers, imagining the journeys that they will
take through your site, keeping track of the real metrics that will
let your organisation succeed, be noticed and achieve objectives.

To sum up: agency people need to be aware that the
elegance of the solution isn't really a measure of success for
their clients, any more than a high number of page impressions
will automatically deliver massive business value. And website
commissioners should be aware that agencies are under a
different kind of time pressure: not the pressure of being there
first, necessarily, but the pressure to ruthlessly cut any scope that
can be done without, to build a quality website within a fixed
budget. Agencies need to be efficient with their time, and focus
on accurately doing work to meet the brief. Website owners are
focused on effectiveness, and making sure that the work done
will support offline goals, including those never articulated in the
website requirements brief.

An obvious distinction, perhaps – but worth keeping in mind,
for everyone.

---

[2] http://www.alistapart.com/ar3cles/web-governance-becoming-an-agent-of-change

Waterfall

A waterfall model is what most people think of when they think about project management (not that too many normal people spend a lot of time pondering such things). Wikipedia's definition is clear enough:

> *"The waterfall model is a sequential design process, often used in software development processes, in which progress is seen as flowing steadily downwards (like a waterfall) through the phases of Conception, Initiation, Analysis, Design, Construction, Testing, Production/ Implementation and Maintenance."* [3]

Waterfall model
of a project

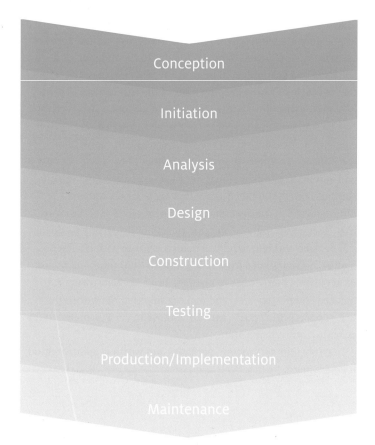

Conception

Initiation

Analysis

Design

Construction

Testing

Production/Implementation

Maintenance

---

[3] http://en.wikipedia.org/wiki/Waterfall_model

The idea is so attractive to organisations because it promises predictability and stability. With each phase distinct, you have a chance to involve all the right people in the review. You can create documents that clearly express the concepts and analysis of your designs, and you can get agreement on each step before moving forward. The classic waterfall model is derived from the project management used in the construction industry, where each step needs absolute agreement so that the proper materials and services can be ordered. Many software consultants over the years have clung to the waterfall model as a way of shoring up management support. The theory is that you can pin down the business stakeholders by making them commit in writing to a description of exactly how the system will work, thus making it impossible to change minds later on.

In fact, I take issue with Wikipedia's statement that the waterfall model is "often used" in software; while it is often the policy of an organisation to perform software development activities in distinct and non-overlapping phases of work, this is rarely the case in practice. Even when the conception, initiation and analysis phases are all done in one chunk and documented carefully, the beginning of the design-construction phase inevitably creates changes in the requirements of the system. But since the analysis phase is already complete and no more effort is planned, the typical result is that requirements are changed only implicitly by changing the functioning of the system, and the requirements documents themselves are left to slowly obsolesce.

The concept seems reasonable: you start by figuring out what you're going to build, then you build it, then you deploy it. What could be simpler? Of course, the devil can be in the details. You won't have a very clear idea of what your users want and need when you begin the engagement. You may not know how hard it's going to be to work with your tools and technologies. There may be other lines of business systems to integrate with that aren't well-understood. And of course, there are very few designs, however wisely created, that long survive contact with users. It is the rule rather than the exception that there will always be problems with your design, there will always be issues you've overlooked, and there will always be parts of the build that are more complicated than expected.

Variations on the waterfall model abound. Most of the consulting companies I've worked for have had their own, branded software development models, and pretty much every one was a variation on the classic waterfall. Drawing a series of boxes or wedges with arrows between them gives a settled, repeatable process, and helps to justify the time to be spent in each phase. Drawing such a diagram can be a way to communicate seriousness and professionalism, and to increase the client's sense of safety and assurance. However, promising completely discrete phases in your work is probably not something you'll be able to deliver. At best, you and the client will both create a detailed, static requirements document and then be willing to ignore it as the design evolves. At worst, you'll be responsible for living up to the letter of a requirements document that neither you nor the client still believe in.

The Rational Unified Process[4]

When I first started working on software projects, the Rational Unified Process was the gold standard of sorts, and still enjoys a lot of popularity. The process (RUP to its friends) combines aspects of the discrete and the iterative, allowing for an overlap of phases and for multiple iterations within each phase. RUP makes a distinction between public and internal releases – you can keep going with a completely iterative process, but show your stakeholders only your finished work.

One thing about the Rational Unified Process: it's a lot more than just a process. While it includes a suggested procedure to follow, that's really just a small part of it. RUP is structured as a series of suggestions, a box from which you can select the tools that you need for each part of the job. RUP covers team roles and what each role might be responsible for. It offers deliverables (documents, mostly) for each phase of work. It also puts forward

---

[4] The Rational Unified Process is a registered trademark of the IBM Corporation.

ideas about the content of your requirements and design deliverables. The thing is, implementing the full rational process is overkill for your average website development project. The system has the reputation of being very documentation-heavy (mostly because there are so many suggested deliverables and so many sections per deliverable). And while the process emphasises the need for multiple iterations, in practice the rigid documentation requirements tend to discourage much experimentation or modification of designs and requirements once developed.

RUP diagram

Inception	Elaboration	Construction	Transition	
				Business modelling
				Requirements
				Analysis and design
				Implementation
				Test
				Deployment
				Configuration and change management
				Project management
				Environment

Agile processes

Everyone wants to be Agile these days. Following on from some successes in bespoke software development, many in the web world have decided that Agile design and development processes will help them save time and money in their projects, and to deliver shippable software and websites with an unprecedented attention to the needs of their users.

An Agile process based on the Scrum methodology

Sprint backlog

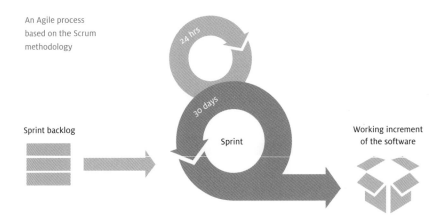

24 hrs

30 days

Sprint

Working increment of the software

So what's the big deal with Agile? Do you need to know how to do it – and what does it mean, anyway?

Though there are some Agile processes that have been defined explicitly (extreme programming, XP, for example), mostly Agile is still used to mean any iterative process that is not a typical waterfall development cycle. Agile means that you'll deliver something small, evaluate it, then go back and refine and extend what you've just delivered, then evaluate it again. The idea is that you can keep following these little cycles until all of your functional and quality requirements have been met. At no point do you need to step back and write down everything about the software or website that you'll be delivering – you can just keep cycling and cycling, and the representatives of the users on your team will steer the final product to something that will be well accepted.

One problem with Agile methodologies is that their project cycle lengths can be difficult to estimate. If you're trying to build a website, for example, you might have a hard time estimating in advance how many weekly cycles (sprints, in Agile parlance) you'll need until the project is complete. In part, that's because in a pure agile approach, you won't really know what complete means until your users agree that it is: it could be after two cycles, it could be after eight. And how are you going to bid on a fixed-price engagement when your own staffing represents anywhere between six and twenty-four weeks of effort per person?[5]

Finding what works

You'll have to find what works well for you as you go, but for most web projects I've found that something like the following cycle makes sense. Plan to spend a fair amount of time preparing, presenting and documenting workshops with the client. These workshops will serve as checkpoints for project progress, as well as being a perfect chance to do some collaborative design with the people who know the most about the organisation, products or services that you're presenting online.

Project initiation

This is about kicking off the project and understanding success criteria. This isn't about compiling everyone's wish list of features – this phase is about being able to finish the sentence, "The project will be successful if..." Workshops during this phase will be about nailing down scope.

Information architecture and user experience design

This is where you do your user research and begin to figure out how the site will work. Within this phase, though, you'll follow quick cycles of sketching and testing. The site will begin to take shape on paper, and you might be able to start to develop working code. Workshops will be about reaching agreement on the shape of your primary user journeys.

---

[5] Usually discussed in accounting terms as person-weeks, or person-days. It's an awkward bit of business jargon, but concise! We'll use it from here on to save space.

Visual design and prototyping

Here you begin to develop a visual language that will express and support your interaction design. Again, the site will continue to evolve in short cycles as new directions are tried, tested and accepted, rejected or modified. Workshops here will help to focus the number and kinds of page templates and to get agreement on common elements, style and tone. The prototype pages that you create will continue to evolve into the final delivered product.

Construct and deploy

This phase will overlap with the previous one. Here you'll get to build the actual site, including the functionality and integration points that you'll need for the final product. Your working prototype will continue to evolve, but you'll now test against the full set of agreed success criteria for the site. Workshops will be about solving specific technical and integration challenges, and to validate the client's acceptance of the website before deployment.

Evaluate

Even after deployment, you'll spend some time looking at what's working and what needs modification. The working website will continue to evolve slightly as you refine, consolidate and split your published content and functionality. Workshops during this phase will focus on retrospectives (seeing what has worked well and what needs to improve), as well as to see how the website is delivering organisational value.

If you have the trust of your client, you can probably get agreement on the rough shape of these phases, and even on the number of person-days required for each one, without knowing exactly which features will be in or out of scope. You promise to take a structured approach, but also to develop directly from sketches and research findings, through to a visual language and working code, without declaring any discrete checkpoint when the full requirements will be written down and agreed. The assurance you give is to deliver a website that delights users and meets the needs of the business, but not to deliver a particular list of pages or buttons.

Developing this level of trust is about showing your past successes, but also about showing your client what they can expect as the project proceeds. And that's what the rest of this book is about.

Certifications

Your clients may ask about what methodologies you use – this may even be a factor in deciding whether to hire you for a project. It's worth thinking about whether you want to study some of these methodologies more formally. That's where a certification comes in. Certifications aren't indications of smartness, or creativity, or dedication as a project manager. They are simply a way of demonstrating to others that you have taken some time to study a formal school of project management methodologies. This may be something that you want to do; it may not.

There are some top-notch project managers out there who don't have any certification or formal study behind them. Having on-the-job experience is great, and I would even argue that you will not be completely successful at minimising risk in your projects until you amass a fair bit of it. But there are some ideas that go beyond intuition, beyond what you hear from others, all the way into structures and vocabularies that you will find useful to expand what you do and how you do it. You might find some of this specialist vocabulary gives you an edge when communicating with people in other lines of business, like clients. You might find some of these example documents and processes spur you toward better planning and reduce the risk of unexpected challenges on your project. You might find that a particular school of thought dominates an industry you'd like to work in. In my current projects in Europe, for example, the vocabulary and concepts of PRINCE2 are ubiquitous, and knowing the words and ideas of PRINCE2 helps me when I communicate with stakeholders.

If you'd like to explore these concepts, great! There are lots of books to read, innumerable websites to follow and formal courses to sign up for. Once you've learned some of this specialist vocabulary, it makes sense to take the test and get the piece of paper. Just remember that no methodology will tell you how to run your project – at best you'll have some techniques and concepts that provide a framework for what you'd like to accomplish. (At worst you'll have a pile of paperwork that adds to your project budget and doesn't reduce any of your risks.) It's up to you to apply these ideas in the real world.

Certification	Description	Accrediting body	More info
PRINCE2 Foundation	The basics and terminology of PRINCE2 methods. This would be suitable for anyone on the project team, including designers and developers, not just managers.	APM Group	**www.prince-officialsite.com** *(www.prince-officialsite.com/ Qualifications/Qualification Scheme.aspx)*
PRINCE2 Practitioner	PRINCE2 certification suitable for lead project managers (formerly highest cert.) This one is probably most useful for project managers.	APM Group	**www.prince-officialsite.com**
PRINCE2 Professional	Highest-level PRINCE2 certification, requiring assessment by observation. The European Commission likes to hire people with this one, for what it's worth.	APM Group	**www.prince-officialsite.com**
CAPM	Certified Associate Project Manager. Basic knowledge (from PM Body Of Knowledge) of terms and processes, and ability to implement them. I've seen this one asked for sometimes in public sector projects.	PMI	**www.pmi.org/Certification/ Certified-Associate-in- Project-Management- CAPM.aspx**

PMP	Project Management Professional. Requires 3–5 years project management experience and advanced training in PM methods.	PMI	www.pmi.org/Certification/Project-Management-Professional-PMP.aspx
CSM	Certified ScrumMaster. Basics of the Scrum process, activities, and team structure. This is the first of the Agile methodology certifications to emerge – there will probably be others. This certification is good for anyone running an Agile business or development process, not necessarily just dedicated project managers.	ScrumAlliance	www.scrumalliance.org/pages/CSM
CSP	Certified Scrum Professional. Highest-level certification, showing experience with and full understanding of Scrum methods and implementation.	ScrumAlliance	www.scrumalliance.org/pages/certified_scrum_professional
CSD - RUP7.0	Certified Solution Designer - RUPv7.0. Knowledge of RUP principles and some experience with iterative development. This comes out of the IBM Rational Unified Process. This was a huge deal in the 1990s when I was starting my project management career, but I haven't seen it in many web projects lately.	IBM	www-03.ibm.com/certify/certs/38008003.shtml

Running meetings

Sometimes it seems like the only task for project managers is running meetings. And since meetings are almost universally reviled as time-wasters, your chances to be well-liked on a project team may seem quite limited, right from the start. Of course, you know that project managers and project liaisons are routinely expected to do everything from negotiating contracts to business analysis, so you'll probably be chairing most of the meetings and workshops for your project. More importantly, you'll probably be the one calling most of the meetings, so it will be up to you to make sure that they are productive and effective.

While entire books could be (and have been) written about the processes of good meetings, we'll start with some shortcuts that will help you out.

The cost of meetings

Don't forget that meetings are really expensive for a project. The simplest way to tally this up is just to take the average hourly rate of the people in the room, multiply by the number of people and by the length of the meeting. This number is scary enough, but don't forget:

- The time needed (for each participant) to find a time on the schedule.
- Time spent on preparation.
- Time spent documenting the discussion or workshop.
- Time getting to and from the discussion.
- Time lost while switching from other work to get into meeting mode, then the time spent getting back into the zone.

The lesson here isn't that meetings are inherently destructive; in fact, when there are multiple organisations at work on a problem (such as an agency and a client), you probably do need to get people together for discussion.

Planning and agendas

The most important part of any meeting is what comes before – the planning and agenda-setting. Don't bother with a meeting at all unless you know:

- What needs to be talked about or presented (an agenda).
- How long each item will take, roughly.
- Who you need in the room, and who you don't.
- Who's going to document actions from the meeting.

Once you know those things, you can find a good time and send out an agenda. Make sure that everyone knows what they're supposed to bring or prepare – there's no point getting together if people haven't read what they need to or made a couple of notes on items they're responsible for.

Documentation and follow-up

Someone needs to be the recording secretary in any meeting. It could be the person who calls the meeting, but it's often way easier if it's someone else. If you're in the chair, your focus is going to be on keeping the discussion to the point and boiling down discrete actions from what people are saying. It's pretty hard to do that if you're also trying to scribble.

Meeting notes are hardly the same as a transcript. Most meetings don't need a transcript – but they do need a few critical items:

- Meeting notes should summarise the information presented, organised by topic.
- Tasks generated through discussion need to be written down in their own section.

Motivation

To understand how web projects play out, you'll need to think seriously about how each person approaches the project, and what they intend to get out of it. From there, you'll have a good vantage point when making decisions.

Our goal: flow

Why do we do what we do? How do you get people to do what you need them to do? How do you keep focus and attention during a project? These are all questions of motivation. There are all sorts of answers, but most of them end up involving money. Unfortunately, money doesn't turn out to be the best motivator.

Especially in professional jobs, it seems that people are happiest when they reach a state of flow. Not unlike the zone that designers or programmers get into, we mostly like to see what it is we're working on, and to feel a sense of progress. We like to know the goals that we're working toward, and see the small steps that we can take towards the larger goal. As a manager, you're in a great position to help this along – just let people know how their bit fits into the larger picture, and find ways to make the small steps visible along the way.

We also all have a well-developed sense of justice and fairness. We like to see that we're being treated in the way we believe we deserve. Part of that is feeling that we're not being taken advantage of, too. When your team is under pressure to meet deadlines, for example, there may be a temptation to keep working late. And while there may be a perfectly good reason to stay a little past closing time, if your team starts to feel put upon, or they feel that they're bearing the brunt of poor estimating or scheduling, any good feeling on the project will quickly evaporate.

Check your gut feeling about what your team will think if you encourage (or just tacitly allow) people to work late. They may volunteer, they may seem happy to put in some extra time, but consider how it looks. It's all too easy to sit there in the dark and think that it's someone else's fault that you have deadlines tomorrow. As a manager, think about making a point of kicking people out at the end of the working day. You'll lose a couple of productive hours, of course, but in the long run your team will probably get more done by pacing themselves. And they'll like you a lot better at the same time!

Combining intellectual and emotional motivations with clearing the path

Asking people to do things isn't hard, but it's not so easy to make people want to do them. Think about it from emotional and intellectual points of view. If you can align the two, you'll have an excellent chance of getting a bright and motivated team going on your project.

Some authors have used the metaphor of the rider and the elephant. The elephant represents our emotions: when the elephant wants to go somewhere, there's really not much that a rider can do to control what happens. Hard to mess with instinct. The rider is the intellect: possible to persuade using reason, and for a while can probably steer the elephant. But only for a while – after a bit the elephant will win through sheer strength. The third factor, and one that gets overlooked, is the path. If the path is smooth, both rider and elephant will be much more likely to follow it.

Your job as a manager is to persuade the rider with reason, to motivate the elephant with emotion and to make the path as clear as possible. Everything that you do on the project to create order and transparency will make the project path easier to follow. Creating a pleasant environment where people feel well-rewarded and listened to will entice the elephant. Explaining clearly where each piece of work fits into a larger picture will persuade the riders.

Rewards and project culture

The client needs to get a website built. It's not wise to underestimate what a big thing this is – by the time you're looking at the particulars, the client has done quite a lot of internal soul-searching, arguing and politicking. The client's business is on the line, and the people involved probably have a personal reputation at risk.

For most clients, there's already a website in place, so they are arguing, and arguing hard, for what might be seen as a facelift, a re-skinning. You may think of it as a lot tougher than that, and it is, but remember what the client has gone through in order to get the project approved to begin with.

You need to respect that. Though the team building the site will be paid for their efforts, and may be working towards steps on their own career paths and so forth, the client's people you deal with will not be primarily motivated by money, or at least not directly. The website builders will probably think in terms of certain kinds of operational flow, but the client is trying to save face, to not screw up. Which means that for the client, the primary motivation is simply to have a successful, launchable website. From your point of view, the motivation of the client is to reduce project risk.

This means that one of your jobs, to make sure that both sides succeed in the project, is to be certain that everyone on the team is following behaviours that reduce risk – which means that the rewards and culture need to be measured against the risk perceived by the client.

- Telling people in advance what is coming up with the project reduces risk, because people have a better chance to prepare.
- Addressing potential problems early reduces risk, because there's a better chance of fixing issues before they make other parts of the project more difficult.
- Getting the right people in the room, even if they are busy and hard to schedule, can make sure that the right kinds of insight are applied early enough to have a big effect.

Transparency and communication, along with constant setting of expectations, are not just measures of how well you do your job. They are also the way you keep the client motivated. With everyone motivated, you have a chance for a great project.

TOOLS FROM THIS CHAPTER

- Project initiation document
- Meeting agenda
- Meeting minutes

FURTHER READING

There's lots of documentation about the PRINCE2 project management process. If you go for one of the certification courses, you'll certainly find that the reference materials you buy for the course will serve well as a reference. The website *http://www.prince2.com/what-is-prince2.asp* gives a good start.

For XP/Agile books and websites, I started with the O'Reilly book, *Extreme Programming Pocket Guide* by Chromatic (2003), which is a good quick reference. That was followed by *Extreme Programming Explained* by Kent Beck (2000). More reference books can be found at *http://www.extremeprogramming.org/more.html*.

Formal methodologies like PRINCE2 put a priority on documentation, and it's certainly true that you need ways to develop a shared understanding with everyone involved in the project. There's some debate, though, about the quantity and nature of documentation needed. The answer depends, of course, but be open to various points of view. See, for example, *http://37signals.com/svn/posts/3073-the-documentation-dilemma*.

SELLING WEB WORK

"Now that we can do anything, what will we do?"
— **Bruce Mau**[1]

What's here: Bidding on projects; some pros and cons of working with big clients; the argument of spec work; creating good work estimates; writing a proposal.

On the face of it, selling work doesn't seem to be a job for a project manager. Technically, that's true – the job of project management formally starts where the business development ends. But there's a problem: in any agency, the project manager tends to have the best estimating skills. The project manager is pragmatic at finding out what needs to be done, forecasting how long it all will take, and seeing risks before they grow too large. As it turns out, those are exactly the skills needed to evaluate and sell web work effectively.

Understanding the real problem and discovering the measurement

Clients may give you general statements about these topics, like "We want to grow our business" or "We want a new website that updates our brand and expands our customer base". In order for you to provide them with the best solution, however, you need to ascertain their specific success markers and their individual problems or obstacles. What you're really interested in at this point is figuring out what would make the project successful, as far as the client is concerned.

Working with big clients

When you build a service organisation, you have to start small. Whether it's your special team of all-stars within a larger group, or you and a friend getting together to make a little web agency, you'll

---

[1] *Massive Change* by Bruce Mau and Jennifer Leonard (2004, Phaidon Press)

be expanding your business. If you come from another agency and you can bring some clients with you, you'll have a good head start, and if your parent company already wants to use you for some particular projects, you could grow pretty quickly.

Landing the account at Coca-Cola or Boeing or some huge public department can be done, but it might cost you. You may or may not have to sign away your soul, but it's pretty certain that you won't follow your usual process of creative chaos. You might have to dress up for some meetings, sure, but more fundamentally than that, to play at such a level you're going to need a solid and dependable process and some strict controls and reporting. It may seem like a lot of overhead, but you'll get to do some great work.

Playing the game
So why am I writing about working for large organisations in a book about managing web projects? After all, I'm assuming that your team is about the same size for every project. You may have more people to deal with on the client side from project to project, but you'll do your work using the same people you work with every day.

As a person with some project management responsibilities, your work pattern and tools will probably change the most if you pursue work with a large organisation. If you're happy walking around your office daily to do status checks, you might have to start writing some things down. (Of course, if you've already set up doable weekly status reports, you're way ahead of things.) If you're used to a quick call with your client counterpart to clarify a requirement, you're going to get used to sending them a query in writing and then waiting for a committee to meet and decide on what's what. No more will you set a deadline for a quick approval of a visual design comp. Instead, you'll be asked to come in for a presentation in front of some important-looking people who will hem and haw and come back to question the fundamental design principles underlying the page.

Why do it

While this may sound gloomy and difficult, you might also get a lot out of working with a large-scale organisation. Big organisations have large customer bases, and the work you do will quickly be seen by a lot of people. The work will be deemed to be important, and some of the large number of internal staff who see your work will get excited about it. When you bring a fresh approach to a mature organisation, you have the chance to reinvigorate the relationships between customers and brand. You'll also get the chance to do work where money is assumed to represent value.

While small organisations in particular struggle to come up with cash to pay vendors, a large organisation doesn't have exactly that problem – they can find the cash if they need it. What a big company thinks about is the value of the investment that it's making. They will expect your project to deliver actual, measurable (and possibly short-term) results. They'll want to know that the money they put in will result in an equivalent increase in revenue – and they're probably more used to measuring this sort of thing than you are.

The proposal phase

When you get to the proposal phase with a big organisation, think value. Small clients are impressed by your skills: they see that you can design and code webpages, and they can't, so they need to pay you for your expertise. A large client doesn't think quite the same way: if they needed a web developer, they'd hire one. In fact, they probably already have some. If they need graphic designers, systems administrators or integration specialists, they'll have some of these people on staff. The one thing that large organisations have been late to the game on is hiring specific user experience expertise, but that's more of a historical problem and is being addressed quickly.

So, why do they want someone like you to bid for the work, if they can already hire all the skills they need, and at a cheaper hourly rate at that?

They want you for your vision. They'll hire you because yours is a lean and focused delivery team which doesn't have to play politics to get ahead. They want a team who can bring an outside perspective, but still empathise with the mission statement and get in the heads of their customers. So play to these opportunities. In the proposal and the presentation, and in the endless back and forth of negotiations and contracts, and even as you get into the requirements development, remember that you're being hired as an expert, a consultant from outside bringing unique insights. Your job is to help show it – you need to connect what you're proposing to the impacts that your projects will have. Don't be afraid to look at published and academic research to justify the value of good usability. Be sure to make some numerical projections about site traffic, conversion rates and expected revenue from sales or donations. Talk about how the project will affect perception in the industry, and in the public at large.

Don't be afraid to claim those big and difficult performance indicators – that's what you're being asked to do.

Certain things might go slower than usual

During the project, you're going to have to abandon your snappy design approval and requirements sign-off cycles. You'll probably have to live with a project that looks a little less like an Agile scrum and more like a classic, stately waterfall. You'll have to write down more, and you'll find that you have to organise meetings with client people to discuss all sorts of things that you were looking for a simple yes or no decision about.

Bear with it. Allow more time in your cycle – double or triple your estimated cycle time estimates to begin with. You're going to have more overhead in co-ordinating with client people, so allow for that, too. Don't be afraid if the project starts looking too big – it's true that some clients will still pick the cheapest shop to do the work, but those aren't the guys that you want to be working for.

With a large client, you have the chance to finally develop the sort of relationship that advertising firms have worked so hard to develop. You can be the go-to guy, the automatic choice, the natural extension of a team. Maybe you'll have to make some changes – move to new offices in a different city, for example – but you can do great work at the same time. Just have patience, and leave lots of room for turnaround of each phase, and enough time for a structured and carefully run testing phase. Of course, the greater elapsed time will end up costing more money, even if you don't have lots of resources working night and day. Those people still aren't doing as much other billable work as they could be, and that opportunity cost is worth charging for. Just think about the project the way your client wants to: as a business investment. If you think about the project from the perspective of the actual value it will bring, you should have no problem justifying the value that you bring to the engagement.

Structuring a brief

This is one of the first points at which having some structure starts to make sense and saves a lot of time later.

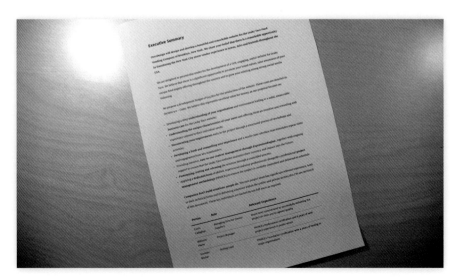

Executive summary

Organisation
- General background and vision
- Key business issues
- Web contribution

Customers
- Main audience
- Key reasons to choose
- Market research
- Pain points

Current site
- How users feel and why
- User groups and functionality
- Site effectiveness
- Content, governance, upkeep
- Scale
- Investment and promotion

Vision
- How you want visitors to feel
- Purpose of the new site
- Content areas
- Required functionality
- Out of scope

Team
- Who will be contributing?
- How many weeks?
- Phases
- Deadlines
- Budget

Internal scoping

As a project manager, you try to figure out the scale of the project, and agree a schedule of work that will be efficient for the build team and satisfies the needs of the client. Unfortunately, you won't start out knowing all of the requirements. Go through a process like this one.

1. Figure out the scale of what you are being asked to build. Before you know who's doing what, you need to know the gross parameters. Is this an e-commerce site? A couple of landing pages for an offline campaign? A big, customer self-service portal? You need to know the rough size of what you're talking about before you go into detail about pages or functions.

2. Figure out what the available budget is going to be. There's really no way to know this except to ask the client. Someone certainly has an idea of what is available to be spent – if you estimated $50 for the project you wouldn't be taken seriously, and if you bid $1,000,000 for a single website you'd probably be too high (for most projects – there are certainly quite a few where a $1m website is quite appropriate).

3. Knowing only the gross scale and the rough budget for the project will give you enough information to decide if you want to continue the estimation and proposal for the project. If the scope of what's being asked doesn't work for you, or if the budget is too big or too small for your team, you should stop here.

4. If you decide to proceed, make a milestone schedule that makes sense. No client will tell you, "Here's enough money for two hundred work days. Go build a website and stop when you've run out of cash." Nor would it be reasonable for them to do so. You'll need to list the major deliverables and workshops for each stage of work, and how much work it will take to prepare, present and refine that deliverable.

If your client requires more specific assurance about what will happen when, try to do the project in multiple stages. Start with an initial budget of probably just a few weeks' work while you do some research and even try out a direction or two. Then, when the research is done and everyone has a better sense of what should be in scope, you can do a proposal for the design, build and deployment of the site. (See chapter 10, an interview with Andy Budd of Clearleft, for more information.)

Product-driven estimation

For product-driven estimates, we make a list of all the work products we think we will need to create to complete the project.

A work product may be any type of deliverable, but it must have some sort of documentation and a specific owner responsible for seeing it accomplished.

Work Product	Deliverable that must be produced in order to complete a project and achieve its objectives
Each WP should have:	Documentation, workshop(s), owner(s)

Writing a proposal

Now it comes to the proposal. At this point, all of the pre-project work that is going to be finished has been finished, and it's up to the project team to work out what can reasonably be accomplished within the project itself.

Here are some things that are handy to know when estimating a project:

- Number of pages and unique layouts.
- Preferred content management system.
- Integration with third-party tools, like mailing list managers.
- Full design and branding specifications.
- Typical user journeys through the existing or potential website.

During the proposal phase, the risks are mostly on the agency side. And while the safe thing to do is to not take the project at all, we know that's hardly the right answer.

There are a few solutions to this dilemma.

First, the agency knows how long similar projects took in the past. This information is invaluable. Second, there's always the possibility of trimming or renegotiating scope as the project commences, should the design and implementation take longer than anticipated. These decisions will be up to the client, but this is why clear communication and good relationships with clients are important. Third, the design agency has the knowledge of what is possible. At this point they can propose just the parts of the website that they know will be needed, even if the client believes that their specific needs go further. Having a consistent and carefully considered proposal is more than useful: it can be the key to negotiating with the client.

Parts to parrot

Proposals are sales tools. They advance a project from the speculative phase of "I wonder whether we could get this done?" to the much more concrete "We can do this much work for this much money, and the work we do will have the following parts." Just because they're sales tools, though, doesn't mean that proposals should read like aggressive used car advertisements. Proposals that are thoughtful, considered and informative in their own right give any agency or web group a great chance to sell the value of their expertise and analysis, right there on the pages.

When writing a proposal, it's important to remember that just because something has been said in a conversation or assumed by two team members, does not mean it has entered the list of project assumptions. Assumptions need to be written down. If they aren't recorded, anyone may challenge the assumption at a later point, when it might be in their interest to do so. Proposals, all about defining the nature of an engagement, are the best and most useful place to document shared understandings. This means when a client commissions a web project and explains their reasoning and business drivers in a meeting, it is perfectly appropriate to repeat these things in a proposal.

Inexperienced project managers sometimes try to avoid parroting any statements made by the client during the pre-scoping phase. They reason that:

- The client will be bored because they see their own words or concepts for the second time.
- The agency will appear unoriginal because they are repurposing the content of another.

The actual state of things is more complex and leaves plenty of scope for repetition.

- Clients, just like everyone else, love to see themselves in print. Any paraphrase of a client's business goal or design constraint is bound to result in a fair amount of self-satisfied gazing and rereading.
- It's important that clients get the chance to see that their own concepts will play a role in the website development process. Many are already afraid that they won't be listened to because they are not themselves web experts. Seeing some of what they have already laid out incorporated into the proposed plan helps to assuage this fear.
- Even if neither of the above points were true, it would still be worth repeating clients' ideas in the proposal. Otherwise, those ideas might never be written down, and important points may be lost.

Proposals say what will be in the project. Proposals also define what isn't in the project – and this half is far more important.

What about mobile?

Mobile (if we include tablets) will be the new rule, not the exception. But budgets and proposal bids are staying the same. So we should be prepared. We can estimate mobile design work as a percentage of desktop web work or as overhead for the project.

Visuals on spec? No

There has been some discussion in the industry about whether it is reasonable for an agency to do a certain amount of visual design on spec during the proposal phase[2]. While clients like to see visuals, working on them at this stage of the project is fairly dangerous and might even be considered irresponsible.

Doing any visual design work before thoroughly understanding the audience and purpose of the new website is likely to lead to the wrong answer. The most insidious thing about visuals is that they tend to be addictive: once you have an image of a page in your mind, it's pretty hard to dislodge. So why would you want to give the client even a tiny chance to fall in love with a design which you think is likely to be more wrong than right?

Doing visual design costs money, either to the studio or to the client. If the client isn't paying for time, then the studio is. Of course, the cost may be indirect: perhaps an opportunity cost, in which a person could have been used in a better way; or a direct cost, where a support or current operation was jeopardised. But, one way or another, there's more cost involved in the project when visuals are added to a proposal and they can't be billed for directly. The only way this works out for the studio is if the additional cost is distributed among the fees of other clients. No one really wants

---

[2] AIGA (formerly the American Institute of Graphic Arts, now just AIGA), has this to say about spec work: "AIGA believes that professional designers should be compensated fairly for their work and should negotiate the ownership or use rights of their intellectual and creative property through an engagement with clients." (*http://www.aiga.org/position-spec-work/*) For them, this means no spec work. You'll also find a strong argument at NO!SPEC (*http://www.no-spec.com*), a campaign started by visual communications designers. Jeffrey Zeldman makes a compelling argument against spec work (*http://www. zeldman. com/2007/08/14/dont-design-on-spec/*) and other designers have taken up the call (*http://www. supernicestudio.com/rfp/*). .net magazine also does a good job of breaking down the various kinds of spec work (*http://www.netmagazine.com/features/should-designers-do-spec-work*). The AntiSpec folks go so far as to call spec work "a cancer within the design industry" (*http://antispec.com*). Strong stuff.

to be paying for someone else's work to be done. So, for the sake of your existing and new clients, hold firm on the visual work. Clients always say that they need to see visuals to gauge whether their agency candidates understand the project. This is a misunderstanding of the nature of design and how it fits into the tasks of research, requirements management and content strategy. If a client wants to know whether their potential agency can create good, beautiful and useful visual designs, they should take a look at their candidates' portfolios. Past work will quickly show whether a designer or studio has a good eye and the required skills to take on the challenge.

That's exactly why industry associations like AIGA have come out so clearly against spec visuals. If you decide not to include them in your proposal, you should know that you have the backing of some of the best designers in the world.

Presenting bids

Each agency's presentation style will be slightly different, but here are a few questions to ask yourself as you prepare to present your bid:

- Is this bid best presented as a written proposal or tender, or a presentation in person?
- Is the style of the presentation appropriate to the client's field and professional expectations?
- Is the information in the bid going to address the concerns of each client-side person in the room (if you're giving a live presentation)?
- Is the presentation going to leave them wanting to see more and excited about completing the project?

See the section on presenting your findings in chapter 6 for a list of some good presentation options to keep in mind.

Tools from this chapter

- Project proposal
- Bid presentation
- Communication brief
- Time and effort estimate

Further reading

My friend Greg Hoy has done a great job of explaining the detective story that is trying to determine client budgets for a project:
http://cognition.happycog.com/article/bloodhounding-budgets

Another perspective on determining budgets:
http://www.thedesigncubicle.com/2010/09/project-budgets-and-secrets/

For a sense of pricing design work, take a look at:
http://l.breandan.org/guild_guidelines

3

Kick-off

"[O]rganizations are collections of human beings. They will perform best and make their greatest achievements when there is clarity, calmness, conviction and collegiality throughout the ranks."
– David Plouffe[1]

What's here: Preparing to start a project; setting up your project communications; definitions of some common terms; using project management software to make your life easier.

The most important time for your project

And, just like that, you're on the clock for the first time. The attendees gather around. Some of them have seen this before; some are a little mystified, but eager to see the art of website-making in action. It's the most important time of your project's lifecycle.

Because the project has just barely begun and everyone is excited, it can be tempting to get through the kick-off period with a handshake and a few encouraging words. There's nothing wrong with that. But if you think ahead and do a bit of planning, the kick-off phase can actually get you some vital requirements.

This is one of the only times in the project when:

- You'll have some of the most senior people from both the client and agency sides sitting around the table.
- Folks are revved up and optimistic about what's to come.
- A healthy (or at least sufficient) budget has been agreed, but none has yet been spent. It feels like there is a world of opportunities ahead!

---

[1] *The Audacity to Win* by David Plouffe (2009, Viking)

A lot depends on these early steps, and getting the tone and tools together. The next time all these people get together could well be the end of the project, and at that point the budget will have been spent. Everyone will be tired, though with good planning and luck there will be a successful website up and running that wasn't there before.

So take advantage of the early high spirits, and get some good work done, right at the start!

Definitions and terms

A few notes on language: web agencies are prone to using a fair bit of jargon. We're all tempted to have that insider edge, to use words that we understand and that we're comfortable with to describe our processes. This tendency can be more than a little off-putting to people commissioning web work. Even when well-meant, misunderstandings can arise when people use the same words in different ways, or just don't define their terms very well.

Since you'll be using some of these words to describe the project plan anyway, the kick-off period is the best time to make sure that everyone's on the same page with the language of the project. Here are a few that might come up.

Stakeholder

Someone with an interest in the success of the web project. These tend to be the people who commission the work to begin with, but also include company directors, chief officers, division heads and so forth. Because stakeholders are the ones most affected by the success or failure of the work, their opinions matter a lot.

Some agencies consider users to be stakeholders in the project, which might be true in some sense. However, since your web-making process is already about the users, you're probably best off using stakeholder to describe the commissioning side of the table.

Deliverable

This word has migrated from corporate-speak and has now become widely used in the web community. A deliverable is, literally, something that you deliver – any work product that is reasonably self-contained. The word deliverable is often used to describe documents: research reports, diagrams, information architectures. Things like weekly status reports are technically deliverables, too, but the word has come to generally mean the bigger stuff. Phase-ending or checkpoint stuff, often – things that you can hand over at the end of a significant bit of work.

It's worth handing these over with a bit of fanfare and explanation. Remember that deliverables never speak for themselves, no matter how carefully put together and beautifully written.

Requirement

In engineering projects, requirements have very technical and specific definitions, which makes them very easy to evaluate and measure. Web workers aren't quite as lucky. Requirements in the web world are notoriously vague, and they are difficult to write down with precision.

When you talk about gathering requirements, then, what you're really trying to do is to develop design constraints – the edges of what your website or application needs to do or support. A requirement could be a type of content that your website needs to contain; it could be a feature of a shopping cart; it could be adherence to a brand guideline document.

Because requirements take many forms, you're going to have a hard time keeping them in a single place. Some projects start off with the idea that all requirements will go into a single spreadsheet, or a set of index cards, or a stack of Post-its. After a while, things start to drift out of sync – ideas are mooted around a conference table and not then updated in a spreadsheet. Content is inventoried but the text lengths don't go into your card deck. It's a lot more practical not to have the expectation that you can keep all requirements in one place. The sensible thing is to keep each kind of requirement in the place where it most belongs.

- Ideas from meetings probably go into your post-meeting write-ups. If there are ideas that need to go into a wireframe deck or a content strategy, send those to the people who own them.
- Content requirements can probably stay in the workbook or database that you're using to manage content. But make sure that you note who's responsible.
- Software features (or user stories, if you're using Agile-speak) probably work pretty well on cards, or in short documents or posts in your project management software.
- User needs uncovered by your project research will probably be buried in transcripts and presentation slides. It's worth pulling these out and folding them in to design principles if you can, or a simple list if that's too hard.

Here's one more useful hint: keeping requirements in email is a really bad idea. There's no medium more likely to get them lost, or not seen by the right people, or not referenced at the critical moment. If you get a requirement in an email, write it down in another form before it gets lost.

Plan

For the more corporate among you, a plan is probably a list of all of the tasks that will need to be done on your project, and by whom. Your plan will include an assignment of responsibility and an indication of which tasks depend on which other tasks. Ideally each task that will need to be done will be quantified in hours, and you may have an optimistic, expected and pessimistic estimate for each item. You may have taken the time to put all of these guesses together into a big spreadsheet or Microsoft Project document. I've made lots of those.

Big plans are hard to follow. I've rarely seen complicated plans of more than fifty steps that still match the real world at the end of the work. A small change on one task leads to a larger change on a subsequent one. A content strategist starts to take responsibility for testing, not normally their area, and then someone else backs them up on the original content tasks. The manager gets involved in scope negotiations, and then the design phase increases from three to four weeks without there being an equal reduction in the time allotted for prototyping. The original list of items (expressed in a gigantic Microsoft Project file) gets followed for the first month or two and then abandoned.

I'm not saying that formal planning is impossible, or that projects should be improvised. But I do think that web project managers need a level of realism when it comes to making a plan. For many successful web projects, an initial plan can be expressed on a couple of slides: you have these people on the project; they do these things; you have this many weeks or months for the whole project. You can divide that into periods for each major phase, with each phase boundary including a sign-off on something major, like a content analysis or a direction for the graphic design. And for all of the little details in the middle? That's what your day-to-day communication will cover. If you decide to start with some guerrilla user testing every week, schedule that in for Friday mornings. If you plan an update call between the manager-type people on the project every week or so, put that into your calendars.

Start with big units of time and work your way down to the specifics: this many people; these job roles; these weeks. Put in the three or four major deliverable points. Remember that your project will be judged (and paid for) based on how it delivers the website you've agreed to build, not by how many rounds of visual ideas you'll go through or how many lines of code you'll write. Think about the end product, do the work that needs to be done, trust the team to do the best job that they can do in the time available. Focus on making a complete product as soon as possible and then making it better. Show your plan up front in a couple of slides, and update managers at critical delivery points. Communicate in a way that everyone knows what's going on this week, and what was finished yesterday. You might find that you don't even miss that big Microsoft Project plan.

Before the start

You may feel that the time between the proposal or bid and the official start of the project is an awkward downtime. On the contrary, this is a valuable opportunity for you to do some homework. Consider creating a checklist for a review of the client's existing site. This will help you to home in on the current strengths and weaknesses of their web presence, as well as identifying any requirements that may not have been introduced yet. This is also the time for you to set expectations for the project kick-off. Make sure that all participants, on both agency and client side, know what to expect to get from the kick-off meeting and what is expected of each of them at the meeting.

Risk and quality registers

Create a list of risks. For each risk, be sure to include individual estimates of:

- likelihood of occurrence
- severity of impact
- ownership and responsibility
- major mitigations

Next, create a quality review with a list of:

- all deliverables
- who reviews each deliverable
- how much time is left before the final version is due
- who's responsible for changes
- who updates the versions over time

Project communications

Here's a quick note about project governance: though you don't need to spend a lot of time on this point, the kick-off is your best chance to set the tone for communication on your project. What communication channels will your team use? How often will you require status reports and team meetings? Patterns fallen into here will tend to continue – so you might as well get them right!

Email

The easiest option is email, and there will probably be a lot of that anyway. However, as most working professionals now know, email can be a big, big time sink. It's really no wonder that inbox zero and more general getting things done methodologies focus so much on keeping a clean and tidy inbox – each message can represent a task not done, a conversation unfinished, a requirement undocumented, information not filed.

I don't mean to run down one of the most useful tools in our arsenal, though. In the context of web building, here are some things that email is quite good at:

- Bringing in people who aren't reachable by other means.
- Contacting people who are outside the project.
- Publishing administrative information to the project – things that are of a reference nature or don't require immediate action.
- Discussing something with a single project member in a reasonably private way.
- Notifying somebody that something needs to be looked at in another tool.

On the other hand, here are some things that email is not great at:

- Discussing functionality or design with more than one person at a time.
- Delivering project documents or deliverables.
- Raising issues bearing on the project as a whole.

- Documenting project decisions.
- Deciding where to go for lunch.

You'll probably deliver your initial proposal via email, and the client will probably send you their project brief (if they write one) and supporting documentation (if they have any) via email. This is fine, and these artefacts can be copied into a better information management system once the project gets going. But don't rely on email to hold important stuff, because:

- Email is hard to archive in a way that the whole project team can search for and find stuff later.
- Email distributes information among multiple points, making a single picture difficult.
- It is easy to jump between topics on an email thread, so searching or scanning the subject line of a threaded conversation can be misleading.
- It's impossible to keep deliverables (attachments) separate from the conversation that goes with them.
- Versioning of documents is difficult, because copies of emails exist in several places (in each contributor's sent items folder and in the inboxes or folders and tags of every direct, copied and blind-copied recipient.
- Every message appears to have equal weight, so it is difficult to prioritise.
- Even though some messaging systems imply that it is possible to retract or edit messages, the lack of standards makes this impossible on a practical level.

Much better, in other words, to rely on a system built to keep and organise information, rather than one designed to copy, store and forward it.

Phone

There's a good place for the telephone as a way to, you know, talk to people, one at a time or in groups. The telephone can be overused, as can email, but phone calls are generally followed up with a written version.

If you have a question for someone, especially a question of any complexity, a conversation either in person or over the phone is going to be the fastest way to get your answer. Be aware of the switching cost of conversations, though – just like going up to a designer and tapping them on the shoulder in the middle of a thought process can be disruptive and interrupt the flow, a telephone conversation stops one train of thought for the recipient and replaces it with another. Once the phone call has ended, it will take some time to come back to the first problem. So, if you're trying to decide whether to call someone, weigh the timeliness of an instant answer against the total amount of time that you are displacing.

Design collaboration is practically impossible over the phone because of the lack of a visual channel. If you have to make or build something together, you'll probably need a combination of co-working in person and writing (via email or IM).

Instant messaging

IM is lots of fun and, when it is extended to include all of our other social feeds (Twitter, Facebook, and so on) the net effect can be exhilarating. IM can be a very effective way to collaborate within a project team, but it does have a few unique drawbacks.

- Most client organisations aren't comfortable using IM at this point. For the most part, you're probably better off documenting client conversations via more formal channels.
- An IM conversation is like a phone conversation – to be useful and timely, it needs to engage most of the attention of two or more participants. Fine, if you mean to have people working together, and sometimes invaluable for teams collaborating at a distance. But it is always, by its nature, a distraction or interruption.

- People can schedule reading their email, they can schedule their meetings. To some extent we've become used to scheduling our phone calls ("Do you mind if I give you a ring at 2pm to discuss? Great."). But IM robs us of the ability to schedule and, therefore, to manage our workload. If you need the instant responsiveness to collaborate on a single problem, IM is great. If you think that IM is less intrusive than a phone call or a tap on the shoulder, you're wrong.

Meetings

We transmit and receive an enormous amount of information when we meet other people. We read body language, gesture, tone of voice, speech tempo and eye contact. We can bring charts, sketches and artefacts with us, and flip through, annotate and present them with a fluidity unmatched by any digital workflow. Just because badly run meetings can take the energy out of a team or project doesn't mean that the concept isn't valid.

Here's what you need to make a meeting work.

- **Agenda:** You have to know in advance what's going to happen. And so does everyone else!
- **Note taker:** Someone has to write up what's discussed, and who's agreed to do what. These notes need to be published to everyone within an hour or two of when the meeting happens.
- **Time frame:** You need to know how much time this meeting is going to take. If you have 15- and 20-minute items to discuss, give your meeting 35 minutes – there's no rule that says meetings need to take place in hourly increments. Google projects a 1.5 metre wide stopwatch on the wall during its meetings – show that you're just as serious about not wasting people's time. Think about making a pie chart of where you are planning to spend the time during your discussion, and hold people to that.
- **Follow up:** If tasks are talked about during the meeting, give each of them to specific participants to own. If you need something specific from someone not in the room, write that down, too. Both kinds of assignments need to go into the meeting notes, and possibly into your to-do or task management system.

Project management software

In the web world, online project management software has become the standard way of managing project communications. A cross between email, online discussion board, network drive, shared calendar and to-do application, such software is an efficient way to keep everyone up to date and all documentation findable.

If you're a fan of Basecamp (or Adept or another platform), you'll want to demonstrate that at the kick-off. As part of your kick-off planning, get the email addresses of everyone who will be involved from the client, agency and subcontractors. Kick-off meetings can be a great chance to take everyone's pictures for the project management system, too – bring a camera and stand people up against a neutral background one at a time. Write up your first meeting agenda using Basecamp, upload the project documents from the client (your proposal and their brief, for example), and then spend just a minute or two running through the project interface at the start of your first project meeting. Spending a few minutes talking about Basecamp will pay off later.

You show right off the bat that you're an organised group of professionals, not an intuitive but vague gaggle of designers. You get people used to the idea that their discussions and documents will be up in one place, so people won't be asking you later on for the documentation that only you possess.

Don't underestimate the ego-pleasing power of seeing your portrait next to a piece of text. Clients are like the rest of us: they like to see their names in print, and they like seeing pictures of themselves. The more you get the client to communicate with the team using the project management app, the smoother a project you'll deliver. The best thing: clients will attribute the smoothness of the project to your management skills, not to the tool.

So, now we have a few things that will go into project communications, and you know how you're going to present and talk about them. The preparation has been done, the workshops have been planned. It's time to get on to the kick-off meeting itself!

Getting things done at kick-off

Best chance for requirements development
Project kick-offs have the potential to be incredibly exciting events. There are usually senior people there, on the website-making and website-commissioning sides. Energy is high – the money for the project has been signed off, and everyone is bursting with ideas for the new website. It's also the easiest part of the project lifecycle to do badly. A bad kick-off meeting looks like an awkward roomful equally divided between client-side and agency brains, with each of those equally divided into boredom, anxiety, and well-meaning bravado.

From my experience, some of the uncomfortable situations you may face look like:

- Going into a first meeting at a big investment bank, only to find that very few of the people around the room knew the purpose of the meeting. The senior vice-president hosting the meeting thought that the discussion was something about colour choices for their new stationery.
- A kick-off meeting for an arts festival where everyone from the client side thought the kick-off meeting was the perfect chance to disagree with each other (loudly) about the programme of events for the next year.
- Showing up with six agency people in full designer regalia, only to be squeezed into the cramped office of one very confused (and very junior) summer marketing intern.

Yet it's an extremely pleasant event. People have the sense that a project is starting, and there's general happy agreement, if only because nothing specific has been broached. Everyone goes back to their offices with a warm and fuzzy feeling, but the project hasn't really moved forward at all. The kick-off box has been ticked.

A good kick-off is something of an art and can actually advance the project considerably. By bringing together some of the most important people at a time when everyone is happy and excited about the project, the kick-off can not only set the tone for the engagement but also generate some key requirements that will define some of the best opportunities for success.

By talking to some of the key people before the actual kick-off, you can get a good head start on requirements, and then use the kick-off itself to refine priorities and work through some real project detail. Doing things in this order means that:

- Stakeholders have the chance to be listened to personally by the web agency and feel a sense of ownership from the very beginning of the project.
- The agency gets to set the tone for a mutual working relationship that depends on the ideas of both parties.
- The kick-off meeting itself is planned and executed by the website builders, which sets the idea of project governance and control.
- The project requirements can be developed early, and any conflicts between the ideas of the various stakeholders can be ironed out before changes are really expensive.

Workshop format
At the kick-off meeting, there's the usual handshaking and fetching of tea and coffee, and then the team gets down to work.

The kick-off agenda should look something like this:

- Introductions
- Newspaper article of the future
- Coffee break and portraits
- Requirements sorting
- Elevator pitch

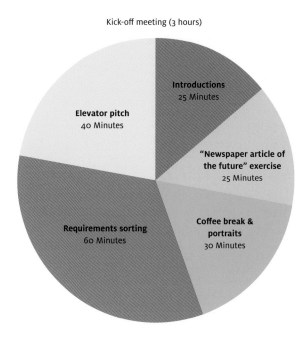

Kick-off meeting (3 hours)

Introductions
25 Minutes

Elevator pitch
40 Minutes

"Newspaper article of
the future" exercise
25 Minutes

Coffee break &
portraits
30 Minutes

Requirements sorting
60 Minutes

Start with the introductions, but since most people have probably already met (at the stakeholder interviews or the proposal pitch), there's no need to take a lot of time. You can assume that most attendees will have read your proposal, so they know the general outline. You can also promise that a few hours of time now will pay off later on.

The first exercise is designed to get people thinking about the real objectives for the project, and also to get them thinking creatively. Pass around some sheets with the outlines of a newspaper article from the future; tell everyone to imagine that the site you're going to build together is a great success. Ask them to write a headline and some copy for a newspaper or magazine article describing the new site. Get everyone to write down:

- what publication the article is from
- the headline
- the first paragraph of the story
- who is quoted in the story and what they say

By addressing these subjects, everyone gets a sense of how the project might create great things – and looking at these future articles will tell the design team a lot about audience, tone and style for the new site. Everyone spends some time on the article, and then they read their answers, usually with gusto and some laughs around the table. The laughter will not only break the ice with people who don't know each other well, but also give people permission to be creative and to work outside of their comfort zones.

After the first round of work, people stop to sip their coffee and chat for just a few minutes. A web team member could use this opportunity during the break to take headshot portraits of each of the client project team members for their (project management software) avatars. Having actual photos will help with the sense that the client people are part of the team, and makes it easier for designers and developers to associate messages with people and roles.

After a short break, people reassemble and you start to sort the objectives. For this exercise, you'll need to bring out index cards with the stakeholder objectives you got from the interviews. Speak briefly about each one, introducing everyone there to the list of objectives in the customer, financial, team or process categories. After you've given a short description of each stakeholder objective, you may want to open the floor for some more suggestions, which you can write on some blank index cards.

Next comes the sorting exercise. Hand some coloured dot stickers to everyone there, both build-side and client-side. Lay out the objective cards on the table. As everyone stands around the board table, they should start to allocate their stickers to their preferred cards. Make sure everyone understands that they can give up to three dots to each idea, and that they should give more dots to the ideas they think are the most important. The result: a series of weighted priorities and objectives created directly by your client.

TOOLS FROM THIS CHAPTER

• Risk register
• Quality register
• Stakeholder interview
• Objective-sorting workshop
• Basecamp

FURTHER READING

Building quality and risk registers isn't so hard if you have an example to start with. Start with the templates at *http://www.prince-officialsite.com/Resources/Resources.aspx* – you can download a zip file of most of the common templates used in the PRINCE2 process, including risk and quality registers, and a bunch of other common reporting templates.

Interviews can be hard to capture accurately. Think about using software like AudioNote (*http://luminantsoftware.com/iphone/audionote.html*) or SoundNote (*http://soundnote.com/*) to make sure that you don't miss anything.

You'll want to read the inimitable Kevin M Hoffman on kick-off techniques for projects, nicely compiled at *Goodkickoffmeetings.com*. This is a seriously useful website when you're trying to turn a kick-off into a creative workshop, especially if the participants aren't as used to this kind of exercise.

A great book on general workshop design is *Gamestorming* by Dave Gray, Sunni Brown and James Macanufo (2010, O'Reilly Media). The authors' website (*http://www.gogamestorm.com*) collects user-submitted games and workshop designs that will help you make certain kinds of decisions or lead a group productively.

The makers of the Basecamp software, 37signals, have started to make some of their internal Basecamp projects public. Following along with these projects is an excellent way to learn: take a look at the projects described on their blog. Not only will you get a sense of how a web-based project can be structured, but you'll see the style of communication and constructive feedback that's possible with such a close-knit team. Watching the iterations of graphic designs, body copy and page layouts evolve over time is also fascinating.

REQUIREMENTS AND SCOPE

*"The greatest challenge to any thinker is stating the problem
in a way that will allow a solution."*
– Attributed to Bertrand Russell

What's here: How to create understandable requirements, perform stakeholder interviews,
process and sort ideas, and facilitate requirement workshops.

There's an art to writing requirements. Say too much, and you
create too many constraints to get a good job done; you can
write yourself into a corner that no amount of inspired, creative
problem-solving can unravel. Say too little, and you're asking for
disappointment; the site will arrive, but fall over at the first hint of
interaction from real users. Neither will do your career (or stress
level) any good.

Understanding, not documents
Most people who have worked in any sort of corporate office
will think of requirements in terms of a very large pile of paper.
Often formatted as one continuous table, requirements lists tend
to follow a format something like this: number, description;
number, description. Slightly more sophisticated lists might
group requirements by area (user interface, database, security),
and might give a priority to each (low, medium or high, or perhaps
Phase 1, Phase 2 and Phase 3).

Category	Requirement Number	Description	Priority
User Interface	3.2.1	The user shall be able to perform a simple search in any combination of author, year, title, or keyword	High
	3.2.2	A rotating carousel of tips shall be displayed on the homepage	High
	3.2.3	The available languages shall be displayed in a drop-down menu on the homepage.	Medium
	3.2.4	The language currently selected shall be greyed-out	Low

Developers and designers are handed these bland shopping lists and die inside. It's not that a long, numbered requirements list isn't the correct documentation for a negotiation with stakeholders – often it's exactly that. And, of course, there are often lots of important details captured that it would be foolish to ignore. But the fact is, typical requirements lists are not only boring to create and read, they are also a long way from being able to define a good project.

Getting to the heart of what a project is, and what it needs to be, is more about understanding than it is about documentation.

Accurate project requirements

Something that tells you what to build

When you start to work through requirements, you may have a list already in hand. Perhaps it was carefully considered by a committee of important people and reflects the priorities of the various departments involved. But no matter how thoughtful and comprehensive a requirements document is, chances are that without the guidance or input from a good web professional it doesn't tell you what you need to build a website.

A website is about communication, emotion, connection, engagement. It's a lot more than a list of screens or a proposed sitemap. If you want to get to the heart of a project, try to work with the website owners to first develop a simple communication brief. Think about the major audiences for the site, and as specifically as possible. Think about how the finished site will make them feel. Think about the activities that these people will accomplish. Don't worry too much about the brand guidelines that you're working with. You're interested here in expressing the values and beliefs of the organisation or service behind the website. If there are major bits of functionality needed, like buying products or customer self-service, talk about these things. But think like an ad man – talk about the benefits of the new website, not the features that it needs.

Your brief should end up being no more than two pages, and one is probably fine. This shared understanding of why you're doing the project and what you expect people to get out of the finished website will be surprisingly useful as you get into building the website.

Communication brief

Whenever you're faced with a difficult feature or benefit trade-off down the line, you can come back to the communication brief and ask yourself, "Is this feature we're arguing about really what the site is about? What role does it play in delighting our customers?"

Not too detailed

It's easy to start making long lists when you're working on requirements documents. However, it's probably best to avoid the longer versions of these, since you can write yourself away from a site that you'd want to build and that will deliver the value you expect.

Why? Well, there are a few things that tend to happen with too detailed communication briefs. You start thinking too much about the expected solution, perhaps including the need for particular controls or page flows. This isn't the time – during requirements phase you should be thinking about who you are building for (the audience) and what will make the project successful for them.

You also start believing that any idea mentioned belongs in the requirements spec, perhaps because it was suggested by an important business stakeholder. Without a lot of summarising and editing, you can list requirements that contradict each other, or just fail to support each other. Furthermore, aspects of visual and interaction design (colours, placement of buttons, number of steps for a given process) can start to become embedded in what will form the definition for the project. The problem is that without having done some research and starting to investigate the nature of your real user challenges, it's too early to suggest solutions.

The communication brief should be aspirational and encompass the major success criteria for the project. It's probably not a good idea to combine this with project governance documents like statements of work or contracts. The reason is, again, the level of detail. A statement of work or contract is a legal agreement, and contains a lot of necessary detail about the engagement and how it will be carried out. Your first crack at a requirements document, though, tells you why you're undertaking the project and who you're making it for.

Mutually agreed: what to do when they differ

Of course, like any artefact made by a web team to be shared with someone in a client role, the document needs to be agreed by both parties. If the communication brief is particularly contentious, you know that you and the client have some different ideas about the project, and quite possibly there are implications for the scope of the work. Disagreements about scope are difficult, but it's far, far better to have those discussions now, before the budget has been spent, rather than at the dangerous 90% point of the project.

You know the point I mean – when everything is substantially or 90% complete, and what remains to do turns out to be just another 90% of work. And another. The real risks for many projects lurk within that final 10%, as all of the ambiguities from each phase of the project development multiply together.

Stakeholder interviews to determine project objectives

So how do you know what to put into the early requirements documents? Well, this is your first real project deliverable since getting the gig, so you want to impress everyone with your knowledge of what's going on, and you owe it to the rest of the web team to commit only to work that can and should be done, and that can be feasibly accomplished within the time, budget or skills constraints of the project.

The best way to build a solid initial requirements document is to interview the key stakeholders. One way or another, these are the people you need to hear from if you're going to build a consensus around what the website needs to do.

If at all possible, you should actually speak to the stakeholders. Arrange a telephone or internet call, or as a last resort ask for responses in writing. Seeing them in person works best, in part because you have the greatest chance to focus the conversation and to ask follow-up questions as you go, looking for stakeholder objectives that are specific, feasible, and measurable. You can do a decent job of gathering success criteria for an average-sized web project through half-hour interviews with the key four to eight people.

I've found that a good approach is to ask questions more or less in this order.

- **What are your responsibilities in this organisation?** Or you can ask a similarly general question for users or other representatives. The goal is to put people at ease, and to understand their motivation for participation and commitment to the outcome of the web project.

- **I'm trying to get a sense of what success looks like for this web project. If you were to think about things from the customer's perspective, what would success look like when we're done?** The idea is to elicit a user-centred view, perhaps a change in perception, a sense of empowerment or a new understanding. If you hear organisational goals rather than customer goals, steer the conversation back again. It's important.

- **Now with your company hat on again, tell me about the financial goals that you personally hope the website will achieve.** Including words like personally will often get you more honest answers because the interviewee doesn't feel that they're being asked just to remember and toe the company line. When asking financial questions, be sure to include cost savings as well as direct income! A lot of projects forget to include time saved for the customer service or marketing teams, more efficient manufacturing or partner relationships – all sorts of saved costs that are just as real as the actual receipts from an e-commerce site.

- **Think about your internal processes some more. How do you think they'll change if this project is successful?** This question can give you some good insights into how the organisation works. Keep good notes on the number of levels of management and on the flexibility of workers to make decisions on their own initiative. These will be important when you're making decisions about site and content governance later on in the project.

- **Think about your own team. Probably your work and skills will change a bit after the site goes live and works really well. Tell me a little about how you'd hope your own work and skills will change for the better.** This question is supposed to discover facts that will go into the governance model for the website, and probably also help to plan content responsibilities. It's not always easy to get good answers to this question, though, so sometimes it's much better to ask direct questions to the interviewee: "Tell me how your own work will change" and "Tell me what else you hope to learn."

- **Just for fun, tell me what a complete and utter failure would look like. Not that we'll let that happen!** This can be a fun question and tends to uncover some deep-seated fears within the organisation or audience. Knowing the big important problems will sometimes lead you more quickly toward the right solution.

- **Anything you've left out? If not, here's how to contact me, and we'll get in touch with you later in the project to get your take on how we're doing.** If you promise to follow up, don't forget to do so! It is just good courtesy to send a follow-up email or card in any case, to thank the stakeholder for his or her time. These people are pretty busy, after all, and the web project may not be their top priority. Everyone appreciates being thanked for a favour.

This interview style is, of course, just an adaptation of the classic balanced scorecard approach to developing business success factors, popularised by Kaplan and Norton in Harvard Business Review (January–February 1992).

As you move into Phase 2, remember that it's OK not to do everything. Each project will grow in a slightly different way, depending on your team and your client. Don't panic. If this site is wonderful, you'll get a chance to refine your process later.

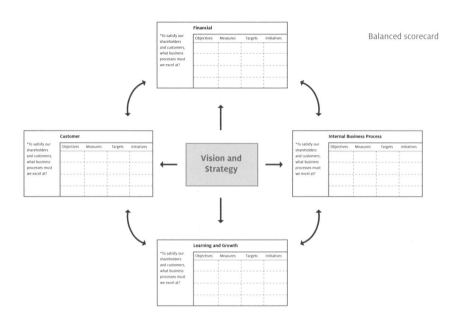

Balanced scorecard

Balanced scorecard

Balanced Scorecard, Kaplan & Norton (1992)

Perspectives	Principle	Example question
Financial	How do shareholders see us?	"Tell me about the financial goals that you personally hope the website will achieve."
Customer	How do customers see us?	"What would you like your customers be able to do that they can't do now?"
Internal business processes	What must we excel at?	"What internal processes will be easier or more streamlined once the website is live?"
Learning and growth	How can we improve and create value?	"Tell me a little about how you'd hope your own work and skills will change for the better."

Expectations

A few tips for setting expectations

- Make sure that every document that goes to the client is an accurate reflection of what the project will look like in the end.
- The important part here is *not* to set rosy expectations.
- Estimates need to be clear and clearly be estimates.
- Workshops are the best way for the client to feel involved.
- Scope and information architecture are not the same subject.
- Clients will want to move toward sitemaps – instead, you should think in terms of users, functionality and journeys.
- It's not about the final page structure.
- The boundaries between pages and components are getting fuzzier.

Post-its

Ah, the venerable Post-it. Not so venerable, perhaps – I don't remember boards full of them in Mad Men – but it would be hard to imagine a contemporary design studio without small dayglo paper shards cluttering up the place. Sure, Post-its can make you seem all designer-y, or Agile, or like a hip project organisation, but what are they for? Why this obsession with a particular office stationery product from our friends at the 3M Company?

Staying loose until the last minute

Post-its are useful (and wildly popular) because of a few salient characteristics of their design.

- They have room for you to express at most one thought, and more likely a single word or short phrase.
- They can be easily reordered or rearranged without fuss or hassle, thus bringing order and structure, while no move or arrangement is permanent.

- They can be presented and worked with horizontally on the plane of a table, or arranged vertically on a wall, poster or window.
- They are very easy to edit – simply write another and replace, or mark through what you no longer want to see.
- They can be easily stacked into portable groups.
- They are relatively cheap.

Does any of that seem obvious? Well, obvious perhaps, but these characteristics are part of why people working with concepts and ideas (like designers and software developers) spend so much time with them. The very impermanence of an idea expressed on a Post-it means that you can always go back later to rethink. You can go back and rearrange a sequence of webpages, or reorder the steps of a user process. You can create new stylistic ideas, or add to a set of goals for one of your key personas. The very editability of Post-it notes suggests fluidity of thought.

Photo by Harry Verwayan, Europeana Foundation. Marco Rendina of Fondazione Rinascimento Digitale presents his ideas

In the world of gathering and documenting requirements, this fluidity is something that you want to keep with you. In fact, you'd rather not commit anything to paper until the very last moment, just so that you can keep thinking through the possibilities. If you've used the intervening time to really think about the qualities and concepts of what you're making, and if you've kept that sense of impermanence, and if you've retained the authority to regroup and reimagine your thoughts along the way, you'll probably find that you end up with a better set of requirements than you would otherwise have.

Why we group and sort ideas
Doing an exercise with Post-it notes (or electronic versions of the same idea) helps you to lump and split. Lumping is about bringing concepts together, finding those duplications and overlaps of ideas that you've put down or gathered from multiple people. Splitting is about seeing that a given idea is too big, or too hard to measure, or just too cumbersome to be an idea in itself – splitting the idea or concept or steps into smaller units helps every bit of your overall system have a similar weight and importance.

Photo Breandán Knowlton, courtesy of Design by Front

This seems abstract, but the need is clear. When you're creating requirements, or a site map, or a wireframe prediction, your ideas need to be clear, distinct and as concrete as possible. The design of the humble Post-it can help guide you toward a better way of working.

Client requirements workshops

Do your homework

If you run the exercise yourself first in the studio, you will definitely learn what works and what sounds awkward, which gives you chance to polish some more for a meeting that you'll only have time to run once. Stage a mock workshop a day or two before the actual workshop, prepare your slides or visual aids and present them, exactly as you'd run the real workshop. It doesn't have to be quite as long – you can probably skip some of the conversation and the detailed discussion. But give it a good hour or two – it's time well spent.

Practice being the client

If someone from the web team sits in for the client at your rehearsal run-through, you'll have the chance to do two things. First, you'll start to see how your presentation flows from the client's point of view. If it's too abstract or too separated from the idea of an eventual website, the client will lose interest and maybe even start to be doubtful about the project. Second, you have the chance to think through the actual requirements for the project, which means that the comments during the meeting won't come as a surprise. Fewer surprises means it'll be easier to anticipate and steer the workshop to get what you need.

Prepare your materials

These sound obvious, but are often overlooked: if the workshop involves a projector and screen, get them warmed up and tested with the laptop that you'll be using. If you are doing card sorting, check your stock of index cards. If you need little sticker dots of different colours, make sure you have them on hand. And don't forget the all-important coffee, tea and snacks order; a tray of nice pastries can get everyone in the right mood and establish a sense of generosity and sharing. Be prepared for the meeting – rushing around at the last minute will leave everyone too stressed and frazzled to do a good job at the workshop.

Get the client involved

It's good to set the scene, and certainly you want to make a good impression with your thoughts and ideas. But this isn't a presentation – remember that the client knows the business and knows what some of these constraints are better than you do. Ask for input in more than a cursory way... and leave pauses in your conversation to make sure you get it. If you stop talking, and are disciplined enough to stay silent, the client will jump in with ideas, questions and clarifications. Sometimes it takes twenty seconds of silence, which will be excruciating, but you will get through it. And once the client engages, they'll stay engaged in the conversation until you do something to lose them again (like talk for too long).

Document quickly and accurately

If you take notes, make sketches and draw pictures as you go: the follow-up will be ten times easier. It may seem that you're absorbing everything in the room, and it all makes sense, but if you don't take good notes (as a combination of textual and symbolic or graphical ideas), you'll struggle to get that focus back later on. Concentrate on actions from the meeting, of course, but also write down relevant adjectives and adverbs that the client uses. These will help generate the emotional road map that you'll need as you iterate your design later. Write down any decisions made – these are the fixed points which your designs will orbit. If you get ideas for good typical or actual users (personas, in other words), start sketching these out, one per piece of paper. It's perfectly fine to give your new personas names right in the meeting, start writing down keywords about them and using these characters to shape the discussion. If you are using whiteboards to draw your ideas, take a good photograph before you erase each board – might as well include these in the follow-up documentation. There's no need to retype lots of things that are sketched on paper, by the way; just scan your pieces of paper, photograph your Post-its and put the whole thing into a Basecamp post.

Talk about success criteria instead of wish lists

The website may seem like a list of wishes – and any brief written by the client will almost certainly sound this way. If the project used a request for proposal of any kind, this document will definitely sound like a wish list. But you're not here to grant wishes. You're here to find the right business problems and solve them using design and technology. For that, you need to know what matters to the client. Frame your questions around what would constitute a success, and you'll hear about motivation and processes. From these starting points you can find solutions. If you ask instead for what people want to see, or what they think you should build, you're asking them to do your job for you and jump straight to a solution without articulating their motivations or the specifics of the problem being solved. Non-experts will develop solutions based on convention, with some radical creativity thrown in. This isn't where you want to start a project – you'd just be setting up ideas that you might have to knock down later. Let the client be an expert in their business; you be the expert in finding the right web solution.

And yes, the run-through is billable time

Like preparation for any workshop, you're not just charging the client for the time you spend in the room. Be sure that your estimates, invoices and project reports account for the time you spend preparing, running, documenting and following up from workshops. If workshops are a core part of your working style (and I recommend that they be a pretty important feature), you'll end up with a substantial part of the project budget represented in workshop time.

It's worth spending some time reading up on workshop techniques – I've listed one of my favourite books for this below. In general, though, you should design your workshops in three parts:

1. Open up the solution space, get people feeling creative.
2. Analyse the options that you have, working out more detail about the potential solutions.
3. Narrow the field again by ranking and eliminating options.

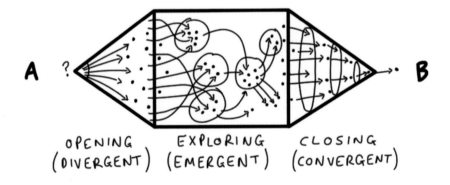

Orchestrating the flow of a workshop – getting from A to B. Adapted from *Gamestorming* by Dave Gray, et al (2010, O'Reilly Media), p12.

TOOLS FROM THIS CHAPTER

• Detailed requirements list
• Balanced scorecard
• Gamestorming workshops
• Post-it notes
• Requirements workshops documentation

FURTHER READING

The *Gamestorming* book is very handy to generate ideas for your workshops. It might take a while to select and adapt the workshop that you need, but you'll get the hang of it after you've run a few. *Gamestorming* by Dave Gray et al (2010, O'Reilly Media).

The book *100 Things Every Designer Needs to Know About People* by Susan Weinschenk (2011, New Riders) tells you about the cognitive biases that your users will bring to the experience, and is well worth looking into if you'd like to create stronger online experiences.

It's well worth reading "Using the Balanced Scorecard as a Strategic Management System", an article by Robert S Kaplan and David P Norton in Harvard Business Review (Vol. 74/Jan-Feb, pp75–85). While the article reacts to a particular kind of business forecasting that you may not be as familiar with, the general approach of eliciting requirements in these areas is quite helpful in getting a true understanding of what matters for the product you're building. I tend to do my stakeholder interviews using these scorecard metrics, as a way of checking that I've covered at least most of the solution space.

5 INTERVIEW: GREG HOY

Greg Hoy is a president of Happy Cog. He's been working in interactive design for seventeen years and has managed studios for eight years. His personal site is *www.greghoy.com* and he has made many contributions[1] to Happy Cog's Cognition.

Greg spoke to Breandán about gathering requirements, kick-off workshops, fixed-price contracts and setting expectations for an engagement.

Day-to-day responsibilities at Happy Cog

Let's start with what you do day to day, running the Happy Cog Philadelphia office.

Primarily, my role these days is defining – that is, helping to define with Jeffrey Zeldman and Greg Storey – the strategic direction of Happy Cog. I'm still heavily involved in business development work, so whenever we do pitches I'm there. Although I'm not writing proposals as much as I used to, I'm still involved in that effort, doing estimates and those sorts of things.

I've noticed that the people doing project management tasks are often not the ones who are called project managers. Often these are business owners, art directors and so forth, and these people perform tasks that are part of the project management process.

I've done PM work before out of necessity. As anybody who knows me understands, I subscribe to a cable tie mailing list in which I get an email with today's cable ties – I'm kind of an organised guy! So being involved with project management was a natural extension of just being organised, and the fact that I actually enjoyed doing it. But it's become more complex as websites and digital design efforts get more sophisticated.

---

[1] http://cognition.happycog.com/author/greghoy

Important proposal-stage activities

You've written about some things that are particularly important in business development, such as getting contracts signed[2] and getting paid before the start of the coding. Do you have any general tips about why these things are important?

One thing that I've learned from previous jobs in consulting agencies is that it's very important to front-load projects and to get paid earlier. You invest a lot of time and energy up front to learn about projects, to get people ramped up and to start working immediately. If you're not funding that effort before you start, you're immediately in a hole. And we don't like one established project funding another, newer project that we haven't received payment for. We like each project, in an ideal world, to be self-sufficient.

We are adamant about clients paying up front. We're not trying to put them in a difficult situation. From a logistical and financial point of view, it really can't happen in any other way. And it shows good faith, too. If a client or a prospect has performed their due diligence and are comfortable with hiring a firm, they should be comfortable with paying that firm in advance. They've done the research, spoken to referees and all that stuff. That's a key secret that I've picked up over the years.

You learn little things, like what I wrote about invoicing[3] – small strategies that you can use to get paid in a timely manner. All these little things you pick up through experience. What cracks me up is, because of Happy Cog's stature in the industry, a lot of people think we have all the answers about everything. We never, ever claim to have all the answers. But one thing I love is using our brand to spur conversation. And I learn stuff from people all the time, and I hope they learn a little bit from us. I think that's something we use Cognition[4] for specifically – to throw ideas out there and see what kind of counterpoints people have to those ideas.

---

[2] Take a look at Mike Monteiro's talk on this topic: http://vimeo.com/22053820

[3] http://cognition.happycog.com/article/the-devil-is-in-the-invoice

[4] http://cognition.happycog.com/, the Happy Cog blog

You've spoken about setting expectations[5], about wanting to be treated as professionals. Are those money conversations difficult to manage?

> *I think you need to set expectations early and be really transparent about it. There are larger organisations that are very used to doing things their own way. Nine times out of ten, if you are consistent with your language and don't cave in or immediately accept what the clients say, they will make exceptions. Don't be a jerk, just say, "Hey, listen. These are the reasons why we do this." I don't care how big the organisation is – you'll be surprised how many times you can get a cheque in five days instead of sixty if somebody walks it over to somebody else, instead of sending it.*

Problems with requests for proposals (RFPs)

Happy Cog doesn't usually respond to request for proposals[6] unless you have already received a completed project planner. Does that always work?

> *Lately we've been getting fewer project planners and more casual contact form-based emails. We want to get more planners, because they are incredibly valuable.*
>
> *When it comes to negotiating logistics and finances, they're typically the last things you discuss in the RFP process. That's unfortunate, because you're trying to prove your worth by pitching and writing fifteen double-spaced pages of very specific information. Then, at the end, if you pass through all of those hoops, you find out that you will get paid at intervals that don't match up to your scenario. They won't tell you their budget because they want your best final price. Then later on you find that their budget is too low, or they won't pay up front.*
>
> *We've learned to ask those questions early in the process, as much as possible. If they won't tell you the answers to those questions, you need to make a judgement call at that point. We've thought about just shutting RFPs off*

---

[5] http://cognition.happycog.com/article/bloodhounding-budgets

[6] http://cognition.happycog.com/article/rfp-advice-from-the-front-lines

completely and saying instead, "Fill out the plan." Or, "Let's talk in person, but we're not going to answer an RFP." We haven't done that yet because we get a few RFPs that are written almost as if somebody has filled out the planner. They're thoughtfully architected with few incredibly ridiculous hoops to jump through. We don't want to completely shut off the tap, because we would not get that kind of thoughtful RFP.

But there are other ones that are ridiculous. Information isn't shared with you up front, you have to submit your responses in triplicate via a nationally recognised carrier, and such. Those we shy away from more and more.

Getting a lot out of kick-off meetings

It seems that Happy Cog is particularly good at the kick-off – actually getting stuff done right at the start.

It wasn't always that way when we started our kick-offs. When we worked with you' we had a very collaborative kick-off. We came to your location, met with everybody and had conversations. There have been other kick-offs that we've done remotely over the phone, going through a questionnaire. There'd be long, awkward pauses while everybody was writing their notes. Ask the next question, move on.

And there was one point in the office when one of those kick-offs was happening, and I wasn't participating, but I was in the other room and I was eavesdropping. Hearing those awkward pauses – I was cringing in my seat. After the whole thing was done, I got up, walked down the hall and said, "We're not doing that ever again. This isn't how we engage with clients." If I was sitting on the other end of that phone, and that was my experience, I would look for a way to terminate the relationship.

---

[7] Greg led the Happy Cog team that built http://comhaltas.ie, a site promoting Irish traditional music.

*Luckily, that's when Kevin Hoffman joined us, and he didn't have to be told –
he just took it! He took ownership of the problem and developed a subcareer
around designing meetings, stemming from that moment. I'm not patting
myself on the back – he did it. He took ownership of it and said, "Look, I
come from an educational background. I've worked in higher ed. I've taught
classes – this should be more like a class experience, where everybody is
communicating, collaborating, exchanging ideas in groups rather than just
one side talking to the other and going through a piece of paper." So, from
that point on, all our kick-offs have really been models of how to engage with
somebody you don't know.*

*I always hated working in small groups in college or in high school. I preferred
just to do things myself. But when working in teams, you're forced to interact
with people you wouldn't ordinarily interact with. Whenever we do that now,
we structure the teams so each team is half client and half Happy Cog, and
everybody is eligible – a junior designer could be teamed with a company
president; it could be a UX person with a developer. You don't know who's
going to be in your mix. But you immediately exchange ideas, get to know
what people's personalities are like, laugh and have a good time. And to me,
apart from going to a bar and just socialising – that's the best way you can do
a kick-off. You come out of those meetings with tons of stuff! Go through these
exercises where people tell you the top ten things that are important on the
homepage. In a kick-off, you can get that input from thirty people, sometimes
in the one room, and you can bring that stuff home. To organise that input
over the phone, or to wrangle that over Basecamp, is impossible.*

You're talking about giving people materials to sketch on and do card sorting?

*We do collaborative sketching exercises where we sketch up the homepage
and try to articulate what's important in the prioritisation of content, with
everybody's input. Then each team presents their ideas to the group.*

*We're thinking about filming them, finding a client who's cool with us filming
the whole thing and posting it for people to absorb. That's the other thing –*

there are no trade secrets. As far as I'm concerned, there's no mystery to what we do. If I hand somebody a Photoshop file, are they going to see the magic we can work with the dodge tool?

The paradox of fixed-price service contracts and internal estimates.

Where do you get enough confidence to say, "Here's a project. We've signed up for this many days of work. We can do those days of work and deliver something good"? How do you get the client thinking in the same way? How do you communicate a sense of solving the problem together – especially when it's a fixed-price bid, so you're solving just this much of the problem together?

We have tried to be very specific about what deliverables and steps we're going to accomplish through a project with a client. But what we've learned is that prior to signing a contract with a client, you're only guessing. You're simply guessing what's going to be appropriate for them, and how long it's going to take.

Our approach now is to say: for each phase of the project, we could do any number of things, and here they are. It's like a menu. It's not completely open to "check the one that you want", but we could do personas; we could do benchmarking; or content genre work; or taxonomy work; or prototyping; or usability testing; or wireframes; or sitemaps. In our contract, it says that based on the project goals, expectations and appropriate use, we could do any number of these things, but we don't commit to any of them specifically.

Then, during project definition, all that specific stuff comes out. We learn so much going through those conversations, from kick-off all the way through to communications briefs and tech approach documents. By the point of finishing that project definition phase, we know exactly what's appropriate during the IA stage. We may say, "We know now that your timeframe is much shorter than you thought it was initially, so we can't afford to go through sitemaps and then through wireframes. We've got to do something nimbler." Maybe it's a prototype that can feed directly into code, for example, and our designers can be designing simultaneously with development, so we can get to the finish quickly.

You use the project to learn about the client, and you trust the client has learned about you prior to the project. You hold your ground and try not to prescribe solutions before you've kicked the project off. You use the early parts of the project to inform what you're going to do in the later parts. And you keep it open. We work with buckets of hours. So, IA could be 600 hours. We can use those hours any way we want. We could iterate a sitemap thirty-eight times if we want to, and say, "That's it. That's IA." Or we could do a prototype in Axure, so it's clickable, and get people involved. We can do testing on it and all of that. But when the 600 hours are up, they're up. If we want to do more stuff, you buy more hours.

So, it's fixed-price, but there's breathing room. There's some elasticity involved so that if clients want to do more, they can.

Appropriate fidelity

That makes sense, as long as they can understand what's on the menu, and know what's actually in the contract and what's not. That's where the RFPs really trip you up, because a lot of them want to know, not just general approach and methodology, but tasks and deliverables. They want to have the tasks exactly in order and to know how one feeds into the next as part of the competitive evaluation criteria.

Yeah, in RFPs there's a lot of language that doesn't really apply to a web design effort: it applies to a software development effort. So that's when you really have to ask yourselves if these are the types of people you want to work with, because there's going to be a fair amount of re-education involved to get them even speaking your language. If they ask for virus scans on everything that you build, they're not speaking from web design reality. They're speaking from a similar IT-related process that doesn't map one-to-one.

It's a different sort of beast. I feel that happens a lot – first clients want all these methodologies, with acronyms, certifications, ISO standards and things which haven't been developed yet for the web. But then they often see the whole requirements-to-build phase as being a definitive stage boundary. They feel that we're going to learn absolutely everything about the project and write it into one giant document that will describe everything. Suddenly, there'll be a thousand numbered requirements with little dots next to them. And only then we'll start thinking about how it would actually be executed. That's one of the mismatches, I think.

I've been involved with both sides of that. I've worked with a software consulting company that built custom software solutions. There were requirements efforts where we would literally deliver a phone book-sized document. And, flipping through the pages, there were just a bunch of use cases: "The system shall do this. The system shall do that." And we didn't do any of that when we started here.

Since then, there have been a couple of projects where we wished we had that documentation. Dave DeRuchie, our project management director, wishes we had some sort of checklist instead of this nebulous agreement. If down the road something comes up when we didn't account for it, then we have to go back and make all kinds of design changes in order to accommodate this new functionality. Because of those project issues, we've been a lot more proactive about gathering requirements up front.

We try to do it in different ways. We're developing a tool that will enable us to work with clients in very common, everyday language, almost like bug tracking for requirements gathering. So we can assign requirements for people to follow up on – you can write requirements down, but not try to nail it all at once, adding to the list as you go instead. That way we make sure that it's all recorded somewhere so we have something that we can fall back on.

This is the area where making websites and building software does overlap to a great degree. Some of the functionality is out of the box; some of it will be built; some will become obvious because of another feature. The integration of those parts can be tricky.

> *The secret is to gather requirements without seeming like a stuffy software developer. People tune out when you show them a wireframe! They ask, "Is the site going to be black and white!?" So gather requirements without looking like you're gathering requirements. Keep it conversational, keep it casual, but keep it. Keep it recorded somewhere, so you have it to fall back on.*

Thoughts for clients

What do you think clients could think about more often as they approach a web agency?

> *Good question. I think it's most beneficial when clients come to us knowing exactly what their goals are. I think that one of the valuable things prospects say, when they have taken the time to fill out the project planner, is that the planner has made them think about both the short-term and long-term goals for what they want to do.*

Setting expectations

What about setting expectations on both the client and the agency delivery sides when going into a web-making project? To me, there's a pretty big gap right in the middle there. What would be the things that you believe clients should think about when they come to engage you? Or things that you should think about as an agency?

> *I think it's tough to expect clients to know what a web development process is. But I wish some of our clients were more in tune with what a project like this entails, from a resourcing perspective and from a commitment perspective. I think a lot of clients believe that we're going to drive the bus through this whole thing, and that it's not really a collaborative process. That mentality means waiting for feedback for a long time, things get dragged out, or they*

won't have the resources on their side that they need to devote to a project like this. We try to ask up front, "Who's involved with the project team? What do they do? Who's going to be a day-to-day contact?", so that they've given some thought to the amount of effort they'll need to deploy to make this a success.

That goes for us, too. When we sign up for a client engagement, we try to make sure we have the resources to do it. We never want to be in a situation where we're scrambling to find someone to fill a gap that we didn't see. We don't overextend ourselves. If a project is going to take too many of our folks, we don't take it. We wait until our schedule frees us before we take it.

You asked that question about both sides of the equation – those are some things I wish clients would give thought to in advance. I think from our side, we should put effort into understanding as much as possible – and this is hard to do – the work style within a client environment.

PART 2

Analysing Requirements

At this stage, you've got the green light and are ready to go forward with the project! User and market research, content governance and usability testing all lie ahead of you and your team. In this section, I'll talk about conducting interviews, creating personas, presenting research, doing content inventories and designing for usability. Planning the integration process and estimating key values in your project are also critical skills in this phase of project management.

User research

Content strategy

Usability

Integration specification

Interview: *Andy Budd*

6 User research

> *"It's really hard to design products by focus groups. A lot of times, people don't know what they want until you show it to them."*
> **– Steve Jobs**[1]

What's here: How to ask the right questions of the right people; techniques for qualitative research; some more interview techniques; presenting your findings.

We're not in academe any more. We're solving a specific problem

Research sometimes gets a bad name. The research that most of us remember was conducted at the last minute for a project at high school or university. But research is vital to any venture. It can be divided into two categories: pure and applied research. Pure research is about developing new facts and new connections in a particular field, with the goal of advancing that field as a whole. There are lots of good things that come from pure research. But when it's time to do research for a web project, pure research data will be one of your inputs, not your outputs.

The research stage of a web project falls under the category of applied research. It's about discovering who the users of your website are going to be and what needs they have. User research in the web context is similar to market research in any other field. It's about customers, needs and preferences. It's not about developing new knowledge or summarising what's already been discovered.

User research is fun, exciting and doesn't need to cost huge amounts of money. It uses skills already present in your team and can be done in your own office or studio. Best of all, good user research can save you oodles of time and money later in the project, and help to focus all of your conversations with project stakeholders.

---

[1] Quoted in Businessweek, 25 May 1998.

Personas

Personas are tools for honing in on the specific market segments
for your site. You will need to create three to six individual
personas through a brainstorming session. Each one should be
represented by a short description that includes a fictional name,
age, occupation, goals, attitudes and desires. These composite
characters, representations of real users, help you to check how
well the site fits its users' requirements. As you compare the needs
and journeys of your personas with the site, take into account
people's inherent biases, such as: reading longer lines of text (100+
characters) quickly, but preferring shorter lines (45–70 characters);
or only being able to keep track of three or four things at a time,
but desiring more than four options when given a choice[2].

Aims and objectives

Creating personas can be fun and enlightening, but don't forget
your goals. Before beginning the user research process, write down
clear objectives. Think about these questions:

- What facts do you want to know that you don't know already?
- What are the three most important questions you would like
  to answer?
- How do you envisage the user research information being used for
  the project?
- What specific problems do you anticipate, based on your
  site reviews?

Qualitative market research

User research isn't going to give you a lot of numbers. Research
in a web context is qualitative – learning things about your users,
how they think and how they behave. It's about getting inside your
users' heads.

---

[2] *100 Things Every Designer Needs to Know About People* by Susan Weinschenk (2011, New Riders); further
reading: *The Inmates Are Running the Asylum* by Alan Cooper (2004, SAMS Pearson Education)

How people behave day to day

Project managers aren't always the ones doing research, of course. But it will often be up to someone in a management role to figure out two important things:

1. How much research is needed.
2. What the research needs to accomplish.

When answering the first question, none is a bad answer, even for the smallest of projects. If you only have time to look at a few competitive websites or talk to a single user, it will be time well spent.

The answer to the second question – what the research should accomplish – is pretty simple, as it happens. User research is aimed at discovering the latent needs and habitual behaviours of the target groups who will use your new website. There are all sorts of other things that you can try to learn. Once you get into a research project the temptation will be to look at too many other subjects. But if you're trying to get the maximum value from your research investment, you'll want to keep the research questions nice and tight.

Use interviews, surveys, questionnaires, books and websites

Your team has many tools available to help you do your research, and almost anyone can do the work. You need someone who is empathetic, able to talk to and understand people. You'll want someone who is a good communicator and can do a decent job of putting together results. You might hire dedicated user experience professionals, of course, but you can also use designers, developers, support people, business development or account managers. Anyone with good people skills will probably get you some solid information.

Throughout the research process, remember to stay focused on your users' needs and return often to the research questions that you want to answer. You have several research techniques and technologies available to you just at your desk.

You can look at the websites of competitors. It's tempting to use competitive websites to make guesses about users, features and needed content – but this is a bit dangerous! Do you really think that your competitors have understood and solved all of their users' problems, and solved them better than you can? If you really believe that, you probably don't have a great business case for your own website. But what you can learn from competitors' sites is quite valuable: you can learn how your competitors see themselves. Are their websites clinical, friendly, professional, humorous, irreverent, authoritative? Knowing how your competitor is planning to compete in the market can help you a great deal when formulating your own answer.

You can conduct web surveys easily. Putting up a survey form, perhaps on the existing website, can be a good way of getting opinions and ideas from your existing users. Think about sending an email to existing customers that invites them to fill out an online form. Lots of people are happy to help. If you can find a small incentive for the survey, your response rate will go way up.

You can look at other published research. Books, websites and market surveys might already have information that you'd like to know about the shape of an industry, people's activities and the technologies or platforms that are popular in your target demographics. Don't waste your budget reinventing the wheel. Buying a good research report or a helpful book may save you many hours of staff time and give you a lot of information.

Output will be personas, not a research report (usually)
The output of your research stage probably won't be a report. There certainly are some projects for which having the research all pulled together in writing is helpful. On larger or more speculative projects you might have the budget to create a report. But for most, the output of your research stage will be fed into the next steps in the process and will be actively used by other people on your team.

You might produce:

- **Persona sketches**
  These little documents, usually less than a page, give a quick pen sketch of an imagined user of your website. Mostly it's helpful to come up with a picture, a name, and objectives and attitudes. These should reflect what you learned from the real people you interviewed.

- **2×2s**
  Simple graphs that map two axes against each other let you summarise a lot of information really easily. How about a graph of the tone of your competitors, arranged on a 2×2 with *friendly* to *cold* on one axis, and *deep* to *shallow* on another? This can give you a good sense of where the new website should be.

- **Value statements**
  Your research can create simple value statements that are useful during later phases of your project. For example, suppose that your research shows that people are frustrated by the process of signing up for your client's service. One of your design principles might be that no sign-up screen should contain more than one hundred words of introductory text, and each step in the sign-up process should take thirty seconds or less to accomplish.

- **Models**
  User research can give you an idea of how your users think, so you could put that insight into a visual form for the rest of the project team to share. Is there a conceptual model that shows a process or structure from the point of view of your users? Such a model can be a great help in everything from visual design to the labelling of form fields.

How to research

While surveys, questionnaires, books and websites can all be parts of your project research, you should think about putting the largest part of your time and money into an old-fashioned technique: asking people what they think, one-on-one. Straightforward structured interviews with potential customers, collaborators or competitors, ideally in person, will always be one of the best ways to figure out what's going on. Just a few interviews can give you insights that you wouldn't find in hundreds of responses to online surveys and questionnaires.

Most of this chapter will talk about:

• How to make sure that you're getting good value from time spent on interviews.
• How to present the results back to the people who need them.

Interview techniques

A lot of interviews look like one of these:

• A questionnaire interview, in which a researcher asks a fixed list of questions from a sheet of paper and makes notes of the results.
• A free-flowing interview, in which the interviewer starts with some general questions and then lets the conversation head out in any convenient direction, recording the conversation for later analysis.

Both types of interview yield insight – and it can be hard to see if there's anything terribly wrong with either of these styles for your research. But when the time comes to put your results together after the interview, you'll start to see some big problems.

The questionnaire interview will give you some specific answers, but may miss whole areas that could be tremendously valuable. You might learn everything about how your user uses the current website, but not see a new potential way of providing customer service that could save lots of time and money for the client.

Free-flowing conversations also yield value, but are very hard to compare with each other. You're certainly learning more about the interviewee, but without more structure you'll have a hard time developing your research into results or principles that you can apply to your project.

The trick lies in the semi-structured interview. You should know in advance what your goals are, and there should be a few things that you plan to ask in a consistent way. For other areas, you'll want to have a branching structure in mind, so that you can ask follow-up questions, going into more depth about each of the interesting things that you hear. When recorded, transcribed and analysed, the semi-structured interview can give you a wonderfully human sense of the latent needs of your users, while still giving you enough specifics to compare and contrast in your analysis.

Establishing questions

People are a bit uncomfortable being interviewed. This is natural – most of us are afraid that we'll say the wrong thing, or somehow fail the interview. Politicians and actors are used to this, and they practise enough that they become pretty good at being relaxed and natural in an interview. Most people don't get this kind of practice, so you'll want to make sure that you do everything you can to keep them at their ease.

A good way to start is with simple establishing questions. Ask the following, even if you already know the answers:

- What's your name?
- How old are you?
- Where do you work?
- How long have you done it?
- How did you get into that?

Even taking three minutes to get these easy questions answered will make your interview subject a little more at ease and a little more confident when you start asking questions that require judgement or self-analysis. And a bonus – you'll be gathering some great datapoints to use in your personas later on. Knowing more about where people are coming from will also help you frame some of your questions and give you a chance to find a rapport with your subject through common backgrounds.

Basic market research questions

Once your interview has reached a comfortable pace (thanks to your establishing questions), start asking the basic market research questions. What is the interviewee's general opinion of the client and their services? Be careful not to ask leading questions! Your mentions of the client and their website (new or existing) should be neutral.

Enumerate tasks and activities

The main question here is:

Tell me about your day

If you're asking about a product or service that will be used mostly by people in the context of their professional lives, ask about their work day, not just about your new product or your competitors. Try to get a sense of what they're responsible for, how the big units of their day break down. If it's a product aimed at the home user, ask about their personal life instead. Remember that it's OK to ask personal questions that would ordinarily seem awkward – you're acting as a researcher, and you've already given your assurance that their answers will be kept confidential. Most people will open up if you look interested, sound sympathetic and give them a chance to speak.

Dive into high and low points of each day

Follow-up questions are good, and help to get the detailed information out in the open. Interview subjects are sometimes too polite to come right out and talk about how their daily tasks and tools work or don't work – probe for the real answers and try to figure out how your subject feels about each task as it is accomplished. Frustrated? Happy? Bored? In control? Confused?

Stressed? At ease? These emotional states can give you the clues you need about how a process could be improved, or a place where a new online tool might help or simply distract.

General questions: ask about industry leaders; good and bad online experiences

Research is really the chance to develop your sense of the industry, not just the specifics that your client thinks about. Take the chance near the end of the interview to ask about competitors, when the subject is already thinking clearly about the topic and imagining how new information sources might help them. Ask about the subject's experience of your client's brand. Ask about what comes to mind when they think about leaders in the industry. Ask general questions about what websites they consider to be easy or hard to use, useful or useless. This last might seem irrelevant, but can actually help you a lot in figuring out how the persona represented by this user thinks about the web. Once you know who's the category leader and what websites seem easy to use, you'll be a long way toward framing the design problem for your client in a way that can be more easily solved.

What you need to do

You won't get a chance to do this research twice – so make the most of it!

As a project manager, you might be taking notes on some or all of the interviews. Get a sense of how by rote or free the direction of each interview is, and don't be afraid to suggest changes for the next one. Also, be sure to maintain the correct consent forms (permission to record and a confidentiality agreement). These should be stored with your interview records and carefully honoured, of course.

Recordings and transcripts

Keeping transcripts of your interviews will help. While it may seem like a bit of a hassle, being able to quickly search through your records later on will help to resolve disputes. Since most web teams don't have a lot of specific user research talent available, as a project manager you may find that this task falls to you, as the de facto business analyst. Not to worry, it's not so bad.

First thing is to get a decent recording. I tend to use an application on the phone or tablet where I'm taking notes. AudioNote[3] for iOS (iPhone and iPad) is quite a good application, and will let you add timestamped notes of the interview so that you can enter keywords as you go. Test the recording in the room where you'll be conducting the interview or discussion, and don't be afraid to move your recording device closer to the person you're talking to.

Once you have the audio file, you can either type it up yourself or send it to a transcription service. I usually outsource this step – there are some excellent transcribers available on very little notice via oDesk, eLance and other online job-finding platforms.

Run through the transcript when you get it back to make sure that you have all of the major keywords. Of course, it tends to be the proper names (people, product names) and technical terms that don't make it across quite as well, so fix these in your copy.

Keep the transcript file where the team has access to it – on your local file server, in a cloud service like Dropbox, or wherever is convenient for the team. Sometimes you may need to go back to the recording or the transcript to check what was said. If the files are recorded in an unusual audio format (.caf files, for example, are more easily read on Mac OS X systems than on Windows), you might want to save them as more standard .mp3 or .wav files first.

Don't forget to estimate and include not only your direct costs in hiring a transcriber, but also the time that you'll spend in managing the process and correcting the transcripts. Depending on the contract, this might be something that you can bill

---

[3] *http://luminantsoftware.com/iphone/audionote.html*

separately (as an expense), but if so, make sure that this is spelled out clearly at the beginning.

Don't over-record. If you only need four half-hour interviews to get the information you need, there's no need to schedule six hour-long sessions. In most cases, thirty minutes of focused questions will be enough to develop the key information that you need.

How to ask without asking

Of course, you sometimes need to think a little past the surface of your questions to get the substantive answers that you need. Think about the following issues.

Frame the conversation
Giving some background about what you're trying to learn will help interview subjects answer you better. After all, people generally want to please interviewers if they can – it's part of our social wiring.

Ask about competitors
Don't be afraid to ask about particular brands that you know about or have learned about. Knowing what other people are doing well and what needs work will help you find a competitive position for your new website.

Assign specific tasks to your user testers
When you're testing something specific, like a set of wireframes or mock-ups or prototype screens, break down your test cases into really small pieces and write down the subtasks sequentially. You'll be surprised how much information you get from apparently trivial and short-duration assignments.

Record a narration of your users' thoughts
Either in person or online, when you ask a user representative to do something, also ask them to keep up a continual commentary

about what they're thinking as they go. If they drift away from doing this, prod them with a gentle, "So, what are you looking for now?" or "What did you expect to see here?" Record these one-sided narratives for later analysis – this can be a great way to back up your findings when you present user research to the business stakeholders.

Notice bias, your own and your subject's

We all come with a wide array of cognitive biases. This isn't anything to be ashamed of, but the more you can learn about your own and your users' preconceived notions and irrational behaviours, the easier it will be to arrive at sound conclusions.

Form open-ended questions to produce informative answers

You know this already: yes/no questions yield yes/no responses, which probably won't help you much unless you're just after a numerical survey analysis. Try to find feelings, emotions, descriptions – this will be the core of the user research that you perform.

Funnel questions from broad to specific

People are happy to talk about what they do and what they care about, but we often can't remember the details when pressed. If you start with the longer tasks and the more general strategies, you can work quite naturally down to the more specific.

End with individual follow-up

Be sure to send your interview subject a short note thanking them again for their time. Give your contact information – users don't often get back in touch spontaneously, but when they do it's because they have something important to say. If you establish a good connection at the interview, you should think about including the user later on in the project to check your results, or to run through your next design with you, or to give you a gut-check analysis of some parts of your nearly finished product. The users who have seen the earlier version will be happy to help.

Talking about personas

Personas are fabricated profiles of people who represent your target audiences or markets. Lots of design firms like to frame work in terms of these composite character sketches. The research is mixed as to whether personas are helpful at all. However, while it may be difficult to measure the exact effects, I find that using concrete personas can help to focus the conversation and to help your client stakeholders to empathise more directly with their audiences. Because they feel like a useful thing to do it's tempting to go overboard with your imagination about these representative people. But, if you stick to the parts that are relevant, personas can help to focus your design and help validate all the other business assumptions that you will have to make about the project.

Questions of detail
Some model personas include everything about the character – their hobbies, lifestyle, clothing and television preferences. While it does no particular harm to think about these sorts of details, they may not help you much when it comes to design. How would you make a web form different for a soap opera fan rather than a regular news watcher? Just because the typical user expresses a preference for soap operas doesn't mean that they want their websites to match the storylines of their favourite television dramas! However, knowing that one persona has a PC in their kitchen which they consult while cooking might be extremely relevant for the cooking site that you're developing.

Aims and objectives
It's quite possible that you find the only thing that's relevant to your persona analysis is that your users want to accomplish a particular task on your new website – there may be nothing about their age, gender, web experience or location that in any way creates different expectations or behaviours. That's OK – and perhaps even expected as the web becomes a more and more

standard tool for entertainment and learning, and as conventions of web behaviour and design become more entrenched.

In this case, you should probably focus instead on the job being accomplished. As one analysis asks, "What is the job that your website is being hired for?" Though it seems strange to ask the question in quite this way, it can be a more useful question than simply, "Who is using your website, and what else is going on in their lives?" The first question invites you to think about a very specific content focus in your design. The second invites a more fuzzy analysis of your users' expectations, and may lead to stereotyping.

Even if you reject the idea that your personas really matter, having names and photographs (pick some indicative headshots to represent your imaginary characters – it helps) can actually solidify your design understanding, and just as importantly serves as a really good way to communicate with your client about the user journeys you're discovering together. Those Polaroids taped to monitors may not represent radically different kinds of people, but staring at them can help you do a better job by envisioning the eventual use of your website.

Mapping to content and functionality

A good way to see whether you're at the right level of detail is to try mapping your personas to specific pieces of content that your imaginary users would need to get their tasks done. If they need to call you, can they find your phone number? If they need to replace one of your products, can they look up a product page using a description or model number? If they want to compare a few configurations of your product, can they create a side-by-side matrix, or perhaps save items for later? A mapping like this tells you very quickly about several kinds of things:

- Where you have multiple types of personas with the exact same content and functionality needs, you've probably gone into too much detail on your personas. Think about merging them.

- When you have a need for a kind of content or functionality and haven't yet planned for it in the website, think about whether this gap should be filled. It doesn't have to be – you can say that a need is unimportant, or will be done in a future phase. But it's good to be aware of.
- When you have content or functionality that doesn't seem to match a user need, think about whether the content area is necessary. This tends to be the case with a lot of obvious content like company histories and other about us text. Companies often assume that this content is more relevant than it actually is. In this case, think about removing the content, or looking at whether you've missed some important user needs.

Persona/Content Mapping

	Family vendor	Festival venue	Food supplier	Company sales rep
User needs	LEASE CART	PLAN FOR LOT, SERVICES		UPSELL EQUIPMENT
	LEARN ABOUT LOCAL LAWS	VERIFY EQUIPMENT SAFETY	SUPPLY PREISHABLES	HANDLE SUPPORT REQUESTS
	ESTIMATE REVENUE	EXTEND BRAND	GENERATE REPEAT ORDERS	IDENTIFY MARKETS
Content	PRODUCT CONFIGURATOR	TECHNICAL SPECS	HEAT/CHILL & VOLUME SPECS	PRODUCT COLLATERAL
	CONSUMABLES CALCULATOR	CERTIFICATION LIST	CONSUMABLES CALCULATOR	MAINTENANCE TICKET TRACKER
	LEGAL WIZARD	PHOTOS OF BRANDED CARTS	CUSTOMER DATABASE	CUSTOMER MAPS

Presenting findings

Now that you have gathered, recorded, and organised the results of the user research, it's time to present the findings to the client. There are several options; choose the format that best fits the presentation style and expectations of your client.

Written reports

Written reports are good for detail, but may not be used as much as you expect. While many clients expect you to produce full written results of your research, you may find that this feeds a formal process, rather than a useful one. The written report is also hard to argue with, which is both a strength and a weakness: it gives your ideas weight, but doesn't encourage revision or the development of new ideas.

Presentations

Presentations are more dynamic than written reports, and they give you a chance to control the conversation. By showing your process and building the pieces carefully, a well-crafted presentation can make a more lasting impression on the client. Of course, they may suffer from seeming to be too much on the surface: you might gloss over important ideas, and your slides or visual aids will certainly not give all of the context that you have uncovered.

Photo by the author, courtesy of Jamie Neely/Design by Front

Workshops

Workshops are the least formal way of presenting your findings, and are most likely to develop new information for you, or let you substantially refine your ideas. Doing a good workshop takes quite a bit of preparation, though, and a workshop that falls flat will just seem like a bad presentation with a lot of pauses. Presenting ideas using a workshop format means that you should do the usual opening, elaborating and closing structure that you would use for any workshop – and build in lots of ways for your client stakeholders to correct or elaborate upon your ideas.

TOOLS FROM THIS CHAPTER

• User research report
• Persona sheet
• Interview recordings and transcripts

FURTHER READING

For questions of developing and presenting design, it's hard to do better than *Communicating Design* by Dan Brown (2010, New Riders). He goes into all sorts of very specific ways to present your research findings, structuring his book in a graduated complexity so that you can start with the basics and get more sophisticated as you become comfortable.

CONTENT STRATEGY

"Simple design, intense content."
– Edward Tufte[1]

What's here: Starting on content strategy; creating inventories; finding gaps and defining a workflow; then recovering from the inevitable content delays.

Content isn't a part of the new site – content is the new site
Even before the research winds up, you need to spend some serious time thinking about the content of the new site. Content is often left to the end – after all, it's the client who's expected to know about their organisation. Even with good research, web agencies generally don't have the budget to rewrite every page. And of course, content management systems are now the norm, so it's no longer necessary that content be semantically marked up and dropped in by web developers themselves. (Of course, many enterprise-level content management systems still allow all kinds of non-semantic markup to be added by department editors, so there's no guarantee that a CMS will save you from the need for good markup.)

Web agencies probably spend most of their time creating templates rather than pages. Templates are the places where content will end up, depending on the value of a field in a database somewhere. Making templates rather than pages is usually a more efficient use of time – templates can accommodate lots of future content without requiring revision, and can potentially withstand a hefty editorial process or even a site restructure without needing a lot of expensive custom work. There's a down side to templating systems, though: it's more and more tempting to leave the content to the end. Bash in some lorem ipsum placeholder text, write some

---

[1] Quoted in "The Feynman-Tufte Principle" by Michael Shermer in Scientific American, 28 March 2005.

fake headlines, drop in some stock photography and call it done. After all, it will be the client's job to upload the finished content at the end of the gig – why worry about something now that will just slow down the process? The budget is already tight, and there are already more requirement wrinkles than anyone thought there would be!

Attractive though it may be, firmly resist the temptation to leave content to the end of the process. Websites and web applications are all about communicating with users, largely through text, but also through imagery, video and other visuals. To design a pretty package without knowing what goes inside won't do justice to the package contents. The content may seem extraneous, but it is the core of what this project will deliver. While the process of managing content may seem difficult, especially on a complicated site, there are essentially only a few key tasks to do, repeat and repeat again:

- An inventory of what's there now, on the website and in the organisation.
- A plan of who will be writing, adapting, developing and uploading content from now on.
- A start to the work cycle.
- A strategy for the organisation to produce and manage its content, using ideas about style and tone as a starting point.

Ready?

Content inventories

Big lists and spreadsheets
Content inventories can seem a bit brainless: make a list of everything on a website. And by everything, I mean everything. For example, a few categories of the things on your list might be:

- a list of pages
- articles on the specific pages
- functions, widgets, boxes and sidebars
- page language versions
- page lengths
- images that illustrate articles
- categories and category navigation tools

For each one of those things you'll need to know, more or less:

- Who was or is responsible for creating the piece of content?
- Are we keeping it for the new website?
- Does the style or formatting match the new site, or does it need to be rewritten?
- On what level is the content in the page hierarchy?
- Is this bit of content shared between multiple pages or widgets?

It can be a bit of a chore. As someone with project management responsibilities, you might get stuck with it. Very few web agencies have content strategists and experts working for them full-time (yet), so this might be someone on the team who usually does business analysis, or design, or development or testing.

It actually doesn't require a lot of specialised skill to do a good content audit, but it does take someone who pays attention to detail.

Your best tool is probably a plain old spreadsheet. While there are some fancy tools out there, a spreadsheet (Excel, Numbers, Lotus 1-2-3 and the rest) will let you:

- Filter your content inventory using the status tags that you've assigned.
- Sort your content by person responsible.
- Sort to let you focus on the longer pages first.

It's rather low-tech, but ultimately a content inventory is just a big list. Oh, and if you know there's a new category of content going up on to the new website, you'd better list that, too!

ID	Page Title	URL	Notes
0	Home	/	
1	Why Leaky Taco?	/why	Global nav
2	Find your Cart	/shop	Global nav
2.1	Festivals	/festival	2nd global nav
2.2	Seasonal	/seasonal	2nd global nav
2.3	Long-term	/longterm	2nd global nav
3	Our Suppliers	/suppliers	Global nav
4	Financing	/finance	Global nav
5	Contact Us	/contact	Utility nav

Content Inventory

How much to sample?

You're probably wondering why anyone would want to go through this exercise at all, especially if the content is in a database and served by a CMS. Here are a few reasons:

- Making a list will give you a better sense of the existing and new websites than mere description.
- You'll figure out whether the client really has a clear idea of what they'll be communicating on their new website.
- The CMS can't tell you much about ownership or development of the content, the source for images, or the workflow behind video clips. You'll need to discover or develop these parts afresh with the new site anyway, so you might as well figure them out with reference to the existing site.

- Asking questions about content will quickly get you in touch with the business people who own each area of the website; if they're not on the project team, you may not have met them yet. If you are going to be waiting for one of these people or business units to provide your content, you'd better figure out which ones are going to be a problem.

That said, you don't need to go overboard with the sampling. If everything is in a database and will be migrated or upgraded in an orderly way, you certainly don't need to complete your inventory. If everything on the site is hand-rolled and will need to be carefully recrafted, you'll need to sample all of it. A good rule of thumb is to investigate the content until you can make accurate, reasonable estimates about how the content will be developed for the new site.

What to keep track of
Your inventory will start with a couple of basic sitemaps and flowcharts, and then rapidly get more complicated. This is when having set up a good spreadsheet will help a lot – you should be able to see how far you've progressed and make a pretty good guess about when the inventory will be complete. If you can't do this yet, you should probably spend a little more time on site structure.

Functional analysis spreadsheet

TITLE	FUNCTION	LOCATION IN PROCESS	TYPE	NOTES
Registration	Prompts user to create a unique user ID and password	First point in account creation process, before profile.	HTML	Records user email, ID and password for account identification
Create profile	Leads the user through the process of filling a profile form	After registration, before billing set-up.	HTML	Fills profile form, with primary and secondary user account information
Set up billing	Tells the user how to set up a billing process	After profile creation, before account activation	HTML	Captures the primary information for recurring billing
Validate email	Check that email address is well-formed	Profile creation	AJAX call, dynamic notification on-page	Follow standard email regex, and check email not associated with another account

A note about clients: lots of clients will tell you to ignore their existing website. They'll say, "No, we're developing a new website, we have a new brand, we don't know how our website got to be such a mess – just start over!" It's not hard to understand why.

More than anyone else, they've seen their website every day, and they're tired of looking at it. Lots of people or business units have had their say in getting content up there, so what's displayed actually is a mess that no longer represents the organisation well. They're embarrassed and plan to do better. Organisational compromises about who gets to say what (or who decides to put what on the homepage) have been fought for years, and embody all the toughest aspects of gang warfare and fire-walking. They don't want to relive it.

Don't let them. Making an inventory of the existing site, even a cursory one, will get you some good information.

You'll learn about the bits of content and functionality that no one wanted to think about when they were writing the brief or talking to you about requirements. But those bits are up there for some reason, and chances are that the reason is still relevant. Ignore it now and it will come back to bite you later on.

If the client really does have trouble organising, writing, compiling and curating their content, you must find that out now. Perhaps some more training or outside assistance would be in order, to keep the new site from suffering from the same disease. And there's no feeling worse than the disappointment that comes after pouring months of your life into a brilliant website which is promptly taken over by dull, colourless, overwrought and inappropriate content the moment your back is turned.

Gap analysis

Check content inventory against personas
The next bit can be kind of fun, because this is where you get to figure out what else needs to be on the website. Content in its many forms is the lifeblood of a website.

Here's how it should go.

- Play the role of each of your lovingly developed personas in turn. For each persona, you should already have a list of primary aims and objectives. List these in columns, one column per persona.
- Draw a horizontal line and below it start to list the areas of content that will support that task, aim or objective.
- You'll find that there are columns with plenty of substantiating content – perhaps even too much.
- There will be areas where the content inventory shows gaps – there just isn't anything to support that task or objective. Mark those gaps with a big X.
- When there's some content that partially meets the need but leaves out something important, make a note of that, too. You'll need to contact the content owners about getting that bit adapted or extended.

For an example of this technique, look back at the persona/content map on page 95. The chart visualises persona needs above the line, and content and functionality below the line to allow gap analysis.

Now you have a lovely bit of information design showing the fit between the site content and the needs of your key users. Aren't you glad you got through the site inventory?

Present back as soon as possible

Once you know where the gaps are, you'll need to plan some time to present and discuss what's happening. The thing about content gaps is that you and the client will both have to spend some time in this area, and it's unlikely that the time has already been budgeted on either side.

One good way to plug the content gaps might be to match personas to needs and content. That can clarify where there's work to be done.

Content development is hard. Yes, there are lots of people who write words for a living, and there are lots of photographers and videographers and photo editors. But creating content for a specific purpose, to tell a story and to represent an organisation or service or idea clearly, without being overbearing or overdone? That takes time. Be very wary of the content estimates that you get from your clients. Most people truly don't know how long it will take to write a good headline or paragraph.

If you're working on a site that relies heavily on content from another source, there are other things to also be aware of. Content pulled in from non-professional sources (such as social media or website user contributions) might well require moderation of some kind. Content brought in from other databases may not be structured in the way you expect, or may simply be off-brand for the website you're creating. There may be translation to do. And, if nothing else, you still have interface copy to worry about – all of the instructions, buttons, navigation, calls to action, about text, even terms and conditions. All will need to be developed, written, scrutinised, edited, posted, and checked periodically for freshness.

You need to get this process going as soon as possible. Towards the end of the project will be far too late.

Don't be afraid to revise estimates

If you find that there's a significant problem around content, don't just barrel through with your original estimates. Step back and re-evaluate.

This isn't a bad or terrible thing. The website builders and the website owners both want the site to be a success. You both want users to be impressed. You both want to write great case studies about the project. If it's worth redesigning a website (or making a new one), it's worth spending time on the development of the content that you need.

Remember that copy is the interface. Show the client what a website looks like without copy. Try a news website, and then something less obviously content-heavy. See how fast the brand values disappear when there's no longer a tone of voice, when there are no longer photographs that evoke a mood or emotion.

If you have to re-evaluate, jump right into it. You might need to get some high-level people involved on the client side – anything affecting time or budget should go right up the chain. But you can find a schedule that works, and a way of evaluating it. Maybe offer your services for a morning a week for a few weeks to evaluate how the client is progressing with the content adaptation. Maybe find a third party to handle the copywriting and strategy. Maybe find a photography firm you're confident will do a good job on the needed imagery.

One way or another, there's no point in waiting until later in the project. Without content, and the right content, you simply don't have a website.

Content governance

Content governance involves making sure that content on your client's website starts out appropriate and compelling, and stays that way. It's a harder job than you might think. As the website builders, you'll probably be asked content governance questions, even if your contract is explicit that all content is the responsibility of the client. It's better to go ahead and plan on developing and delivering a content governance strategy. This might just be a couple of conversations and then a workshop, but it's best to get this planned and budgeted early in the project, before the lack of content starts causing any problems for the delivery team.

As an aside: I'm assuming that you don't have a full-time content strategist on board for the project – most web shops don't. But content is more and more important, and if you don't look at these governance tasks as part of your project plan, no one will. And that just leads to bad websites.

Chain of command

If the website owner already has a great process in place for making website updates, you have a good start. You'll need to make sure that you have filled the following roles.

Editor-in-chief

Someone ultimately responsible for the content of the website. Other people and departments can certainly have responsibilities for their areas, but one person must be assigned overall responsibility for what goes up.

Writers

People to develop the textual content for each page. This might be a trivial task or a complex one, depending on the organisation, but whether you're adapting a product catalogue or writing company blog posts, there must be people assigned and time set aside.

Video and photo editors

If you have a site that requires original audiovisual media and images, you'll need to have people in place to handle this. It's pretty common to hear organisations talking about making corporate videos, training manuals, podcast interviews with the CEO, all without thinking at all about who will produce, edit and transcode the files for the website. Video, especially, can be a very engaging platform, but be wary of an organisation trying to make good videos for the first time without outside help.

Setting a production schedule

The most obvious part of a content governance platform is the
schedule. Each piece of content identified in the audit, along with
those pieces named in the gap analysis, will need to be assigned
and scheduled for the initial site release. You'll also need to
determine the cycle of updates and additions to what you start off
with – someone needs to write those blog posts.

It helps to take the general approach of the publishing industry.

- An editor assigns a content task, along with a deadline.
- The writer or curator writes and collates what's needed and sends
  back a draft by the deadline.
- The editor does whatever prodding is necessary to meet the
  deadline, but can renegotiate due dates if necessary.
- Drafts with the editor's comments are returned to the writer, who
  makes any revisions.
- The editor looks over the second draft and either uploads the
  content or forwards it on to the person who will.
- On a regular schedule, an editor reviews the content for accuracy
  and freshness, and a new set of assignments is made.
- Every now and then (every month or two, perhaps), editors report
  to the manager with responsibility for the website, indicating how
  deadlines are being met, what content is out of date and flagging
  up any snags in the process or extra resources needed.

This shouldn't be too much overhead, but bear in mind that people
who are assigned to develop content for most organisations
have other jobs that don't involve writing or editing. Their line
managers need to take into account the time that working on the
website will entail, and build that into the department workloads.

Building in a workflow (using a CMS)

Most good content management systems have some important tools to help you manage your content, and you should keep these capabilities in mind when you're working on the content governance plan.

- You might consider setting expiration dates for content; that is, dates on which content will cease to be relevant and be automatically removed from the site.
- Similarly, you could queue up content in advance, to appear on the website on a regular basis after being edited in a batch, for example.
- You can create workflows such that a writer can start an article but mark it as in progress, then an editor can review before the content item is published to the site. Sometimes two or more people might review content before publication.
- You can take advantage of automatic resizing, transcoding and embedding of video, audio and images as part of the content publication process.
- In many CMS tools you can integrate content into various marketing campaigns, based on email or social media for example. Some CMSes will give you a good set of tools for both publishing such campaigns and for measuring the results.

Thinking about all of these things will give you a head start on the content process. Many of the tasks in setting up content governance systems aren't exclusively within the purview of content strategy experts; most of content governance is a combination of people and task management, and marketing expertise. If you find yourself doing much of the work, that's fine, but be sure to include your time as a schedule and budget item.

Figuring out how content is going to be published, withdrawn and distributed or syndicated on a new website isn't just a project management overhead activity – it's something to be planned and assigned. Once you do, though, you and the client will be glad you did, and your new site will have a much greater chance of success.

Managing the content process

You've completed the content strategy, but now comes the actual process of managing what's really at the core of the site – words and images. Of course, it would be pretty rare to completely understand all of the possibilities of your content before you start writing or adapting, so leave some time in the schedule for another round of content strategy revisions once the writing, adapting and sourcing of content begins in earnest.

I hope that you have a chance to work with one of the up-and-coming professionals who think about content strategy and development full-time but, especially with a smaller agency or client, you might do content-related tasks with someone who spends some of their day doing something else. This isn't necessarily a bad thing – subject matter experts and line professionals in most businesses can do a great job of writing and sourcing material for you. You might even do some of this job yourself as a project manager, though if you do, don't forget to include your own time estimates in the project budget!

Whether you're working with seasoned professionals, part-time draftees or writing neophytes, it's handy to have an idea of some of the project risks that you'll face in the content development process, and what you can do about them. So, here are some of the common ones, and what you can do about them.

Promises

Everyone over-promises on content. With the best of intentions, people tend to overestimate their velocity in writing and adapting content for the new website.

This can be frustrating. Knowing that this is likely to be a sticking point for the project, you'll want to set deadlines that allow some time for slippage. You should also get to the content development really early in the project – the first couple of weeks isn't too early. If you and the people writing content both discover that pages are taking longer than expected, you should still have time to adjust schedules.

If you think that you'll need to do some convincing in order to get the client-side content resources lined up, be sure that you put this into the contract as a hard deadline, and that as a consequence any lateness on the client's part will incur daily change fees until the target is met. This can seem pretty harsh, but is, in fact, fair: if lack of content delays the visual design, testing or deployment of the new website, your team will be kept from meeting important delivery deadlines.

Content risks

Content presents several risks to your site design process. They need not be fatal, and can be turned into strengthening exercises. First of all, consider this question: can you design or develop at all without content?

The first content risk is that there isn't any content. The second content risk is the consequences of the mindset that believes there's no such thing as too much content. Content may take over the site structure in a blizzard of words, menus and image galleries.

Multimedia production is especially dangerous. It is easy to underestimate, requires a lot of people to execute, and often the necessary skills aren't in-house (unlike basic text development and editing).

We're still waiting

When the content stalls (and it will), what do we do with the rest of the project?

If there's one thing that can be said consistently about website content, it's that it will probably be late. Even when you're rewriting an existing website (which is the norm these days), most of the time you'll be left without content at the time you expect to have it.

The reasons are many and mostly boil down to the following:

- Text needs to be written with someone intimately familiar with the products and services offered by the client. If it isn't the primary job of this person, website-writing tasks will tend to be pushed to the end.
- The people writing your content aren't used to creating text for lots of people to read. This can lead to a kind of stage fright and paralysis, with version after version being tried and then abandoned as the writing is polished and polished again.
- Writing is assigned to a committee. While groups of people can get a lot done in focused problem-solving sessions, writing text usually requires a consistency and voice that can't easily be tackled by groups. Shared responsibility in this case can easily lead to no responsibility. This also accounts for a lack of deadline-sensitivity for content: with no single person responsible, no one feels a strong sense of urgency.

	Pros	Cons
Option 1: Press on!	Stay on schedule Develop ideas in other areas	Push content aside Create a division between design and content
Option 2: Stall	Keep to the project sequence	Lose time Lose momentum
Option 3: Cancel	Save future money/time	Lose money/time already spent

TOOLS FROM THIS CHAPTER

• Content strategy
• Content inventory
• Content gap analysis
• Content governance plan and production schedule

FURTHER READING

Fortunately, content strategy is becoming a much more accepted and well-documented discipline by the day, and there are some excellent books, blogs and other resources. The increased professionalisation of content strategy means that this area is less likely to be neglected, and also means that web groups are more likely to have some of these skills available in-house. However, it can still be a bit of a chore to explain to a client (especially one not already in a traditional publishing industry) exactly what it is that you're proposing to do during this phase of work.

You'll find the following books quite helpful making this case – and interesting reads, besides.

There are two books on content strategy with which everyone should become familiar. One is *Content Strategy for the Web* (2nd edition, 2012, New Riders), by Kristina Halvorson and Melissa Rach. You can read more about the book at *http://contentstrategy.com* or read their blog at *http://blog.braintraffic.com*.

The other essential book is *The Elements of Content Strategy* by Erin Kissane (2011, A Book Apart). Erin writes at Incisive.nu and her articles for A List Apart are well worth reading (*http://www.alistapart.com/authors/k/erinkissane*).

Usability and accessibility

> *"Beauty and brains, pleasure and usability – they should go hand in hand."*
>
> **– Donald Norman**[1]

What's here: Making usable websites (including some myths); understanding accessibility standards; and presenting your findings.

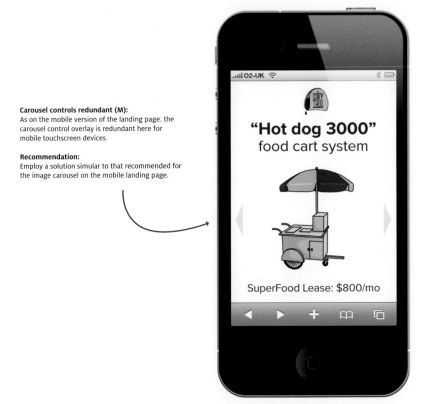

Carousel controls redundant (M):
As on the mobile version of the landing page, the carousel control overlay is redundant here for mobile touchscreen devices

Recommendation:
Employ a solution simular to that recommended for the image carousel on the mobile landing page.

[1] "Emotional Design", ACM Ubiquity, January 2004.

When we think of examples of usability failures, we think about hasty assumptions exposed by everyday wear and tear. Usability needs to be planned out. If you've waited until the wireframing portion of your project lifecycle to start thinking about usability, you've waited far too long. Don't jeopardise your client's web success and their website's user experience quality by pushing usability to the side.

Why usability?

Most websites have usability problems. Most of those problems keep people from coming back. Yet such problems can be easily avoided by implementing usability assessment in all projects. If the goal of your site is to help people form a relationship with an organisation, product or service, then meeting their expectations is the first step.

Making usable sites

One aspect of usability is about reducing the number of choices in a project – refining a design. No design is created perfectly the first time. But the second time will be better, and improvements will continue as long as you are willing to make the necessary effort. Also, if usability is included in your project success metrics, it's easier to justify. Sometimes, though, you will have to dispel a few myths before getting down to your usability work.

Usability myths

Every occupation has its myths. The scariest stories are the ones that feel like they have a grain of truth. If you work in an agency, understanding a few of the myths that have grown up will help you set your clients' expectations. Perhaps you can even defuse negative feedback before it makes life hard for your people. As a client, it's best to be aware of some of the current thinking – after all, you want your website to be as effective as possible, so there's no point in clinging to outdated beliefs. Listen to each side's concerns and take note of any expressed fears or reactions given without specific reasons. Stay current with research in your area, so that you can be informed and effective.

Above the fold: a myth about how people read on the web
Assuming that all of your important content needs to be above the fold ignores the fact that users are perfectly used to scrolling. Entice, by all means, but there's no need to cram everything into the top 600 pixels.

Two views of reading. The first assumes that the focus of the page needs to be at the top. The second, more realistic view assumes that a page can build to a conclusion. Image adapted from Paddy Donnelly at *http://iampaddy.com/lifebelow600/*

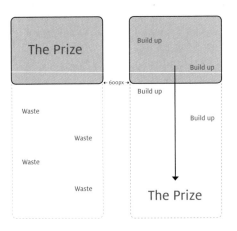

Understanding accessibility standards

There are a number of accessibility guidelines out there – what do they really mean for your project? Most derive from the W3C WCAG guidelines, so I'll give a bit of detail about those. Despite the popular conception that these guidelines are incredibly difficult to meet, most of the accessibility principles, guidelines and techniques not only are applicable to every web project, but also articulate straightforward rules of thumb for any designed interaction.

Web Content Accessibility Guidelines

The Web Content Accessibility Guidelines (WCAG, currently at version 2.0[2]) were created by a group within the W3C (World Wide Web Consortium), and are a standard reference for accessibility and usability[3]. Quoting from the documentation[4]:

> "The guidelines and Success Criteria are organized around the following four principles, which lay the foundation necessary for anyone to access and use Web content. Anyone who wants to use the Web must have content that is:

1. **Perceivable** – Information and user interface components must be presentable to users in ways they can perceive.

   > This means that users must be able to perceive the information being presented (it can't be invisible to all of their senses)

2. **Operable** – User interface components and navigation must be operable.

   > This means that users must be able to operate the interface (the interface cannot require interaction that a user cannot perform)

3. **Understandable** – Information and the operation of user interface must be understandable.

   > This means that users must be able to understand the information as well as the operation of the user interface (the content or operation cannot be beyond their understanding)

---

[2] http://www.w3.org/TR/WCAG20/

[3] http://www.w3.org/WAI/WCAG20/quickref/

[4] http://www.w3.org/TR/UNDERSTANDING-WCAG20/intro.html

4. **Robust** – Content must be robust enough that it can be interpreted reliably by a wide variety of user agents, including assistive technologies.

This means that users must be able to access the content as technologies advance (as technologies and user agents evolve, the content should remain accessible)

If any of these are not true, users with disabilities will not be able to use the Web."

These guidelines do not create a rigid system of dos and don'ts, which is why there isn't any way to automate testing for accessibility. But you can perform an automated audit by choosing to look at a few obvious points, such as including alternative text for all images.

For each of the four general principles there are a series of guidelines, adding up to twelve in all. Each guideline has success criteria which can be tested. The success criteria come in three flavours: A, AA and AAA, representing increasing levels of compliance. What you might find particularly useful, though, are the "sufficient and advisory techniques" that are provided for each guideline. The sufficient techniques are ways to code webpages so that they just meet the guideline, and the advisory techniques are ways to go even further toward best addressing each guideline issue.

Using WCAG is fairly straightforward on the surface – you take the recommended techniques, apply them, and go on your way toward developing a site that works for all users. Of course, this process can take a bit of work. For example, the guidelines recommend that for all non-live video content you provide audio descriptions of what is occurring, preferably in multiple languages. Conversely, for recorded audio content, the guidelines suggest that you provide video files of sign language interpretation in various dialects. This sort of provision is expensive and gives the impression that complying with accessibility guidelines is hopelessly cumbersome.

However, most of the guidelines are simpler to follow, and often they represent best practice for contemporary web development. For example, much of the craft of web design is about meeting guideline 2.4: Navigable: "Provide ways to help users navigate, find content, and determine where they are."

Keep it cheap and cheerful

While usability is a big field with its own practitioners, it's quite possible that you won't have a dedicated usability person on your team. That's fine. Lots of graphic designers, information architects and user experience designers are quite familiar with usability principles. You'll find the right talent to do meaningful usability work, as long as you are able to focus and structure the usability activities. Doing a good job on a usability analysis project does not necessarily require fancy equipment or massive amounts of time. In most cases, the cheap and cheerful method will get you most of the way there. Here are a few tips for running and presenting usability tests.

Estimate time spent on usability activities for later reference

Usability can give you real results that improve site performance (and revenue) significantly. But it's not free. It's easy for usability (and accessibility) work to take up a lot of your design-phase time. Make sure that you keep good time logs for everyone involved, including travel, set-up time and, especially, time spent on analysis. Make sure that on your next web project you'll be able to estimate and bill for this time accurately.

Write task scripts for usability tests

If you imagine a few of the journeys that users will take through your website, it should be straightforward to come up with a list of tasks and functions that you need to support. The simpler the better. Once you have some tasks in mind, ask several people to take a look at your site and watch how they accomplish the assigned tasks.

Ask some friends to help

You can learn a lot about what's working (or not) with an inexpensive and fast walk-through presented to a few people. It's better if the people giving feedback aren't actually involved in the project, since the "insider" perspective won't represent a typical site user.

Create clear testing comparisons

It's important that you show the expected vs. actual time and complexity levels in your reports. If you expected a task to take 10 seconds and it took 60, you should say so in your presentation.

Use web testing services

UserTesting.com, VerifyApp.com and other similar services can help you get feedback quickly. You can pay to recruit particular kinds of people to perform your tests, or send invitations to people you already know. You'll get the results back in a very easy-to-use format.

User task

Annotations

Playable video

Explore A/B tests

Sometimes the most interesting questions come down to a very simple choice. You might find that there's a preponderance of preference for one option.

A/B testing going past the design phase

Once the site is live, you can continue to measure the return rate of each of your choices.

Show your findings against a range

Numbers don't mean much in isolation: always give context for your statistics. For example, talk about number of seconds spent on a task and your expected time, but be sure to also show the minimum and maximum times from your group of users.

Present user testing videos and screencasts

If you're able to collect them, these audiovisual results are are the most effective ways to convey points to stakeholders who were not present at the tests, while maintaining group objectivity.

With some relatively inexpensive testing and analysis, you can learn most of what you need to know in order to make your website easy to use. Go in without too many preconceptions and with a sense of humility, and your design will improve a great deal.

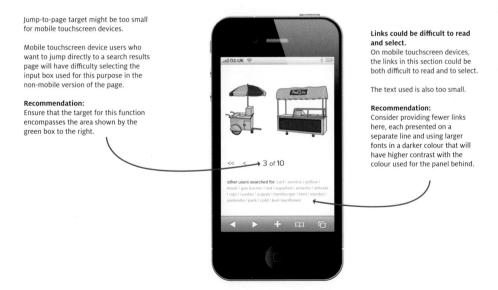

Jump-to-page target might be too small for mobile touchscreen devices.

Mobile touchscreen device users who want to jump directly to a search results page will have difficulty selecting the input box used for this purpose in the non-mobile version of the page.

Recommendation:
Ensure that the target for this function encompasses the area shown by the green box to the right.

Links could be difficult to read and select.
On mobile touchscreen devices, the links in this section could be both difficult to read and to select.

The text used is also too small.

Recommendation:
Consider providing fewer links here, each presented on a separate line and using larger fonts in a darker colour that will have higher contrast with the colour used for the panel behind.

Tools from this Chapter

• Usability test setup
• Usability test report
• Accessibility guidelines

Further reading

When the stakeholder asks for everything above the fold, you'll want to be prepared with some numbers and experts to reference.

Of course, a web usability discussion isn't complete without the opinions of Jacob Nielsen (*http://www.useit.com/*), who has written some of the most influential books on the subject, such as *Designing Web Usability* (2000, Peachpit Press) and *Prioritizing Web Usability* (2006, New Riders), with Hoa Loranger. However, you should probably be aware that plenty of people take issue with some of Nielsen's findings, on everything from font face selection to handling of mobile platforms. Something you will find extremely useful from his research are his quantitative findings; he does a great job of showing how relatively modest increases in system usability can deliver strong financial return on investment. He's also good at demonstrating how to run good usability studies with a minimum of equipment (*http://www. useit.com/alertbox/simple-usability-lab.html*).

As mentioned earlier, what Steve Krug (*http://www.sensible.com/*) writes about usability in his various books not only makes sense, but gives you some precise, practical things that you can do to improve the usability of a website. A bit more down-to-earth than Nielsen, perhaps, but then he doesn't talk about such big projects at extremely large scales (and budgets to match). Krug's *Don't Make Me Think!* (2nd edition, 2005, New Riders) is a standard reference with very accessible, friendly writing.

You should look at the videos and whitepapers from Human Factors International (*http:// www.humanfactors.com/downloads/whitepapers.asp*). This group does some very good research and consulting in the usability area.

You might also take a look at Paddy Donnelly's essay at *http://iampaddy.com/lifebelow600/* – it's a bit of a rant, but I'd be surprised if you didn't end up sending that link to clients from time to time.

9 INTEGRATION SPECIFICATION

*"The architect should strive continually to simplify; the
ensemble of the rooms should then be carefully considered
that comfort and utility may go hand in hand with beauty."*
– Frank Lloyd Wright[1]

What's here: When things must talk to other things, you'll need to do some integration; using patterns, making estimates and matching them to lightweight agile techniques.

This is the part that many web agencies miss. If you're a client or an agency, you need to know some of this, at least enough to ask the right questions.

Integration isn't the easiest thing to get right. While much of the software development industry is well-versed in the nature of data communications, database-backed systems and client-server communication, a lot of web development shops are just now coming to an understanding of how these things work. Web shops have learned about databases because they're used by content management systems. They've learned about web services and XML formats because they're indirectly used by Ajax-style dynamic page behaviours.

But increasingly, meaningful websites need to do a fair bit of old-fashioned software integration, either via web services or using home-grown solutions. If you're feeling a bit lost, not to worry – there are some straightforward things you can do to reduce uncertainty in your integration activities.

[1] "In the Cause of Architecture." Frank Lloyd Wright. Architectural Record. March, 1908. Reprinted in Frank Lloyd Wright, Collected Writings. vol 1. pp 87-88.

Integration patterns

From the discipline of software development

The first things to think about with any integration problem are specifying end points and specifying messages. While there are a number of different integration patterns that you can use, the essentials of what you'll need to figure out will be consistent.

In a web project, you'll be looking at a webpage that takes input from a user, mostly through some kind of form. Information will be collected and sent back to the server, either right away (using JavaScript or Ajax), or after the form is submitted. That information will be checked against another back-end system within the organisation, or a web service which could be inside or outside the organisation. That request will result in some sort of information being sent back, and often some part of the information will be displayed to the site user.

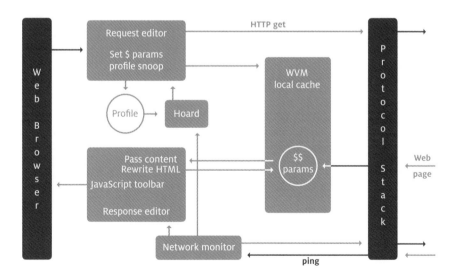

Integration block
diagram for a website

- How will you handle authentication (who is the user?) and authorisation (who can do what?)
- What will the request look like? That is, what information will be collected on the webpage and sent to the server-side component?
- What will come back from the server, and how will this relate to what you actually display to the user?

Software architecture textbooks will contain quite a few patterns that you can use to think about how these integration problems will play out in your system.

Using software design patterns

You might want to start with the so-called Gang of Four – four authors of the book *Design Patterns: Elements of Reusable Object-Oriented Software.* The patterns they outlined have been heavily implemented on a variety of systems. Unified Modeling Language[2] (UML) is a visual diagramming style that you'll see if you dive into software development handbooks. If your team isn't already using

Example of UML sequence diagram

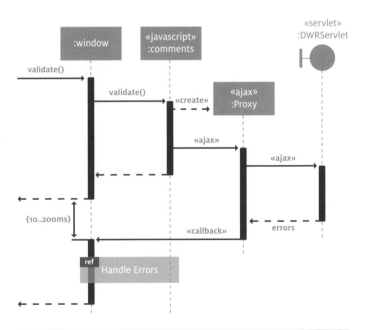

[2] Unified Modeling Language is a trademark and UML is a registered trademark of Object Management Group.

it, you could encourage someone on your team to read up on it – you might find the sequence diagrams (flowcharts) and activity diagrams (swim lanes) to be particularly handy as you work out communications between two systems.

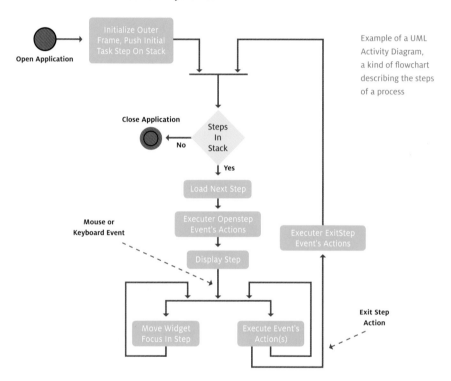

Example of a UML
Activity Diagram,
a kind of flowchart
describing the steps
of a process

Software vendors are quite aware of the interconnected nature of the web, and so most are publishing straightforward application programming interfaces (APIs) that can be used to send and retrieve data. You might find that your back-end system or web service has a well-documented API, or perhaps the mechanics of interoperability are a bit more murky – you'll need to leave some room in the schedule to figure out which kind you're dealing with. If there's a simple API you can use, you might be able to find examples from other projects or from reference implementations created by the software manufacturer.

Synchronous versus asynchronous patterns

It used to be that computers and mainframes were essentially batch system command processors – there was no such thing as immediate communication. Later on, machines got powerful enough that we came to expect data transfer immediately over fast networks. Now that the web has expanded so much in scale, there are more and more services that require some requests to be batched in order to preserve resources for the most important live requests.

The biggest decision your team will have to make will be whether to handle every website event as it happens (synchronous), or allow things to happen over time, and then batching up the communications between server and client (asynchronous). Of course, there are a few ways that this can play out in practice, and the technique you choose will depend on the details of your project.

Synchronous communications are needed when:

- There are security or other important considerations that absolutely must be handled right away.
- The user's input is time-sensitive.
- Your database or other system doesn't support anything except real-time access.

Asynchronous communication might be needed when:

- You're caching or prefetching data that you might need.
- There are operation efficiencies to sending batches of data all at once.

Most importantly, think about an asynchronous mechanism when you're waiting for a response from another system and you can't determine accurately the time it will take. For any long-running query or request that might take a while, you're better off thinking about the problem as an asynchronous query and updating the user once the data comes in.

Making the user wait for a page because you're waiting for a web service to return data isn't a great plan, and your website will get the blame when the service is slow. Better to come back with what you can and update things later on when you can.

Hardcore estimating

For any project, you'll need to spend some time thinking about how you're going to come up with numbers. You need numbers to win the project or to know if it's worth doing; you need numbers when you assign people and resources; you need numbers to know how long to spend on each type of task. Work may expand to fill the time allotted, but allocating the time in the first place, and then allowing the time that you might need to run over is a project management function.

This may seem so obvious that it barely deserves a mention, but if you estimate the resources needed for your tasks accurately, you have a better chance of project success, and the converse is also true. A lot of thought has been put into project estimation over the years – companies, military services and non-profit organisations of all sizes have tried to find the perfect way to estimate work, and thus to improve the chances of the work's success. And while there are now some good models and lots of formulas to apply, the secret is still what it always was: get to the point of least uncertainty, look as far ahead as you can and at whatever historical data is available, and then guess. For good or for ill, your guess will determine not only whether the project will get done, but what the quality of the outcome is likely to be.

You really need a proof of concept to estimate

Project schedules follow cycles of expansion and contraction. First you explore, research, think about the strategic possibilities, and watch the possible number of projects you could do open up. Then you refine, reduce the number of open possibilities, and increase your understanding of the actual solution to be delivered. You might then build consensus around a direction and begin to open up the design again, looking for visual and technical platforms and concepts that will fit the shared project vision. After that, you refine the designs and technical choices, make decisions, find the right options, and the possibilities contract again.

The more possibilities are still open to you, the more nebulous your estimates will be. To give a good estimate for a task, you have to have the end in sight. There are only really two ways to know this one. One way is when you're on a cycle of contraction, where the possibilities are diminishing rather than expanding, and you can look ahead to the shared concept of the project and see something concrete emerging. The other way is if you've done something similar enough in the past, then you can look back and evaluate how long something took the last time. Any useful estimate will be based on a combination of these two things.

The point in the project when you have the most assurance around what you're going to build is right after you've achieved consensus around a good functional prototype. You'll have completed the exploration phases and the research, and you'll be looking ahead to a specific product that you can build in a specific way. You'll have ironed out most of the risks associated with your approach, and you can say with assurance how many designs, pages, configurations, environments and tools will be involved in the final product. Unfortunately, in most web projects, this point in the process comes way too late to get an understanding of what is yet to come. You need other tools, other ways of estimating.

Estimating software development is about function points

In the world of software development (a field which sort of, but not entirely, includes the work of building experiences on the web), projects are generally estimated based on what they do, which means function points. This is certainly one reason that software requirements are generally expressed as a long, long list of function points, rather than in the form of a conceptual model which gets more and more detailed (as design projects are often created). With a function point list handy, you can assign work hours against each task that the software needs to fulfil, then add some overhead for project management and other things. In a function point list, there is often not much of a distinction between what the software does and what the user does; that is, the project is defined in terms of the software acting as a sort of agent on behalf of a user, rather than in terms of actions and decisions that will be made by the user. As such, estimating the user interface for such a system is often also expressed as a percentage of the time to develop the software functions.

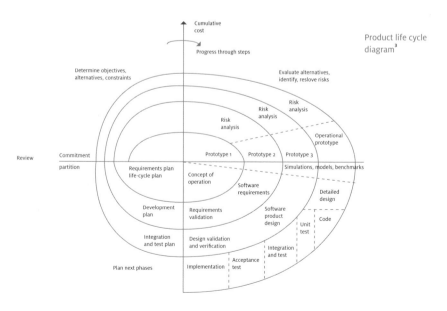

Product life cycle diagram[3]

---

[3] Adapted from Barry Boehm's "A Spiral Model of Software Development and Enhancement", ACM SIGSOFT Software Engineering Notes, ACM, 11(4):14-24, August 1986.

The Agile way to do this kind of estimation is to build your schedule around sprints: short periods of work (usually a week or so) during which you will select requirements, design the new screens or features and implement them, coming back at the end of the week to test your new work against your requirements. This is a great way to build because you have a chance to see your work progressing, day by day and week by week. To use this method, though, you'll need to agree with all of the client stakeholders at the outset that you'll accept requirements and enhancements at the start of each sprint and execute them, and then accept a new set. However, if you have a fixed-price engagement, or a fixed time schedule, you might know in advance how many sprints you'll have to staff and work on, but you won't have a sense of how much functionality you'll have time to build, because it depends on how fast you manage to take on and execute each new set of requirements.

If you've built agreement on this Agile-style method of building, you still need to measure progress and estimate the remaining time. Given the inherent uncertainty around requirements, it's probably more important that you find a way to estimate the remaining time for each task as you work on it. A good strategy here is to ask the people doing the work (the most granular level of task assignees) to continuously record both the time spent per task, and also to update the task record with an estimate of remaining time to completion.

By putting together the progress you make with requirements and looking at that list against the overall set of project requirements, you can start to develop a sense of the project velocity. Using a burn down chart[4] along with your velocity measurement, for example, you can make some pretty accurate predictions about how long a given group of tasks is going to take your team, and thus let the project owners know what will get done and within what budget.

---

[4] A burn down chart is a graphical representation mapping work left to do against time.

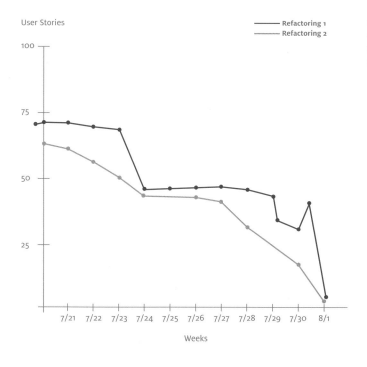

User Stories

———— Refactoring 1
———— Refactoring 2

Example burn down chart showing velocity/progress over time

Weeks

Content management systems and customer relationship management

CMS, CRM and other enterprise systems can be effective tools, but they introduce several risks and roadblocks of their own. These platforms don't necessarily have clean interfaces and aren't always easy to understand or modify. They look like out-of-the-box solutions, but they usually aren't. In fact, your CMS probably needs to be treated as a software development problem. CRM integration also promises great things, but most integrations fail. Testing your chosen system a little bit at a time will reduce a lot of this risk.

Light-touch integration

One strategy for dealing with complexity is to break it down into small, simple steps. Keep people in the middle of the process. Sometimes it is actually more efficient for a person to batch and act on groups of data, rather than trying to automate everything. A person will see abnormalities in the information and can make certain corrections to ensure consistency. Even if you don't retain a person for data processing, starting this way may give you the information that you need to make a more automated solution later on. At a small scale, using people may actually be easier and give you a better chance for a positive customer experience. For example, I remember a project where the managing directors of a start-up were terribly concerned about the possibility of not being able to meet user demand for their new service. They insisted on an incredibly complex IT infrastructure to support the imagined future demand for their product, which never materialised. A few years later, their astronomical hosting bills were actually higher than revenue, and the company closed down. Take some cues from from Eric Ries's book, *The Lean Startup* – build what you need, when you need it. Deliver, learn, improve. The necessary technical automation may not be as big a problem as you think.

TOOLS FROM THIS CHAPTER

- Product life cycle diagram
- Function point estimate
- UML diagram
- Agile development velocity

FURTHER READING

Take a look at the classic book about software patterns, usually called the Gang of Four book[5]. Using the Unified Modeling Language, the four authors work through some of the common system templates that show up again and again in software design, no matter the programming language or platform. This is definitely more of a software development read rather than web design – but that tends to be the nature of integration projects.

Enterprise Integration Patterns by Gregor Hohpe and Bobby Woolf (2003, Addison-Wesley Professional) is one of my favourite books for laying out some of the specific problems of getting systems to talk to each other in a robust way. Some of the examples are a bit system-specific, but the principles will come into play no matter what the environment.

Thinking about the real needs that you have right now might keep you from over-building a solution, which is always a temptation in integration projects. Take a look Eric Ries's book, *The Lean Startup* (2011, Crown Business). Think about the integration project in phases, and build for what you will need next, deliver, learn and then see what the next phase needs to be.

---

[5] *Design Patterns: Elements of Reusable Object-Oriented Software* by Erich Gamma, Richard Helm, Ralph Johnson and John Vlissades (199...

10   **INTERVIEW:** *ANDY BUDD*

Andy Budd is one of the founding partners at the user experience design consultancy Clearleft. His book, *CSS Mastery,* has sold over 60,000 copies and has been translated into a dozen languages. He has been blogging about design and technology since 2003.

   Andy spoke to Breandán about the role of a design studio principal and the early phases of a web project. He also discusses why you might want to warn off a client rather than take the gig.

The role of a managing director in projects

I'll start off with a bit about you. Tell me about what you do, day to day, at Clearleft.

That should be the easiest question, but it's actually the most difficult. I am the managing director of the company – in America, I would be the CEO. Because we're a very small company, that means I end up having to do all the kinds of things that the rest of the people in the company don't do, because they're busy doing the work they're paid to do, their day jobs.

A large part of my day-to-day activities involves the sales process and responding to potential client requests. That might be fielding initial emails from clients asking about our services; it might be filling in request for proposals, invitations to tender, or various documents involved in sending proposals to clients. I do quite a lot of travelling to clients and talking them through our services, explaining how the culture of the company works and outlining how we approach design problems.

For example, five minutes ago I got off the phone with a client; I was explaining what Clearleft does and essentially asking them not to use us because I didn't think we were quite the right agency for them. I think in that respect I'm quite unusual. I believe a lot of agencies try to hoover up every single project that comes along because they see it as extra money, whereas I'm very selective about the kind of work I do, or the kind of work Clearleft does. That is partly because we want to do interesting, fun projects, but also because I don't think it's fair for the client to be sold on an agency that it can do something when it turns out that it can't, or isn't the best agency for the project. In this instance, I recommended a competitor. I suspect that few competitors (or at least that one) would ever think of recommending us in return. But I prefer the client to be happy.

I do a lot of sales. I also help manage the office and help plan events. For example, I'm very heavily involved in the UX London[1] project. I used to be more involved with dConstruct[2], though Jeremy Keith does a lot more of that organisation now. I generally make sure that the team and the staff are happy. I oversee projects, but with a very light touch. I'll be in touch with a project manager to make sure that the project is going well, that the clients are happy, that timelines are being met and that clients are getting what they want. I occasionally look around at the work being done, and I check in with the staff to make sure they're happy and that they're making progress. Generally, I have a coordinating and nurturing role.

But on top of that, I do all the bits and pieces that nobody else does, whether that be changing the water cooler or making sure the office gets cleaned properly – all the bitty things. At the moment we're looking for new office space, and I've spent the last nine months running around various places in Brighton, looking at new offices and talking to estate agents. So, basically everything that a company needs behind the scenes.

My friend Eoghan McCabe, CEO of Intercom.io, wrote in his blog[3] that the definition of a CEO is "everything else".

Yes. If I'm honest, I think that the role of the CEO is a bit trying – to lead by example and to set the culture of the company. A lot of what I do is making sure that the people we employ are really happy here and that they understand what's expected of them. A lot of tasks come from making sure that the office is a nice place to work, and making sure that we do things as a team. For instance, soon we're having a team day out. We have one every six weeks

[1] http://uxlondon.com

[2] http://dconstruct.org

[3] http://blog.intercom.io/welcoming-macey-jeff-and-frantisek/

or so. This time we're going up to London, and we're going to look around a
bunch of design-related exhibits. I help to organise those types of things. We
do monthly or six-weekly movie nights when we all get together. A lot of my
role is invisible and is about making sure that the culture of Clearleft is the
culture that we want and produces the results that we look for.

Early project phases

Moving into some of the practical work that you have been doing on projects, tell
me a bit about the early activities that come after you've decided to do the job, but
before you present something to the client.

There are usually a good couple of months between those phases. A lot of
design agencies are very design-led, and the first thing they'll do is take a
brief, go into Photoshop and start producing designs. That's definitely not
what we do, and it's definitely not the user-centred approach.

The first problem with designing or speccing out a product is actually knowing
what you're being asked to build. Pretty much all the time, clients come to
us with a very loose idea of what they want to have created. They're coming
to us for our expertise, asking us to help them define and solve some of the
tricky problems that they have. An issue with that is that until we've spent
time helping them solve the problems, we don't know what we're going to be
building, and we don't know how much time it will take or how much it will
cost. So we have this weird circular problem of deciding how we're going to
quote for something, if we are being paid to figure out what the thing is that
we're building, so that we can come up with a quote.

Sometimes clients will come to us and they will give us a fixed price, and we'll
work on a flexible-scope basis. They don't really know what they want, but
they're bringing us in. Because they've tackled projects of a similar size, they
can estimate that it will take four months, at so many thousands of pounds.
They will then work with us to define what the scope of the project is. We'll
match the scope to the budget that they have.

Business context research

If it's the other way around – if clients want a very well-defined project before they start working – then what we usually do is recommend a four- to six-week pilot project. The first couple of weeks are usually just spent understanding the context in which the problem exists. That involves reading any background research that the client might have done, reading any papers on the client's industry or profession, and reviewing their existing service or competitors, so that we understand what this business is about.

To be able to tackle design problems, we need to solve them from a position of knowledge. We need to be as smart about the client's business as they already are to be able to make design decisions. Otherwise, we're just making really badly informed design solutions.

Stakeholder research

Once we've got a better understanding of the context, we undertake quite a bit of stakeholder research. We used to do less stakeholder research, but it's increased over time because we find it more and more useful. We might spend a week setting up one-on-one meetings with various important parties around the organisation. Those might be everything from one-on-one interviews with the CEO or the head of marketing – people who have very detailed business objectives – to the person involved in SEO, or the person looking at the analytics. Often, great places to find this sort of design intelligence are in the areas where people interact with customers. The telesales department or the tech support department are great people to ask about any problems that they may have.

The reason that we do this is, if you just take the brief or initial meeting notes as gospel, you will miss a lot of needs. These sources tend to all focus on one area. Often, that area is what the CEO wants. But projects are a combination of a lot of different needs. We like to unpick all those needs, figure out the different angles and put all of them together. Then we can create a solution that meets as many of those needs as possible. The reality is that our solution isn't going to meet all of those needs. We also need to know whose needs we're not going to satisfy, so that we can manage those stakeholders and let them know that their solution is not going to happen. The other benefit of doing a lot of stakeholder research is it makes people feel they've been involved, it makes them feel they've been listened to, and it makes them feel like part of the project.

User research

Let's say we've done an initial week's worth of stakeholder research. We might, if we're lucky, spend a similar amount of time on user research – all of this could be different, but we're talking about an average project. We might spend three or four days talking to users and doing one-on-one interviews. We sometimes set up some quantitative surveys online to ask specific questions. If we feel that we don't fully understand what's wrong on a site, we might do some initial usability testing. Usually, though, we save usability testing for a little bit later. Normally, when clients come to us asking for our help, it's obvious what the problems are. It seems like a waste, from our perspective, to do usability testing too early.

Now we've got the big picture. That's the understanding phase, the research phase, done. Then we start exploring possible solutions. We'll often have a client workshop, perhaps initially with some of the more senior stakeholders, in order to set a vision, direction and design guidelines that we can refer back to when we're making design decisions.

Client/agency misconceptions

Is the biggest misconception that you've seen between a client and an agency a misunderstanding of what it actually takes to do this work of making websites?

I think it's that there's a misunderstanding of how much work goes into designing a good website. Often people will see the web as a cost centre, and a cost centre is something that businesses try to minimise. They try to find the cheapest possible suppliers to do the work. When that fails, the initial assumption is, "Oh, it must be one bad supplier. Next time we'll get a better supplier."

After a couple of rounds of being cheap and hiring bad suppliers, the penny drops that they need to get someone who is better and charges more. I'm seeing that clients have bigger budgets now, after being bitten a few times. They're starting to realise that to do this right they need to do all the consultancy work that I suggested. Because if you jump straight into the visual design side of things, a lot of the business reasons behind doing the website get lost. You get a pretty thing, but a pretty thing that doesn't really generate any business value unless you have been really, really lucky. So that's that.

PART 3

Design and Prototype

The wireframing phase brings up lots of questions of fidelity, organisation, and presentation. In this section, I review taxonomies, paper prototyping, layouts and design constraints. I'll also discuss a few of the many facets of visual language and graphic design, as they relate to your project management process, including the difficult comps question, user journey sketches and choosing the right tools. With plenty of sketches and annotations to represent your team's work, you'll be able to move through the visual design phase with confidence.

Wireframing

Graphic design

Initial prototyping

Interactive wireframing

Interview: *Rob Weychert*

Wireframing

> *"My drawings have been described as pre-intentionalist,*
> *meaning that they were finished before the ideas for them*
> *had occurred to me. I shall not argue the point."*
> — James Thurber[1]

What's here: An introduction to sketching at appropriate fidelity, and why it matters; presenting wireframes; and taxonomies.

Detail and agreement of scope

From my experience, wireframes are sometimes a bit controversial in the website development industry. I suspect that they come to us from the world of software engineering, where seeing a user interface in sketch form gives engineers something to talk about and a way to collaborate on a project.

The rationale behind creating wireframes usually takes the following form:

- They give you a chance to demonstrate and develop a page without having to use difficult tools.
- They are easily changed, so can be used for iterative designs
- The lack of colour and texture means that decision-makers can focus just on the functionality, and details of the visual design will not be distracting.

True enough, as far as it goes. However:

- Making wireframes isn't always that easy – they often require the same page design and graphic design skills that a more traditional design comp would take.

---

[1] Life Magazine (14 March 1960)

- The speed of wireframe software relies on common libraries of user interface widgets. Using such widget sets encourages the designer to continue using existing conventions, even if they are out of date or inappropriate for the particular problem.
- Most importantly, clients have a very hard time understanding wireframes. You can say, "This is just a page schematic: don't worry about the fonts or spacing or layout, just the relative hierarchies of items on the page", but very few of us are experienced enough to see wireframes as schematics without unconsciously assuming that the visual design of the page will be some kind of coloured in version of what we're seeing.

I'm not saying that you shouldn't make them at some point in your design process – wireframes can not only document scope with clients, but be a great way to explore the options open to you as website makers. Be aware of their limitations, however, and don't forget how incredibly weird they look to someone who doesn't deal with them frequently. Three dangers to keep in mind:

- Wireframing in the UX phase of a project is speculative and divergent. It can go in several directions at once and isn't about refining ideas at all.
- This phase is quite different from wireframing during the visual and prototyping phase, which is about refining ideas to find the right solutions for your set of design constraints.
- As a project manager, your biggest problem will be to manage the amount of time that goes into various solutions, and to keep internal and external stakeholders from buying into a particular direction too early.

Presenting wireframes

Most people (including clients) don't understand wireframes. Creating wireframes is a specialist skill for producing a technical schematic of functionality and content hierarchy. Clients cannot be expected to understand wireframes without any training or explanation. This is especially important since wireframes have nothing to do with the final visual style and layout, and yet appear to be a sketch of how it'll look.

Talk about your wireframes in person, taking time to explain their function. Use a combination of sketches and full wireframes to emphasise the draft or blueprint nature of these documents. Clickable is good, but so is paper!

The concept of appropriate fidelity

Enough detail and no more

When wireframes work well, it's because they follow the principle of appropriate fidelity: they show enough detail about your solution to be useful, but don't show too much. This is important – getting this wrong can derail any web project by either:

- Getting clients invested in practically finished visual designs that just aren't ready yet (because the wireframe is too detailed).
- Creating an endless wireframing stage of work because there's no way to quickly update all of the details needed (as the wireframe is too detailed).
- Increasing project risk because important elements aren't specified or discussed early enough in the project (as the wireframe isn't detailed enough).

Any of these things would be bad for the project. It's also important that the wireframes you're developing stay at a relatively low level of detail at any given time.

- Don't work on the gradients for your button shading while other big chunks of the page are still in the form of cross-filled boxes.
- In fact, working on things like shadows and gradients at the wireframing stage is too much detail. Don't let the black and white nature of wireframes trick you into producing just greyscale versions of your final page layouts.
- Don't repeat lots of details just for the sake of convention. If you haven't thought about the page footer yet, leave it as a big unknown area, not as a standard-looking footer with a few terms and conditions links. Wireframes are supposed to present and solidify design decisions, not serve to reinforce tired conventions about what web pages look like. It's OK not to know yet.

Time management, detail and the wireframing process
The wireframes your team is working on can end up taking a while. Be careful of sending revisions back and forth between the designer and the client; either of the following features of a wireframe can end up being huge time sinks.

Wireframes that try to show interaction on a page, such as a logged-in state versus a logged-out state: if you find yourself starting to implement clickable wireframes using tools that involve lots of page variables and dynamic behaviour, you might be spending more time on the tool than on the solution. There's a place for demonstrating interactivity, but your goal at the wireframe stage is to show your thoughts about page structure, hierarchy and flow of functionality.

If you're seeing wireframes that are too good, with pixel-perfect alignments and lots of shades of grey, you might be spending too much time creating a black and white version of the web site. If you really understand the design challenges well enough that you are ready to get into visual design, then by all means get into visual design. You don't always need a wireframe. In fact, if the page structure is obvious for whatever reason, the step of creating a wireframe for the unique layout may just take time and budget away from refining your other design decisions.

Of course, it's the less obvious aspects that you need to look out for in the process. If there's a logged-in state for the app, go ahead and show what this would look like. Is there a dashboard for any kind of data? Show what this would look like, and how you'll present real numbers. Do you have error conditions to think about, based on external data services not being available, for example? You might want to show these in wireframes – this is the time to decide whether an error pop-over window is going to be useful or annoying.

The point of a wireframe is to document and get agreement on features and specifications. If you only need to worry about a small rectangular panel that has to do something fancy, then wireframe just that little panel. If you need to see how the whole page is going to work, show the whole page. There's nothing that says that you need to wireframe entire pages or entire websites, if there isn't anything useful to say about most of every page. Think about the wireframes as a communication tool, something for people working on requirements to use when liaising with the people doing the building. If you're not sure about the level of detail, just ask a developer who will be doing some of the implementation of the page. If he or she doesn't need a detail (because it's obvious, or because it's been specified in some other way), leave it out.

Show more detail as the project progresses
For any pages that need to be wireframed, plan at least one round of revisions into your schedule. Clients mostly don't fully understand wireframes the first time they see them, so plan to present not only the work you've done, but also the concept behind wireframe development. And if the page or page area is complex enough that you need to model it with a formal wireframe (as opposed to another low-fidelity sketch), it's probably tricky enough that you'll need to refine your initial solution.

As the project progresses, you can show more details as you gradually ramp up the level of fidelity. Knowing the general structure of a page might let you make some more decisions on size and contrast and rhythm for the next version. Reaching agreement on the rough length of an article in one wireframe version will let you put more into the sidebars and pull-quotes in the next round.

Just be ready to call it done. By definition, an abstraction of your page design will never be the page itself. So, once you have all of the decisions and documentation that you need from a wireframe deck, call that good and move on to the next step. You can get into visual design, or functional prototyping, or do some usability tests – whatever makes sense for the project. You don't have to flow your changes through a massive wireframe deck, showing every unique layout, just for the sake of completeness. The wireframes are there as a tool for you and for your client.

Oh, and never step back and bring your wireframes up to date after the fact unless you're prepared to redo work or to extend time and budget. They're not magic – they're just supposed to help you document your thoughts so that you can get to the next stage.

Do you have low (or appropriate) fidelity?		*This allows you to go back, if needed.*
Are you looking for the right solution?		*Love (for your work) makes you blind.*
Have you checked with other people?		*Ask for constructive feedback.*

Taxonomy

Making sense of your content and functionality will lead you pretty quickly into the realm of navigation. There are plenty of standard conventions for navigating through systems of pages and information, including all of the top horizontal navigation bars, roll-over menus, and the like. Don't get so caught up in the standard models that you don't think about the other ways information is organised on your site: you might have to design category tags, archive structures, product hierarchies and tag clouds. Making sense of information means putting your pages and content into some sort of structure.

Organising information

Much could be written (and has been) about how to organise information – and I'd refer you to Donna Spencer's book on information architecture as a good starting point[2]. Moving pages into a sitemap is generally considered to be information architecture, and has to do with grouping together what's closely related and separating that which is not.

But that's a very simplistic way to think about your content. What about the content that belongs in multiple categories, perhaps because it's useful for different kinds of people? What do you do when you're trying to leave room for future content, but don't know exactly what it will be? What about information that needs to be presented in different ways for different people, but is still conceptually related? How do you distinguish between the classification needs of new and returning users?

There's actually a lot to this, and it's probably best to keep as open a mind as possible and remember that convention is not always your friend. Most clients will want their site's homepage to go first in the primary navigation list, for example, followed by an about us section. But studies show that the attention of users falls off rapidly when glancing down a menu, and about us content is not really important for most users. So here you already have a conflict between how you would rank and group the information to be presented and what the client has asked for.

Hierarchical taxonomies

You need to think in terms of rank or importance, which is why hierarchical taxonomies (like most organisation charts, or top-down sitemaps) work so well. You get a chance to say, "This piece of information is important; this less so; and this should barely be

---

[2] *A Practical Guide to Information Architecture* by Donna Spencer (2010, Five Simple Steps)

mentioned, if at all." Once you can say that a group of information is important, you're able to break it down into the pieces that would be most significant within that grouping, and so on down to the level of content not important enough to get its own page at all.

Don't be afraid to create lots of levels at this point – you can always go back and lump some of the levels together. And you might decide later on that multiple parts of content can coexist on the same pages, just at different levels of prominence. This is where the hierarchical decisions made by newspaper editors every day are a good model: just look at the various amounts of space, sizes of headers and amount of illustration given to different pieces of information on the front page of a newspaper. Decisions have clearly been made about grouping and importance.

Faceted taxonomies

The hierarchical model will break down at some point. While newspaper articles can only exist on a single page at a single size, with any interesting site you find information that could be useful for multiple kinds of users, or reached in different ways. That's where faceted taxonomies come in.

Think about organising a clothing product catalogue. You might want to organise by price. And by fabric, size and colour. These are all facets of the information that you have to organise. Navigation will have to be attached to each of these facets in order for them to be discoverable and useful, whether that means multiple menu items or just a drop-down filter. The same will go for any other list of facets that you can come up with for the information and functionality of your new website.

List the facets. If you know them, list the options within each one. List the big categories and their subcategories. List the types of information needed by each of your personas. List the information needed by experienced users and by newcomers. It's really only when you put these various lists together that you'll have the chance to boil them all down into the (inevitable) compromises that will let you design the navigation and page hierarchy of your website.

Paper prototypes

Sketching interfaces on paper is the fastest way to develop and evaluate concepts. The process provides low fidelity (for easy changes), high collaborative potential, low record-keeping pain, and high presentation value (sketches that look like real sketches are easier for clients to grapple with at this stage).

Snapshots of wireframe paper prototypes

Co-creation

Because paper prototyping is low fidelity and uses basic materials, this is the perfect task for live, workshop-style co-creation with clients. Whether in Sharpie on paper or in marker on whiteboard, sketching wireframes in a client workshop will help both sides of the project to clarify their information architecture ideas in a collaborative environment. It also reduces the possibility of the client introducing many significant changes to the architecture after you present the prototyped wireframes.

TOOLS FROM THIS CHAPTER

- Wireframe
- Taxonomy
- Paper prototype

FURTHER READING

Of course, the ever-useful Dan Brown book, *Communicating Design*[3] has some great examples of wireframes.

For some more philosophical thinking about the nature of taxonomies, Weinberger's book *Everything is Miscellaneous*[4] goes into the various hierarchical and non-hierarchical schemes, including the much less-structured "folksonomies". His more recent book, *Too Big To Know*[5] is perhaps not immediately relevant, but great fun to read if you're interested in the nature of internet-age information.

Morville's book about navigation and the web, *Ambient Findability*[6] is definitely worth a read if you'd like to consider the nuts and bolts of navigation, and orientation and wayfinding systems on the web. Where Weinberger speaks generally about the nature of information and understanding, Morville talks about the specifics of how to keep your users oriented to where they are and where they can go.

If you'd like to think about wireframes in a very visual way, McCloud's book, *Understanding Comics*[7] is a very interesting read. McCloud goes into the conventions of visual storytelling, which wireframes are – if you can think of your wireframes the way Scott thinks about his comics, you'll go a long way towards communicating effectively.

---

[3] *Communicating Design* by Dan Brown (2nd edition 2010, New Riders)

[4] *Everything is Miscellaneous* by David Weinberger (2008, Holt Paperbacks)

[5] *Too Big To Know* by David Weinberger (2012, Basic Books)

[6] *Ambient Findability* by Peter Morville (2005, O'Reilly Media Incorporated)

[7] *Understanding Comics* by Scott McCloud (1993, William Morrow Paperbacks)

12

GRAPHIC DESIGN

"I've been amazed at how often those outside the discipline of design assume that what designers do is decoration. Good design is problem solving."
— **Jeffrey Veen**[1]

What's here: Graphic design, and the difference between visual design and art; sketching user interfaces; dealing with design constraints; web typography, layouts and comps; and presenting graphic design.

Visual language and design systems

Graphic design is widely misunderstood. People think of visual and graphic design as a sort of colouring in between the lines, or skinning, or making something pretty. Honestly, ideas like those do a great disservice to the professionals who develop the visual language of websites. For example, here's a definition from the UK Usability Professionals' Association: "Visual design, in the context of web design, is the practice of applying corporate identity, style, imagery, iconography, typography and animation to an interface."[2] To me, that misses the point a bit – visual design isn't really a process of "applying" brand colours to an interface. Here's a definition I like better:

"Visual Design is the field of developing visual materials to create an experience. Visual Design spans the fields of Graphic Design, Illustration, Typography, Layout, Color Theory, Iconography, Signage, Photography, etc. and any medium, including online, broadcast, print, outdoor, etc. Visual Design is concerned with the elements of visual expression and style. It is often an integral step in Information Design and other communication design disciplines."
– **Nathan Shedroff, An Evolving Glossary of Experience Design.**[3]

---

[1] *The Art and Science of Web Design* by Jeffrey Veen (2000, New Riders)

[2] http://ukupa.org.uk/resources/glossary-of-terms/

[3] http://www.brycecorkins.com/about/glossary/

Visual design is about problem-solving, about figuring out how to communicate with people using a pictorial language.

Where you come in

As a project manager, it's your job to get work done efficiently in this area, where clients are most likely to express their own aesthetic opinions. This can create a huge challenge for you. The website has probably not been commissioned for purely aesthetic reasons, but you'll hear everything from personal colour preferences to wistful soliloquies about competitors' websites as soon as you start gathering feedback. Some of the comments will be legitimate cases of misunderstanding on the part of the design team. Some of the feedback will be well-grounded in user experience research and validated with users.

It's also your job to help your designers be full members of the project team with ownership of their work and their concepts, rather than mere technicians. You'll need to keep designers in touch directly with clients, giving them the chance to understand and develop good concepts and guidelines. You'll need to keep the team focused on delivering a solution, rather than letting the exploration phases spin further and further from the end-product. And you'll need to find the right balance of time spent exploring new ideas versus time spent coming back in with a refinement of a design.

Sketching user interfaces

I highly recommend Bill Buxton's book *Sketching User Interfaces*[4]. Beyond serving as a primer to sketching itself, the book gives a solid overview of the processes involved in bringing a design to fruition.

Even as a project manager you shouldn't be at all afraid of getting out a piece of paper and beginning to sketch ideas. Having dealt with the client at each stage of the project, you may actually be in a good position to act as a solid proxy for the goals and experiences of the client and of the website audience. So your

[4] http://www.dustinkirk.com/2009/04/04/bill-buxton-sketching-user-experiences/

sketches may well bring insight to the table, whether or not you are a visual person. If you need some inspiration or ideas on getting going with your own sketching, try reading *The Back of the Napkin* series of books from Dan Roam[5].

Besides being a powerful spur to creativity, visual sketches follow appropriate fidelity rules. By bringing in the right level of detail at the right point in the process, your sketches let you explore the problem before you have invested too many of your limited resources of time, effort and budget.

The sketches that you make during the visual design phase can feed directly into wireframe development, and technology prototypes you're working on will inform your sketching. But the point of doing sketches isn't to create finished work – it's about getting the ideas down on paper in a way that can be discussed as a group.

Presenting sketches is a great way of getting feedback on designs in progress. Because your work is still unfinished, you're much more likely to receive feedback that is honest and creative. A finished, high-fidelity drawing or design tells the audience that the essential decisions have been made, and that feedback should adjust the tiny details. A rougher, more sketchy presentation signals to your audience that you are still working through the basic concepts and constraints, and that you need feedback on the design as a whole, including the more fundamental assumptions. The higher the level of polish on your presentations, the more you'll get feedback that is essentially nitpicking. The lower the fidelity, the more you'll get feedback on underlying concepts. This can be extremely useful to take advantage of early in a design cycle.

---

[5] http://www.danroam.com/the-back-of-the-napkin/

Constraints

Design is all about constraints

One way to develop design requirements is for both parties to assume that the client knows exactly what they want to get built. This confuses two issues: while the business stakeholder certainly does have an excellent idea of why a site needs to be built, and even what it should accomplish, they are not experts in the how of making the design actually work. When designers encourage clients to specify too much of the how, the conversation about design ends up being fairly brief.

As a basic starting point, it makes sense to treat the visual design of a website not as something that will be specified exactly by a client and then painted in or polished by a designer, but rather as the outcome of a series of conversations, informed by the designer's experience and sensitivities to audience. Many web shops now approach design in just this way, scheduling workshops to elicit the requirements of content and audience that will determine a good set of visual solutions. But there's a hidden danger here.

We've all seen design-related discussions and meetings that lead to disagreements – and there's little as frustrating as an argument between client and designer about whether a design needs more or less yellow. Because clients and designers can sometimes have these creative differences, it's tempting to downplay disagreements by just asking open-ended questions, being agreeable, and trying in a nice way to learn about the real requirements for the product being built.

There's nothing wrong with being civil, but in an effort to avoid imposing their design aesthetics on people or having arguments about colour, designers can sometimes create an even more difficult situation – absolute ambiguity about what's being done.

This is where a project manager often needs to step in. During these conversations, it's your job to constantly steer from the general to the specific, and to get rid of the edge cases that can't be easily addressed. Your job is also to immediately push back on requirements which sound good but which will have enormous knock-on effects when it comes to implementation.

The goal of requirement and design discussions should be to develop the constraints that designers need to do a focused, thoughtful job in solving the problem at hand. Your job as a project manager is to make sure that this happens, because the natural tendency of such engagements is to drift off into territory where you attempt to make everyone happy and cover all bases. You need to make sure you leave the meeting knowing whom specifically you're designing for, what you're going to be telling them through the design and how they will read and act on your communication. The more constraints you can develop (and the more things you can agree not to do), the better and stronger the design that you'll be able to produce.

Here are some of the tools that you can use to bring that focus. Most them involve making a guess and then refining along with the client, rather than going into an open-ended discussion prepared to discuss all sorts of things in a freewheeling way.

Mapping the mood

Think about creating a mood board representing what you're building. Look at other websites, of course, but also photographic images, typography, packaging – anything that helps to communicate the idea of the project visually. Make a collage of these images and ideas, and bring these to the first visual design meeting with the client. The conversation will then turn to the right design solution, not to the many combinations of possible audiences. For a slightly more structured approach, think about style tiles.

Style tiles can communicate options for a visual brand without designing a full page. You can download a PSD style tile template at *styletil.es*. Image courtesy of Samantha Warren

Integrating with existing brand guidelines

If there are elements of the existing brand that you think will work well on the web, bring them along. Whether it's a brochure, flyer, poster, or something else, focus on the things that will present the right emotional or conversational tone, and do so in a clear way. Bring examples of printed materials, or make quick snapshots of some of the physical environments, products or offices of the client that you feel will extend well to the screen. Like the mood board, examples of existing brand expressions make it easier to focus on the qualities that have already proven most important and worthy of notice.

Using 2×2s

There are many cases where you need to answer the questions: "More of this quality or that one?"; or "How do I balance these two aspects of the personality or design?". When answering these questions, or when mapping a competitive space, it can make a lot of sense to show the axes against each other, and pinpoint where you think the client's current market offering fits. The discussion, then, is wonderfully focused because it comes down to two simple questions: "Is this where you want to be? If not, which direction do you want to move on which axes?"

Snapshot of a 2x2 example

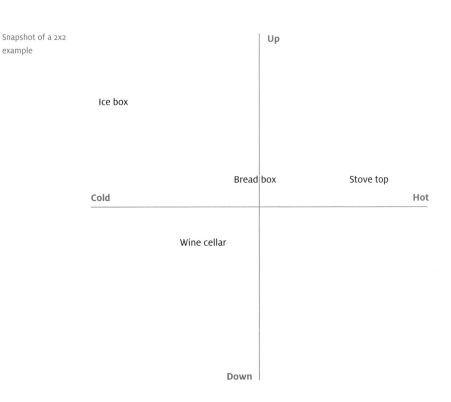

Up

Ice box

Bread box   Stove top

Cold   Hot

Wine cellar

Down

Managing typography

If the designers in your agency aren't already adept at web typography, you should make sure that they read some blogs, buy some books and go see a good speaker or two. (There are lots of helpful ideas in the further reading sections of this book!) Not only is good web type beautiful, and not only does it finally make one aspect of the web as subtle and finely controlled as parts of print design, but good web type will help your sites live longer, attract more readers and fulfil their missions more easily.

Here are a few useful web typography tools:

- Typecast (*typecastapp.com*)
- Typekit (*typekit.com*)
- Fontdeck (*fontdeck.com*)

Key layouts

When the visual design gets going, your first question will concern estimation. How many pages will need to be designed for the website? This can be a complicated question these days – there's no longer a one-to-one correspondence between pages to be built and pages that are displayed. The work of content management systems in slicing up and recombining bits of layout and content is certainly the biggest factor here; often when the question of how many pages is asked, what is actually meant is how many CMS templates.

In the visual design phase of work, it would be handy if the needs of the CMS were known, but this shouldn't determine exactly the work to be done. The important part is to determine how many kinds of information need to be displayed. Work out a rough hierarchy of information, and then work from there to the key layouts that need to be developed.

Counting variations

One of your key numbers will be the number of unique layouts; that is, the number of actual templates that will have to be designed and coded. There's a big multiplier effect going on here. Each of these layouts will need to be designed, sure, but also implemented in markup, adapted or rethought for smaller and larger screens, considered for touch interface elements, reworked at different resolutions and colour spaces, considered for a mad plethora of browsers, tested, iterated, refined, redeployed, integrated with your content management system and versioned.

Of course, that makes it tempting to reduce your design to as few templates as possible when you're doing work estimates, and that's fine – as long as you stick to it.

What you really need to watch out for is accepting variations in pages during the first design review, or during requirements discussions. Even if you estimated the variations accurately to begin with, the person in the room presenting designs to your client may not be thinking through the full lifecycle of each change. If the client gives you a new requirement for a special feature on any of their pages, something that means you can no longer use your generic two-column or product detail page layouts, the designer may put forward their estimate to redesign that special module within the page, without thinking through the implications for the rest of the process. It's OK to add layouts if you really need to, of course – that's what change requests are for – but you should be sure to take changes back with you and re-estimate fully, involving all the same people (designers, developers, sysadmins, information architects, and so on) whom you used for the estimates you built your proposal around.

Getting buy-in on the important pages first

When looking for agreement, it's easiest to start small and build. Whether you've used style tiles or some other mechanism to demonstrate your design system, seeing pages come together into partial or full comps is one of the danger points for web projects. Seeing real content, in context, is one of the points where you are likely to see the difference between the client's interest in design against their skills in visualising design solutions. An experienced designer can think through many of the ramifications of design decisions before committing them to Fireworks (though you might be surprised how much Moleskine sketching is still done as part of the process, and by how many approaches are routinely discarded by very experienced designers).

When you start to present your designs, you'll probably get the best feedback if you can show the reasons for your design decisions. This will help avoid the purely subjective aesthetic judgements that can derail the conversation. When you plan the presentation, step through the process, from small elements and building, to modules and out to the page level. This way you can show the logic of each step, which will help get agreement. In the first round of feedback you may not want to show the homepage, but you do want to present any pages containing elements that affect other designs. Pages with forms, with different kinds of content, pages with video, imagery, purchase or sign-up steps all contain a lot of different modules, and getting agreement on the basic look and feel of these elements will help when building consensus later on. Starting with the more workaday or functional pages will also help with the critiques that you get inside your shop or from the client: because the pages are clearly designed to do something, it's easier to imagine seeing them from the point of view of your audience.

How many comps?
You don't want to spend forever doing comps, nor do you want to go in lots of directions at once. While it may make sense to try a couple of different treatments for smaller elements that will make up the surface design, don't commit in advance to three (or five, or any particular number) distinct designs to choose from. You'll end up putting a lot of effort into each, and then discarding a lot of the work. Also, having completely different directions on the table will make it easier for the client to pick some of one, some of another, and make it harder to present a single, coherent visual system.

Multiple approaches in parallel might help a client make a decision, but start with smaller elements of text, graphics or navigation – no need to create whole pages just to get a decision. But beware of 'frankenprojects': you don't want to end up with approval for elements that conflict with each other. Try really hard to develop a single, coherent visual language that reflects the tone and emotional values that you've agreed.

One set of comps is gutsy, but might be effective. If you start at
the page level to present your designs, clients may feel that they
don't have enough choices to make. Starting with smaller textual
or visual modules will make it easier to elicit the feedback that you
need. Present the full pages once the overall visual direction has
been established. This way you'll only spend the time building one
set of pages, not three.

Responsive and adaptive designs

You've certainly heard about responsive design and adaptive
design lately, along with liquid layouts, flexible grids and
content-out techniques. All of these ideas are based around
making your webpages and applications more portable, more
accepting of smaller screens, different workflows and a variety of
non-desktop devices.

Clients are starting to ask for these things, just as they might
ask for a mobile version of the website. It's tempting to treat
this as a separate design project, and to charge separately for the
desktop version and the mobile version of the website.

Don't insist on a false dichotomy of desktop versus mobile.
After all, what is an iPad? The screen resolution is high, and fits
more pixels than many desktop devices, but the interface is based
on touch. A modern smartphone can browse desktop websites
perfectly well... and often more easily than some mobile-only
versions. Mobile websites optimised for a single version of a
single kind of phone often look awful on the next version of
the device.

There are ways that you can develop websites that work well
on a variety of platforms and devices, without having to know
your users' exact contexts in advance. The technologies that
enable this more flexible development style are also changing
rapidly, and the changing landscape of browser support adds
yet another wrinkle. As a web-building organisation you should
invest some time in learning how to handle these questions.
Eventually, adaptive design won't be an extra at all, but simply part
of your way of working, and probably a competitive advantage for
your team.

Presenting visual designs

There's something of an art to presenting visual designs to people who need to make decisions about them. You need to get agreement, of course, but you're really trying to create a shared vision, even a shared excitement about the website and the way you've decided to solve design problems. In this, designers and clients tend to have different ways of thinking.

Clients
- Focus on designs that reflect their overall brand.
- Look for continuity with print and other offline brand expressions.
- Often think of a website generally as a marketing vehicle to build excitement around the organisation or service.
- Want to be surprised and excited by what they see.

Designers
- Focus on solving visual problems of contrast, space, hierarchy, texture and flow.
- Want to exploit the unique possibilities of screen-based digital interactions to create new experiences.
- Think of a website primarily as a tool to serve a set of user needs or facilitate a set of journeys.
- Want to create transparent clarity and usability around what they build, to reduce any potential barriers to use.

Neither approach is wrong: both are valid approaches to the purposes and uses of a website and how to build one. But there is an obvious chance for miscommunication here, and because it relates to the actual purpose of the work being done, there can be frustrating ripple effects. If you want to get useful feedback about the work you're doing, and if (perhaps more importantly) you want to get sign-off, you should proceed very carefully.

Walking through visuals in person

The first presentation of visual designs to the client is a crucial step in the project – a lot can fall apart if this process isn't managed carefully. Because this is such a critical milestone, you should present in person if at all possible. There are a few reasons for this.

First, you can present your ideas in a controlled, ordered way, and gradually reveal your solution rather than trying for the concentrated effect of a complete set of visuals to be instantly digested.

You can also manage the feedback more carefully in person. If a stakeholder says, "That doesn't really work," or "That's not strong enough," you have the chance to follow up. You can ask not how a page should change but rather find out more about the goal that you're trying to solve with that part of the design.

Finally, you can schedule time for some co-designing activities in person when things aren't clear to you. For example, if you think that you've nailed the top and second-level pages of a product hierarchy (1 and 2), and have a good approach to the detail page (4) but still need some more thought on the mid-level page (3), you can present pages 1, 2 and 4 in a sequence, then work on page 3 with the client right there to help guide your work.

You should practise this, of course – like any workshop, you'll need to practise your pitch an hour or two in advance for every hour you are going to spend in the room presenting it. Use other people from your web group, especially those with a business focus, to stand in for the client, and run through your presentation exactly as you plan to run it on the day. Keep careful notes of what worked well and where there might be a gap in logic or presentation that deserves some more time to refine and prepare.

Start from small elements, build the picture

Your goal with the visuals presentation meeting is to develop a shared understanding of the design constraints and goals affecting the visual language of the website. Activities that support this shared understanding should be prepared and rehearsed; activities that don't support this goal should be jettisoned.

You should also accept that what you've learned up to this point, even if well-founded in research, might in fact lead you in an unproductive direction. Of course, something that isn't working at this stage isn't necessarily a bad idea; all you can really say is that this idea isn't the right one for this client, for this time, for this phase in the project. Keep track of what you throw away – there may well be a time, even within a future phase of this project, when your approach starts to make more sense.

To build the right understanding, present your visuals in more or less the same way that you conceived them. By starting with the smallest elements (small blocks of text, icons, colour swatches, logo treatments and choice of images), and then only gradually building to the big reveal – your pages or style tiles – you have the chance to get agreement at each point, and to help the client see the design problem against the same constraints and ideas that you've been working with.

Building on this idea of progression, your workshop to present client visuals might go something like this:

1. Introductions, setting the stage: 5 minutes
2. Tone and intent: 20 minutes
3. Type and colour: 20 minutes
4. Choices of imagery: 15 minutes

Take a break

5. Page or tile approaches: 20 minutes
6. Co-design with the client: 25 minutes
7. Documenting and wrapping up: 15 minutes

Refining the user journey stories

If you can find a way to relate the user research that you've done directly to the visuals, this will be an even stronger presentation. A few ways you might do this:

- Keep referring to your personas by name, as a way to reinforce that actual people will be using this site to accomplish real things.
- If you can, present a sequence of activities that correspond to one of your stories.
- Always use real text in your presentations, even if you have to rewrite it yourself based on the existing website. You may not get the details quite right, but you can show headlines, items and navigation in a real-world context of use.
- It might make sense to present the mapping between personas, content and functionality that you developed in the persona phase. Doing this and then switching directly to a specific content item highlighted during the persona work can show the effects of your decisions.

As much as possible, think of the visuals presentation as a way to zoom in and out. At the high-level view, there are your user groups, your research and the results of your content analysis. At the closest, most detailed view, there are the many small choices around text, colour and space that make up your design. Connecting the small decisions with the larger themes of the project will result in a much smoother process of decision-making for all concerned.

Get agreement and immediately document

Like all of the workshops you run, the following up that you do will determine how effective it was. The most important step is to begin building consensus while people are still in the room. Be sure to leave enough time in the agenda to wrap up the session, show what you've come to agreement about and what remains to be resolved. This documentation should be public – on flip-chart or whiteboard or projected mind-map or note – not just on a notebook page of the person taking notes for the meeting.

Posting your agreements and concerns publicly and at the time will help cement the hard work that you've already done to the point at which you can talk about visuals. If there are misunderstandings, now is the time to know about them. If tensions emerge between competing points of view within the client team (which is extremely common), now is the time to bring everyone together. If there are particular avenues that you've promised to follow up, now is the time to get these commitments on paper and ready for action.

Presenting visuals is an important step, and from now on the project may start to feel more coherent. It's an inherent problem of the design process that things just won't feel concrete until there is a visual system to talk about. Everyone involved will feel proud to have come this far – and the client will feel just as proud to see a real manifestation of the work they've put in to defining and developing the project. There's a long way to go from here, but having those visuals posted on the wall (and you should definitely post them on the wall of your workspace) will help show everyone a great sense of progress and shared ownership.

TOOLS FROM THIS CHAPTER

- 2×2 matrix
- Interface sketch
- Mood board
- Brand guidelines
- Typecast/Typekit/Fontdeck
- Layout comp
- User journeys

FURTHER READING

There have been a few influential books in this area lately. Luke Wroblewski's book, *Mobile First*[6] certainly reflects a lot of current thinking about this approach to design, and gets into some of the front-end development techniques that you'll need.

Other important books in this field include *Responsive Web Design* by Ethan Marcotte (2011, A Book Apart) and *Designing with Web Standards* by Jeffrey Zeldman and Ethan Marcotte (3rd edition, 2010, New Riders).

Kim Goodwin's book, *Designing for the Digital Age*[7], goes into great detail about how all of these pieces come together, and not just in the graphic design phase of work. She goes into all sorts of useful details about user research, project and client management – almost everything you need to execute a web project, with lots of illustrations and examples. Perhaps better as a reference than as a straight-through read.

Sketching User Experiences[8] by Bill Buxton has had a lot of influence over the iterative nature of today's design environment. Using some very good principles distilled from experience in product, packaging and graphic design, Bill does a great job in convincing the reader of the need for a culture of sketching and refining.

---

[6] *Mobile First* by Luke Wroblewski (2011, A Book Apart).

[7] *Designing for the Digital Age* by Kim Goodwin (2009, Wiley).

[8] *Sketching User Experiences* by William Buxton (2007, Morgan Kaufmann).

Initial prototyping

*"I suppose it is tempting, if the only tool you have is a
hammer, to treat everything as if it were a nail."*
— **Abraham Maslow**[1]

What's here: We'll see some pages actually working; developing, testing and presenting
wireframes and early prototypes.

Reasons for prototyping

Prototyping is an activity that might come at a few different points
in a project. Some people start prototyping before the engagement
formally starts. This is a bad idea, because you won't have a good
idea of what's going to be needed, and you might talk yourself
into a false sense of security. Some people leave prototyping to
the end, or even skip it altogether because it's easier just to design
and then code the finished product. Also not a good idea: there
might actually be risks that you don't see until too late and don't
have time to fix. One of these risks is a communications risk: the
client may not see some piece of functionality until it's too late to
be changed.

In general, as soon as you're creeping up on having the
website requirements figured out, you're in a good position
to prototype. It's worth spending a little time to get the CMS
implemented, to get a staging server set up, to get the basic
navigation of your site in place – these are all things that you have
to do eventually, so doing them earlier than you need to gives
your client more of a chance to see how things will work. And
transparency is good for your project and your stress levels.

How deep do you go? Start on a version of the whole site on
the target platform as soon as you can. This gives the whole team
confidence and makes things real earlier in the process. After

[1] *The Psychology of Science: A Reconnaissance* by Abraham Maslow (1966, Harper & Row).

that, think about specific features that should be worked on and demonstrated. You probably don't have finished page layouts or designs yet, so don't spend time implementing things that will go away – but at the same time, a prototype of risky pages and features is an insurance policy that's worth having.

You prototype any time when you're trying to make a decision about the feasibility of something. Maybe your website is supposed to retrieve artist information from Last.fm; you know it has an API, but you're not sure whether you can get the information you need. Write a prototype that connects to the service and spits out the raw data required. Maybe you have an idea for a new kind of online Ajax wizard to step your users through a process, but you're not sure if you can implement it smoothly. Make a prototype that models that specific page behaviour and see how it works. Learn to know what you don't know yet.

There's another time when you want to make a working prototype: when you've made a technical or design decision that can't be easily shared with the client any other way. This is a somewhat wasteful way to prototype, unless you write your prototype in such a way that it can be rolled directly into the final product. But there's no arguing with code. Either a page does what it's supposed to in a way that's acceptable to you and to your client, or it doesn't. Neither a sketch, a comp, a mock-up nor a specification document can replace a working demonstration of a feature or interaction. If it's something you're not sure about, better to spend the time and get broad agreement. Even if there's some controversy, you're definitely better off having the argument now than when you're testing the site as a whole and getting ready for launch. Prototyping is about showing feasibility and documenting decisions.

Tools and platforms

Generation tools

There are a bunch of tools to help you out. Like any professional activity, knowing the right tools to use is another part of your craft that you'll need to practise and develop. And the right tool for your last project may be the wrong tool for this one.

When you're wearing your project management hat, you need to keep an eye on which tools your team decides to use. Even though there isn't a single right answer, we're all creatures of habit, and it can be tempting to reach for whatever tool feels the most familiar. As a leader you'll need to help push past that urge from time to time; it's OK for you to suggest to a developer that they might be better off starting in a text editor rather than using the latest gadget. You should ask your team to evaluate what works for them, and for the project, as they go along.

Wireframing tools like Axure[2] have become pretty complex, and there are some kinds of prototyping that can be done within them. You start to have access to clickable menus, pop-up boxes, integrations with other data sources and page-level variables for you to use if you want them. Similarly, you can do some quite fancy modelling with Fireworks and other modern graphic design tools. You might want to be careful with these, though.

Remember that the point of the prototype is to show that a certain interaction or feature can work the way you plan on implementing it. If you put time into a fake version of the interaction, you'll have something that you can test with users to see if it works cognitively. This is a valuable kind of prototype. But it's valuable when the question is: "Will my user accept and understand this interaction?" It doesn't bring you any closer to using a real data feed or implementing a new library.

The visual fit and finish of graphical interfaces can disguise some critical components of user acceptance. Using a graphical tool may not tell you if an interaction will work on non-desktop

---

[2] http://www.axure.com/

browsers, for example, because code generated by a tool will not be responsive or adaptive. You won't be able to measure the real-world performance implications of making a certain kind of network connection. You won't have a sense of the compromises you'll have to make to accommodate users with visual disabilities. There are all sorts of reasons why the real thing is sometimes the right choice, even if nothing else on the page looks or feels right.

Practical CMSes
If you're using a content management system for your site, you might as well get an instance up and running early, even during the inception stages of the project. Installation can sometimes be tricky with these tools – you might as well get some of the work done early. And once you do, prototyping the basic site is pretty straightforward, usually. You'll have tools available to set up the basic page structure, perhaps generating simple but working navigation along the way. For example, if you're using ExpressionEngine, you can turn on the membership or user modules so that you can start seeing the difference between logged-out and logged-in states of the website. You can start to make the configuration changes that you need to make to the administrative interface, or even see where you'll need to spend time later on, making up for the shortcomings of your CMS.

There isn't any good reason not to create a shell version of your site as soon as you have the basic information architecture figured out. Having that platform to play with will make it possible to test all of the specific interactions that you're going to need. You can give a head start to whoever will be doing content training with the client, use the prototype to collect real content (in the structure that will go live), and get a real sense for what text lengths are going to work for different content types. You can get going on your test plan, using the prototype as an evolving blueprint of how the final site will work. Anything that shows up as an issue when using or administering the prototype site might well be something to consider for the project's issue log, as well.

Hand-coding

Prototyping doesn't have to live at the level of the visible page. There could well be integration, messaging and data validation that will be completely invisible to the users. But if you haven't done it before, or if you're using a tool or resource for the first time, or if your client isn't sure how something will work with the in-house system, you're better off prototyping and testing early.

In fact, if any of those things start to show up during the requirements phase (new tools, integrations, and so on), as a project manager you should immediately ask yourself and your team how you're going to verify that whatever it is works as advertised.

For many of these prototypes, you may well have interactions that don't yet belong on a page. Perhaps you need to do a side-by-side comparison of two JavaScript libraries, and only one can be installed at a time. Make two little HTML pages, embed your code and test away. Or maybe you want to prototype a stored procedure to get data from a back-end database. Write the procedure, export the query results and check that you're getting what you expect. Maybe you want to ensure you can make a particular network call to include some data from an internal client server. You could write a little Perl script to pull the data and print it to a file, then set it up to run in a server configured like your target production server.

Prototypes aren't about being pretty, or about impressing people – they're not software demos or vapourware. Good prototypes are about reducing technical or project risk by showing something working in the real world. Figure out what the risks are, and make sure you have a prototype to test it, before you get into the actual build phase of the project. You'll be glad you did, as soon as you find that area that's just a little bit harder than you thought it would be. And if you don't find any issues – great! You're coming in a bit early on the build phase, and you haven't even really started yet.

Don't forget

A few things to keep in mind in the prototyping phase:

- Use version control. You should check in designs, code, clickable wireframes – anything that you're working on, not just completed, production code. This gives you a way to compare versions, recover from failures and keep assets in sync within your team.
- Make backups as you go. You will be going fast, so it's likely that you'll make a mistake or break something. Backups give you security to move at the fast speed of good prototyping.
- Use real content. Lorem ipsum and made up or copied content won't give you a sense of what you're building. It doesn't have to be every page, or every real image, but do make sure that you have actual, real content from the client's content owners. Using real content will give you the emotional and logical context you need to evaluate your prototypes.
- Document your assumptions. It's fine to assume that a certain kind of file isn't needed, or that a user will perform a particular action, or anything else. But you should try to write these things down. Because it's a prototype, clients will assume that you've considered everything, and because it's a prototype, you'll assume that you left things out deliberately. As far as possible, write down what you're covering and what you're not.
- Keep a feedback log. You'll get reactions from the team, from the client, from user testers, from anyone else you show your prototypes to. Don't wait until final testing to learn and address these issues – capture feedback now (good and bad), and feed this into the next phase of development.
- Don't be afraid to fake some of the product. It's a prototype, not the final product, so you don't need full coverage. If you want to fake some functions, go ahead. You shouldn't let the lack of full integration keep you from making a good prototype as long as you document your assumptions!

- Use graphics from your sketches or wireframes. It seems obvious, but it's better to use a sketch from an earlier phase, even if it's not finished, rather than make something up or use a stock image. Be sure that the designers are talking to the developers in this phase.
- Do some quick checking to avoid disappointment. Prototypes have a way of breaking the moment you show them to someone outside the team. Avoid some stress by giving everything a quick once-over within the office first. An hour or two of playing and fixing can save some major embarrassments later on.

Prototyping can be tremendous fun. Prototypes will also give you your first real idea about what's going to work. If everyone stays talking, you'll learn a lot while reducing project risk. Enjoy!

Tools from this chapter

- Prototype
- Wireframe
- Content management system
- Frameworks

Further reading

If you want to get better at sketching and generally thinking visually, you should check out Matthew Frederick's book, 101 *Things I Learned in Architecture School*[3]. He goes over the bits of drawing and sketching, perspective, space mass and balance that might come in handy when you're working on initial prototypes.

Since prototyping could use almost any combination of tools, I won't list specific ones here – use what you're comfortable using, and select appropriate platforms to make rapid and iterative changes. If you use particular prototyping tools, you can probably find resources related to them, for example Axure[4].

For a general overview of prototyping, take a look at Todd Warfel's book, *Prototyping*[5]. This book can help you to test the feasibility of your prototypes using your internal team.

---

[3] 101 *Things I Learned in Architecture School* by Matthew Frederick (2007, MIT Press)

[4] *Axure RP 6 Prototyping Essentials* by Ezra Schwartz (2011, Packt Publishing)

[5] *Prototyping: A Practitioner's Guide* by Todd Zaki Warfel (2009, Rosenfeld Media)

INTERACTIVE WIREFRAMING

*"Design is a funny word. Some people think design means
how it looks. But, of course, if you dig deeper, it's really how
it works. To design something really well, you have to 'get it.'
You have to really grok what it's all about."*

— Steve Jobs[1]

What's here: Seeing designs come to life through interactive wireframes and prototypes;
adapting the wireframing process to include time-based interactions.

As websites get more complicated and move further away from
brochureware, web builders are asked to incorporate more
and more time-based interactions, more complicated on-page
functions and a more immersive experience.

A client project is hardly the time to be trying out brand new
preview techniques (at least, not on the client's dime), but if you
want to eliminate one of the bigger risks of your project, you'll
want to find ways to look at on-page interactions in an intelligent
way. If you're really trying to figure out what's going to work and
what's not, it's probably time to put together a combination of
preview techniques that will let you explore the possibilities of
today's web. The build phase of the project is going to be too late
– you'll have already decided on page layouts, so any additional
functionality will start to feel forced or bolted on.

Of course, sometimes the best interactive prototype of HTML
and CSS is, well, HTML and CSS.

---

[1] Quoted by Gary Wolf in "Steve Jobs: The Next Insanely Great Thing", Wired, 4.02. *http://www.wired.com/
wired/archive/4.02/jobs_pr.html*

Showing interactions

Persona-based development of user journeys

The designs that you're working on now are designed for people. Even though search engines may be some of the bigger targets for your website project, people have to use your site to perform actual tasks. Sounds obvious, but thinking too much about you and not enough about your users will leave you with a site that's strangely maladapted.

Ask your interaction designer to print out pictures of your major personas, and tape them to their monitor. At the meeting when you plan the development of your pages, go through each persona. Write their names up on the board, and ask your team to describe the typical journeys that they'll follow through the site.

Persona Journey

Al opens the Leaky Taco site on his mobile, logs in.

He sees the supplies he has associated with his cart.

Al selects onions, mustard and hot dogs, hits "order".

Site confirms delivery tomorrow morning at 6.00.

The cost of his supplies are added to his balance.

Al is emailed a confirm code for the delivery truck.

Al
Chicago food car vendor

Example user persona journey, with persona picture, name, and bullet points describing a particular user journey

Ask to see some sketches of the pages and parts of pages encountered by your personas. This isn't just a designer activity – as a business analyst, and as someone heavily involved in defining the project, you almost certainly have insights into the users' journeys that aren't yet shared by the design team. Don't be afraid to play a bit. This is the last time in the project when you can really define new pieces of functionality.

Sketching first

Just as with visual design, you should start with sketches. These might be thumbnails, but it's a great start. Try this with your team, just before people go away to work on the interactions or to take another pass through the interaction specification.

- Tape up a picture of your persona, and write down the journey you're describing.
- Make a list of the pages or states that they'll encounter, drawing rectangles for each one.
- Put up some Post-its with content or features clustered around each rectangle.
- Start to sketch in the rectangle, just roughly – enough to show the intent of how the interaction might work in real life.
- Draw a new row of rectangles representing errors or unexpected events that might happen on each page or at each step.
- Sketch in the error or unexpected things that might happen. Branch out into new little trails of rectangles if you need to – errors and unexpected turnarounds are part of your user experience, and you'll want to include these in your mock-ups.

At the end of the workshop you probably have most of the website or web app covered, and you're ready to make some mock-ups that can be used.

Sketched wireframe

Have to have something clickable

While paper is a great place to start with prototypes, and sketches are a crucial first step, to really get a sense of utility you're going to have to have something clickable. Think about a stack of Post-its. You might have a list of brilliant ideas there, but if you flip through the pile like an animated flip-book you're going to miss most of what makes those ideas great. (Of course, making flip-books is fun if you have some extra time.) It's the duration, the sense of time and interaction that make a webpage, and why things like page load speeds can turn a great design into a terrible one.

You have some tools already that can help. The various wireframing tools available are getting pretty good at exporting websites that you can click through. You can mock up clickable interactions using PowerPoint or Keynote, perhaps using a UI interface library toolkit like Keynotopia[2]. You can mock up sites quickly using WYSIWYG design tools like Adobe Muse or Dreamweaver.

---

[2] http://keynotopia.com/

The most promising channel for these interactive prototypes, though, is learning to make good mock-ups using HTML and CSS. You don't have to keep all the code when you're done, but you will almost certainly keep some of the concepts. And your feasibility confidence should go way up – if you're using CoffeeScript[3] to create something interesting, or if you're relying on node.js[4] or the html5shiv library[5], you'll know that what you make will actually work as advertised, and your testing will be uniformly valid.

This may not seem like your problem as a project manager, but remember that managing risks is your primary job. Being someone who can check your team's designers and developers on their strategies to get their ideas out into the open is a role that you shouldn't shy away from.

Annotating wireframes

Your project's wireframes will probably become the de facto functional requirements spec, even if you write a long report to go along with them. More than just a tool for internal discussions or client demonstration, those wireframe decks will end up being the obvious, go-to place referred to by everyone doing work in the build stage of your project.

Out-of-date wireframes are pretty common in this business. So are wireframes that are overspecific, and ones that leave out entire areas of vital importance. While not every deck will have the same level of granularity, as someone dealing with specification and quality control it will be up to you to make sure that the wireframes you create and keep have a uniformly useful level of detail. That's where the annotation comes in.

---

[3] http://coffeescript.org/

[4] http://nodejs.org/

[5] http://code.google.com/p/html5shiv/

Focus on the important stuff

Designs never speak for themselves. Seeing a rectangle on a wireframe with an accompanying label saying "Log in" doesn't solve the problem. That text box, even with a label, might be used to input an email address, or perhaps some kind of username. It might be used as the first step in a registration process. It might be a search box to look up other users in a system. It might be a way to check if a particular user handle is already taken in a web application, or a way to claim a name for later use.

If an element is important to the function of a design, you need to provide an annotation. If an element is part of a widespread pattern or convention, you probably don't. There isn't much call to write against that login box:

> "A text box that accepts the login of a user of the system. If the user supplies a valid login and then proceeds to type a correct and matching password and then submits the HTML form using a submit button labelled 'Log in', the user will then be logged into the system."

That's obvious, and doesn't communicate value. You certainly don't need to label and annotate a repeating widget or function that appears on multiple pages, assuming that it behaves the same way on each page. But both of these problems (obviousness and redundancy) are a frequent feature of wireframes.

The net result is to reduce the amount of useful signal within the noise of a webpage. Aircraft designers are probably asked to specify exactly this level of detail (and considerably more) when they specify systems. But life or death engineering isn't being asked of the designers of most webpages.

Show anything unexpected or unusual

A wireframe needs to show the edges of a problem, the expected and the unexpected. But it doesn't need to be tedious, or redundant. If you see wireframes that seem too detailed to be useful (yes, there is such a thing), or wireframes that leave off needed interactions (out of laziness, or because of time pressure), you should stop and rethink.

- Knowing that a login box contains a login isn't useful. Knowing that it will only take twenty-four unaccented Latin ASCII characters might be. Document places where a technical or business constraint results in a behaviour that wouldn't be clear to someone seeing the page.
- If a bit of data is supposed to update in real-time, you need to know that. If a bit of data should be rendered in a bold face, you may or may not need to know that. The more important thing is that a piece of information needs to stand out from its peers – the hierarchy of importance on a page.
- If an error condition will result in the page being redisplayed, you should find a way to show how the page will look. Will there be an alert area at the top, or perhaps indications of problems proximally located near the inputs of a web form? Don't forget those non-straight user journeys, and alternative page states.

Let developers own their annotations

It's tempting for wireframes and their annotations to be assigned to the business analyst who worked the most on requirements, but there are some other choices.

Bringing in the developer who will create a coded prototype or the site itself has a lot of advantages. They will have a chance to work in depth with the pages that you'll be asking them to implement, and the questions they ask will help you to refine the project requirements. Ideally, a lot of the functional specification (the annotated wireframes, plus commentary) will be owned by the person doing a lot of the coding work.

You might also see the visual designer, or creative or art directors getting involved with wireframes. These people will bring an appreciation of content and feature hierarchy and contrast as well as a detailed knowledge of online conventions. Again, involving people who will be integral to implementing the designs for your unique layouts will improve the specification and prepare them for their client presentations.

A dedicated interaction designer probably spends a lot of their life inside a wireframing tool, and can create them quickly and well. Make sure that you've given a good sense of all the alternative paths that a user might take – designing for the unusual or edge case will often strengthen the core, standard path through a website.

There's no problem with jumping in and making some revisions yourself, if there's time and if you have the right requirements background. Increasingly, tools like Axure are integrating directly with version management systems like Subversion or Git, and that assurance not only simplifies multiperson requirements development, but means that changes or groups of changes can be easily rolled back. So even if your ideas don't work out the way you expect, just creating a good starting point for the other members of your team can help to establish the level of fidelity that you need.

TOOLS FROM THIS CHAPTER

- User journey
- Flipbooks
- Wireframes, annotated and otherwise
- HTML mock-up
- Mobile sketch

FURTHER READING

Check out Des Traynor's excellent article on wireframing: *http://blog.intercom.io/wireframing-for-web-apps/*. Do what this man tells you.

A lot of what you need to know about wireframes you can learn from books. However, the more dynamic flavour of interactive wireframing is a new thing, and not as well documented. Still, there are some good standard references that might help you and your team get into the right mindset. Alan Cooper's *About Face 3: The Essentials of Interaction Design*[6] lays out much of the thinking that you'll need in constructing wireframes of all kinds.

Ethan Marcotte's *Responsive Web Design*[7] is an excellent, short book that has rapidly become an industry standard – I see this on desks around the world when I visit development groups. Like any technical book, the specific techniques, technologies and browser support can change quite quickly, but the philosophies embedded in this text are quite sound, and well worth learning. Similarly, Aaron Gustafson's *Adaptive Web Design*[8] gives you what you need to know when implementing progressive enhancement.

Mobile First by Luke Wroblewski[9], another in the A Book Apart series, is also an important book in the field. Of course, mobile browser capabilities are shifting even faster than desktop browsers, but the principles are easily applicable to new platforms as they evolve.

Mark Boulton's conference talks include a lot of information about this topic, as well. I suggest you follow his lead in beginning to think about design in ways other than the traditional page metaphors.

---

[6] *About Face 3: The Essentials of Interaction Design* by Alan Cooper et al (2007, Wiley)

[7] *Responsive Web Design* by Ethan Marcotte (2011, A Book Apart)

[8] *Adaptive Web Design: Crafting Rich Experiences with Progressive Enhancement* by Aaron Gustafson (2011, Easy Riders)

[9] *Mobile First* by Luke Wroblewski (2011, A Book Apart)

15   ## INTERVIEW: ROB WEYCHERT

Rob Weychert is a Brooklyn-based freelance graphic designer, striving to create layouts and interfaces that are organized, intuitive and easy on the eye. In recent years, he has shared his design expertise as a creative director at Happy Cog in Philadelphia and as an interaction designer at Harmonix in Boston. Today, still wanted by the government, he survives as a soldier of fortune, slowly piecing together a plot for world domination with his cohorts at Studiomates.

Rob talked to Breandán about his design process, prototyping and testing, including some parallels to his work in print.

Could you start by talking a little about what you're up to these days?

After I left Happy Cog, I took about a year and a half detour in the games industry[1], doing interaction design. That turned out to be not exactly for me, so I decided to move to New York and start working for myself, which I've been doing for about a year. Honestly, it's been kind of slow to start. Not for lack of interest – I've received a lot of referrals from friends, which has been really helpful, but I've just been slowly acclimatising myself to running a business and figuring out my pace, what I need to do and how I do it all.

Does your business have a name?

It's Rob Weychert Design, LLC. Real simple. I tried to get cute and clever about it, but then decided to be straightforward.

Over the last year, there have been a handful of projects, including a couple of websites that I designed and did the front-end development for. I've helped design pages for a start-up. I was working on a project with a publisher about an article prototype, a responsive design prototype. Now I'm finishing up with the latest A Book Apart books, doing print production and composition.

---

[1] At Harmonix, maker of the popular "Rock Band" video game

Back to print again!

> *Yeah. And there are a couple of potential web projects in the pipeline.*

Visual design in print and web

Since you come from both print and web – one reason I wanted to chat with you – can you tell me, when you're building up a visual system, do you take a similar approach for both?

> *I do take a similar approach – of course, taking into account the factors inherent to each medium. There are certain aspects of the visual approach that are better suited to print than the web. Do you start with type, colour or something else? What do you do, in what order?*

> *It's funny – since I got clued into web standards, I've changed my whole process, even for print stuff. I've gotten back to thinking about design as interpreting meaning, as opposed to dressing things up. So when I work on a print project now, I tend to mark things up as if it was a web project, even though the end product will not be marked up. Since there's already an established hierarchical language which I can use, and do on a daily basis, that's become my standard for doing print projects. I tend to use that approach even for A Book Apart. There are different heading levels – you can see them as HTML's heading 1 and heading 2 – block quotes and all that sort of stuff. I see it through a veil of web markup now, which is kind of weird but is helpful.*

So you're like the geek in those movies, when the guy is out and the code is flashing?

> *Yep, I can see the matrix.*

Presenting designs and prototypes

That's pretty cool. But people who can't see the matrix quite as well, like clients, can have a different idea about what design is. What's your general approach to communicating with them?

> I try not to just present stuff and say, "Here's what your site will look like –
> isn't it great!" I try to go into a little bit of depth without getting super-nerdy. I
> explain how the hierarchy works, why it's set up the way it is and all that sort
> of thing. So I might not get into "Here's how markup works", but I do try to
> explain the separation of structure and appearance, why that's important and
> how it's dealt with. When there is a system in place, I take pains to describe
> how that system works.

Do you ever come back with multiple directions and ask people to choose between them?

> Yeah, I still do that a lot. That was the way we did things at Happy Cog. It's
> one of those things that works great for some projects and not for others. But
> when I give multiple directions and ask which one they like best, I do talk
> through the benefits of each – beyond saying, "I like green!"

Do your clients ever end up saying, "Well, I like green, so this design is better"?

> It depends. When I present multiple options, I explain the problems with
> 'frankencomping' or 'solutioneering' or whatever you want to call it. I make
> it clear that each one is a holistic approach so smashing them together is not
> necessarily going to create success. We can still arrive at something the client's
> satisfied with – with one of these things as its foundation. And the end result
> may be substantially different from any of the foundational approaches. It's
> just a matter of seeing the potential in something – seeing a nugget of what
> you want in one of those directions.

> I don't just throw them a bunch of stuff and say, "Hey, here are some designs:
> pick one."

Can you explain things remotely, or does it need to be in person?

> *Actually remote discussion works best for me. Speaking off the cuff doesn't work as well for me as Basecamp threads or something like that, where I can put my thoughts together really carefully. Conversations in person certainly help the feedback aspect, though. People want to see designs up on a big screen and point at things, but for my initial presentation, it helps me just to write it out.*

Using frameworks for prototyping

A lot of standards guys seem to really like hand-coding stuff in TextMate because they can. Since you are working with web standards, you've also talked about wanting to have that level of craft. Do you use any of the frameworks out there as a starting point?

> *Nope. I'm vaguely curious about the 960 grid system[2].*

Seems to be a popular one, and you can tell just by looking at the websites.

> *Yes, there's that. I feel that making extensive use of those sorts of frameworks – even though a lot of them are really flexible – can set you on a specific path right from the beginning, whereas I'd rather be restricted by the content than by the layout options that I have. I want the layout to do what's best for the content. That's not to say that those sorts of designs and frameworks are always mutually exclusive, but I don't like working with other people's code. You know the saying, "Hell is other people's code." Well, frameworks are other people's code. Plus, most of the frameworks that I know of haven't accommodated the way I've always done things, although that's changing with responsive web design exploding all over the place.*

---

[2] http://960.gs/

It's not always possible to start from scratch. When you're talking about jQuery and stuff like that, for somebody like me who is far from being a JavaScript aficionado, plugging in that stuff is a different story. But when it comes to straight-up HTML and CSS, I like to have as much control as possible.

Content, design and interactive wireframing

Does your print experience play into the way you approach design? In print you tend to have the content at hand when you're starting a print layout, not just a placeholder for a flyer or a poster so the words can be put in later.

Most content-oriented web design is akin to print editorial design, where systems and flexible templates need to be designed. But there is a lot more contingency and templating in web design, where you need to know as much as possible about the content that needs to be accommodated before you design. And that's tricky.

In the new version of my site, for example, I've got this ridiculous blob of code that basically handles all kinds of nested lists. I guess some people would have boilerplate stuff that they use for lists – I should probably do something like that, but it's so tricky because it's so circumstantial. Some sites will never have to deal with video, tables or things like that, while some will have all different kinds of content. That aspect is definitely different from most print design. In print design there's a thing: you make it, you made it, and then you're done. But editorial design definitely has similar challenges, where you need to have a solution at hand for lots of potential problems.

Client education

Do you find that you have to educate your clients to get content delivered early in your projects? Perhaps it depends a little on who you're working with?

Yeah, it does. Certainly at Happy Cog that was a challenge, even though we had a lot of very smart people who knew what was going on. I think there's still a prevailing attitude of "We'll get to the content – eventually." People can get so excited about the design and the process that they forget they actually need to do something with the site.

Honestly, in the last year or so, I haven't run into that problem so much. I did a blog design for this guy who was writing all the time, so there was never a shortage of content for me to work with. I've been fortunate to not have to chase people for content so far, but I'm sure I'll be in that situation down the line.

Designing for mobile

To what extent are you considering non-desktop browser environments for stuff that you're working with on the web?

I am excited about responsive design, and I hope to do a lot more of it. It proposes new workflow challenges. Am I going to design four different versions of a comp to show people how it would work on these different screens? Or am I going to convince them to trust me to make the baseline design look just as good in all four instances? I ran up against that dilemma while doing something for Adobe recently. I think the way we ultimately went about it was a mistake, so I've learned from the experience. Basically, for the first round I gave them a desktop layout, and for the second round I gave them three different sizes based on different screen sizes. I gave them the opportunity to have revisions on multiple screens, and it was a mess. So I'm still figuring that process out, as are a lot of people.

Ethan Marcotte touches on it a little bit in his book, Responsive Web Design[3], but I think it's such a new concept that there is a lot of exploration to be done. Never mind the fact that there are a million different devices that handle things in a million different ways. Luke Wroblewski's book, Mobile First[4], really gets into a lot of that discussion.

[3] http://www.abookapart.com/products/responsive-web-design

[4] http://www.abookapart.com/products/mobile-first

So does Mark Boulton's *Designing for the Web*[5].

> *Yeah, it's a tricky issue, but I'm definitely not ignoring it. I spend more and more time online on my phone or my iPad, and there definitely are a lot of desktop-centric user paradigms that don't work in each environment. I try to shy away from using a lot of hover effects and things like that, for example. I try to shy away from those effects anyway, just because of accessibility for people with disabilities. So in that way all this mobile stuff has been really helpful for accessibility.*

Is it yet possible as a designer to think about the elements of your page as a hierarchy that can flow or manifest in different ways? Or is it still a question of saying, "I've got a screen this wide and another screen this wide – they each need to be rethought"?

> *I'll start with one single design approach, and then adapt that. For now, it's usually the desktop – I start there. When I get that design the way I want it, then I figure out how that changes to accommodate other sizes. Whether or not it's useful to plan for specific sizes, some people using media queries have their breakpoints at popular device widths, usually 480 pixels, and so on. For now, I think that starting with one size makes sense, so long as you're using a flexible approach that isn't based specifically on pixels, though the visual design itself might be based on pixels.*

> *When it comes to code, however, I do the mobile-first thing. I don't want the mobile users to have to load all kinds of code that they're never going to use.*

---

[5] http://www.fivesimplesteps.com/products/a-practical-guide-to-designing-for-the-web

Time to test

How do you test the designs or early prototypes?

> *That's something I'm ashamed to say I don't do. I really need to work with a team to properly test that. When I'm redesigning somebody's small site, unless they have infrastructure in place to deal with testing, it doesn't really get tested, beyond my showing it around to a handful of people.*

Which can be complete testing – you don't need to be in a soundproof room with eye-tracking software.

> *That was one of the most valuable things I learned from Steve Krug[6]: that you don't need a million-dollar testing lab to do proper testing. At the same time, I feel that some things don't get quite the testing they deserve, so that's something I need to do better.*

Understanding clients, understanding designers

This book is about the expectations gap between the process of making and the process of commissioning. Can you think of a few things that you wish people commissioning web projects would be more aware of? And then things that you, as a maker, wish you thought of earlier in the process?

> *The best projects are the ones where both sides, the commissioner and the producer, have an 80-percenter mentality. Where whatever team is making this thing has a well-rounded knowledge of the whole process from both sides, and the same is true on the commissioning side. For example, at Happy Cog, when we worked on the Maryland Institute College of Art website, the guy who hired us, Kevin Hoffman (who then went on to work for Happy Cog'), knew exactly the sort of thing he was going for. So his decision to go*

---

[6] Steve Krug is the author of the popular book about web usability, *Don't Make Me Think!*

[7] Kevin Hoffman is now working in the Philadelphia area as a freelance information architect, writer, speaker and facilitator.

with Happy Cog was a very educated one. He used Adaptive Path[8] to do user experience studies and so forth. Whatever success there was in that project had to do with a really good understanding on both sides of what it needed to be.

Getting that kind of understanding can be hard as hell. In Design Observer a few years ago, Michael Bierut said: "Not everything is design. But design is about everything."[8] To properly design for something, you have to know all about design, but you also have to know about the thing you're designing for. And that onus isn't necessarily on the other side, the side of the people commissioning the project. They need to know intensively about their thing, and so do you. But they're putting it on you to use your design expertise.

Sounds as if we designers need to be experts in everything?

In a perfect world. But that never happens.

If you had a client who wasn't a Kevin Hoffman, and you could hand that person a book, manual or checklist and say, "Read this stuff to get a glimpse of what this process will look like", what are a couple of things that would be in it?

I'm going to point to Happy Cog again. We worked really hard to explain things right from the pitch. We would go into depth about our process and why it was the way it was, right down to explaining what web standards are and why they are important. We did our best at the outset of the project to say, "Here's how it's all going to break down. Here are the milestones. Here is the schedule. This is going to have to be flexible because there's always a dance, an exploration. But here it all is." Then at the outset of each specific phase, we would come back with more depth of information. We would say, "We're going to present these designs. You're going to have the opportunity to give your feedback. We're going to revise them." Without getting into too much jargon or getting too nerdy, we gave them the vital information they needed.

---

[8] http://observatory.designobserver.com/entry.html?entry=4137

What kind of information would you like to get from the client?

What's key to get are things like, "Here's what we're trying to accomplish" and "Here's why this is important". We'd do our best to structure our questions to get the best answers that we could in the beginning of every phase. It's all a question of structuring those communications properly. You can have some boilerplate stuff, but it's not always about smashing things into a mould – it's about having a flexible mould. Not treating every project in exactly the same way, but instead trying to get at its idiosyncrasies and specific challenges.

I believe in avoiding templated approaches, but there's one example that deviates from that, at least with Happy Cog. Instead of giving an ordinary response to an RFP, they would submit a project planner that did a good job of asking the right questions, things like: "What are you trying to do?"; "Why are you trying to do it?"; "Who are you trying to do it for?" That's the definition of boilerplate, right? But it worked.

So, I guess the key is finding that balance between relying on a standard structure or adapting a structure that makes sense for each specific project. How hard is it to strike that balance? Short answer: it's fucking hard.

PART 4

Construction and Testing

Content management systems and integration present project managers with an array of complicated decisions. In this section, I discuss your CMS options and explore the maze of integrating with enterprise databases and customer relationship systems. As you move through the build and deployment phases, I'll help you focus on change and risk management. I'll also discuss some of the testing and Agile development techniques that will help your team through the project.

Content management systems

Some thoughts on integration

Time to build

Time to test

Interview: *Niek Jansma*

CONTENT MANAGEMENT SYSTEMS

"Innovation in process may trump innovation in product.
But innovation in both trumps either."
— **Bill Buxton**[1]

What's here: Deciding how to build or select the content management system for your website; CMSes are often selected early in a project – managing them is an art in itself.

Rolling your own?

When you go hunting for a good way to get your beautiful designs and content on to the web, you will quickly run into the classic question: buy or build? You can buy (or license) a commercial content management system that promises to deliver your content, designs and functionality using some sort of database-backed templating engine. Similarly, you can adopt one of a number of open source CMS projects, getting the underlying code for free but probably paying for support. Or you can just build your own, as simple or complicated a system as you want. Evaluating existing CMSes and projects is so complicated that the last option may seem the most tempting – after all, you have a database guy and a programmer and a front-end developer, so why not just build the system that you'll use to get your work on the web? Still beats coding and managing the whole site in plain HTML, right?

Maybe. There's nothing wrong with building a CMS if you have the chops and the time. But think really carefully about what you're getting into.

Estimating development time to build a content management component

It's tempting to build something that will publish your pages. As you go through the incredibly long list of available CMSes, you'll get the impression really quickly that there's no one system that

---

[1] *Sketching User Experiences* by William Buxton (2007, Morgan Kaufmann).

really does everything you want. This one is friendly for designers, this one is more developer-orientated; this one makes updating news articles a breeze, but is inflexible when it comes to static layouts; this one will generate clean, lightweight, standards-based code, but takes a lot of black art knowledge to customise, while this one is easy to use but generates an impenetrable forest of invalid markup.

That's the nature of the industry, unfortunately: no one has come up with the perfect way to publish content on the web, in part because no single project is going to balance all of those factors. So the temptation to build your own is going to be there. If you succumb, you'll probably see some advantages:

- It's your code, so you're not at the mercy of other companies or projects to fix a bug or answer a configuration question.
- You can charge for the service that you're offering, recouping your investment in building a CMS across multiple projects over time. You can eliminate all of the features that you don't care about, focusing on a lean, mean system that does *exactly* what you want.

Of course, you should be aware of some potential complexities, as well:

- It's your code, so no one else is going to be able to help you much when it comes to making changes or figuring out a new configuration option that will let your system scale to multiple clients.
- The temptation is going to be to customise your system a bit for each client; after all, each has a different workflow and different needs. You should resist this temptation: you'll end up forking your own codebase in a way that will not make your developers happy after a couple of projects. When you fix a bug, you're not going to want to go back to ten projects and remember the ten ways that you found to do something, just so that you can fix the same bug on the websites of ten clients.

- Don't underestimate the requirements of workflow. Making a system that takes text or markup from a web form, combines it with a PHP template and outputs an HTML page is pretty straightforward. But there are other requirements that will creep up on you, like workflow.

Here are some workflow questions:

- What happens when you need someone to approve the content first?
- What if the approver shouldn't have permission to delete the page, but only update it?
- What about when the template changes – can you still use the old form data to build the page?
- What happens when you need to roll back to a previous version of the page – are you keeping track of that?
- What about when some pages should be behind a registration wall?
- What about when your registered members want to delete their accounts?
- What happens when an editor deletes their account? What about the things currently assigned to that person in your workflow?

The complexities and wrinkles can multiply quickly – those questions were just about workflow. What about date-based displays, map or form integration, social data integration, multiple languages, mobile device detection and optimisation, account management and sitemap reorganisations?

If you're going to build your own CMS, great! Have a good time. But be sure that you know what you're getting into. Talk to the potential editors of the system – they're your primary users for a CMS. Figure out what you'll need to know about workflow, roles, permissions and security (hint: these are the bits most often overlooked). Think about the user journeys of your content writers and editors, and design and map these out just like you're figuring out what the users of the site need and want. Put it altogether into a reasonable project plan, with plenty of time for iteration and improvement. And don't expect a single client to pay for all of the work that you put in – this sort of internal software platform is an investment that you're making as a web-building team, and you should think about how much capital you want to put up in the form of lost billings and overhead, and when you expect to recoup the investment through license fees, or as a competitive advantage in bidding for web work.

If you decide that the whole thing is too daunting, not to worry. You have some incredibly good tools and platforms out there to choose from, and with a bit of training and configuration work you can get a system that probably meets most of your needs (and those of your client) pretty well. And a lot of CMS products can be branded or styled to match your agency identity, so the client doesn't even have to think too much about where the system came from. The important thing is that it works, and lets you express your visual language and your client's beautifully crafted content as fluidly as possible.

Consider if you're integrating with another system

One area where off-the-shelf CMSes are quite weak is when it comes to ingesting data from other system. It stands to reason: there are so many possible line of business systems that hold data about customers, products, services, billings, customer support and sales pipelines, how could any standard package really know how to get the information that you need to display? With any larger client, you'll inevitably find that there is important information that should be published via the project's website that now resides in some other system.

Product documentation is a biggie – for most organisations that sell things, there's already going to be some sort of inventory management in place. Same for technical specifications. And customer databases and customer relationship management systems (CRMs) are a big deal as well. Your client has spent a lot of money and effort getting these systems in place, and it's only natural (and quite correct) to want to use this information to improve the user experience of their website.

Most web CMSes, of course, won't really know what to do with these data stores. A CMS usually has its own database, its own user management system, its own communications tools. And CMS platforms that are better at talking to big business systems (sure, there are some) tend to be so complex that the headaches of integrating them may not be worth it. So what to do? Does having a big organisational data store to deal with mean you can't use your favourite lean and mean CMS platform, the one with the template system that your front-end developers can configure in their sleep? Not at all.

Talk to the client's database administrators, or to the owners of the CRM or inventory system. You'll probably find that these systems can spit out data in a form that's not so hard to deal with, probably plain delimited text (the venerable CSV file!) or as some kind of XML. The requirement for data integration might be one-way only – you need a list of products and categories, but don't have to write anything back to the inventory system in return. And the requirement for integration probably doesn't mean moment-by-moment, or in real time. Think about whether a nightly dump from the business system could be picked up by your lean CMS. Maybe all you need is a little script that reads the file and makes some updates in the CMS's database, leaving the PHP and control panel interface alone completely and none the wiser. Maybe you can generate a simple email from your CMS that will be picked up by the account management system, without having to be something complicated or to use a web service.

There's no shame in finding a simple solution for integration. And if you're figuring out file formats and workflows anyway, why not use the web publishing tool that you're most comfortable with? For the long-term, consider the direction of the CMS provider and make a plan in case you need to get your data and assets out later.

Tools from this chapter

• Project plan
• User journeys

Further reading

For a list of content management system platforms, you could start with CMSMatrix: *http://www.cmsmatrix.org/*. With more than 1,200 platforms (as of this writing), it's not for the faint-of-heart!

If you're interested in ExpressionEngine, a CMS that I and some of my friends rather like, you could take a look at the EE docs at *http://expressionengine.com*.

If you haven't spent any time with the Markdown syntax as a simple way to get your thoughts on the web using a simple text-based format, you probably should. Look at the documentation at *http://daringfireball.net/projects/markdown/* and you'll find a very powerful idea there about publishing valid web markup without an in-depth knowledge of HTML. You should probably look for Markdown plug-ins for whatever CMS platform you adopt – this can be a nice way to include a variety of users in the publishing process.

SOME THOUGHTS ON INTEGRATION

"Making the simple complicated is commonplace; making the complicated simple, awesomely simple, that's creativity."
— **Charles Mingus**[1]

What's here: Legacy systems are explored; a bit of a history lesson; what web shops should know about integration patterns; creating a good technical specification; and managing change.

Web shops aren't great at integration, but more sites are starting to behave like applications, so we should learn about web app integration.

There are a lot of designers out there. And it's not terribly surprising: the costs to create a digital agency have gone down, and down again. One or two people can work out of their homes using their college laptops and create websites that are sometimes the envy of agencies with millions in revenue. That's a good thing: one of my favourite things about the web is its openness. Anyone can use tools, many of which are free, to create beautiful designs and well-functioning web sites.

The thing is, the web is being asked to do more and more things. If you want to integrate a website with the existing mailing list of your client, you're going to need more than a copy of Photoshop or GIMP. You have to communicate with enterprise databases and CRM systems. You might have to take data captured on the web and put it into an accounting system. Making a timetable change on the city bus company website you just built might require that you feed data to a layout tool so that the bus signs can be reprinted.

---

[1] Statement in Mainliner (July 1977) as quoted in *Creativity and the Writing Process* by Olivia Bertagnolli (1982).

These sorts of integrations have become pretty common, and they require more special handling than a standalone website. If you come from a software development background, you're in luck – but even those of us with programming backgrounds find it hard to estimate and manage back-end integration stages.

Interoperability Services

Web Services	3rd Party Tool Plug-ins	Metadata Management	EDI and EDI-INT

Integration Services

Transformation	Routing	Data Management	Query Management

Adapter Services

Service Handling	Event Handling

EDI & e-Biz Adapters	Terminal Emulation Adapters	Transaction System Adapters	Technology Adapters	Touchpoint Adapters	Application Adapters	Data Adapters

Line-of-business applications such as order management or customer relationship management systems interact in a complex way with other services present in an enterprise

A history lesson

Mainframes

A computer used to be a person who sat at a desk and calculated things. Wild, right? You'd send your computing task to a room full of people who would sit there, do the calculations, and send you back the answer on paper. When we developed electronic computers, the iconic room-sized machines of not-so-ancient history, you only had a few more options than before. You could add and subtract large columns of numbers. You could multiply numbers and do basic sums, as long as there weren't too many digits. You could calculate things like compound interest, and you could get a computer programmed to give you logarithmic tables.

Soon computers became a bit more sophisticated, and could start to handle memory and symbols. Some were configurable enough to be programmed and reprogrammed on the fly, so you could set up your own programs. Often a single, central computer would do all the work while lots of people tapped in using simple typewriter-style terminals, in a structure not dissimilar to the server architecture of the web today.

Eventually computers became the best technology for storing large amounts of information, processing it and sending it back out again in other forms. Programming languages started to get more sophisticated, and the instructions given to a computer looked more and more like natural human languages, in terms of syntax and grammar. The direct descendants of some of these giant computers are still in use in a lot of insurance and manufacturing companies – and they're still great at counting things.

Client-server

Once processors got fast enough, the computer you could have on your desk was fast enough to handle its own inputs and outputs, in real time. But since a lot of the data remained in still larger computers, buried somewhere in the organisation, your computer needed to talk to the bigger one to get the information it needed.

It would look like you were working with your information directly, but behind the scenes a lot of chatting was going on between the little computers on the edges and the central computers that kept all the good stuff.

Data exchange formats started to become important, so that you could write programs for your desk computer in a standard way and know that you would be able to get your information back in a structured format. Each computer manufacturer, it seemed, had their own standards for databases, for files, even for network communications. You'd buy into the electronic ecosystem for the manufacturer you liked best, and there you were – writing software designed to run on the client computer, matching up with more software running on the server computer.

Up to the distributed cloud – simple formats rule, again.
Deskbound and, eventually, handheld computers got faster and faster, and now you have enough computing power in your phone to make the early space program jealous. But the big data still lives far away from the desktop – for information that we really want to keep safe, we mount expensive servers in bombproof, climate-controlled buildings with elaborate physical security measures and backup diesel generators. We shuffle our data around very quickly, now; we have dedicated fibre-optic lines that can move those ones and zeros faster than you can imagine. But we're still writing software for our client devices, greedily sipping at the stream of precious data served forth magnanimously by the big machines at the centre of our information web.

Since so many people are moving so much data, the standards for exchanging information have become both important and complex. We now have XML schemas to define precisely the structure of the data that we're sending, and we can check that what we get is what we're expecting. We have protocols to make sure that every byte of information we put on the wire gets to the other side and reassembled, in order, into the perfect copy of what we flung over. We have standards to identify people and machines, and we have complex systems of codes, descendants themselves of military communications, to keep our client-server conversations safe. It's a complicated world, but our standards keep us on track.

Building with a CMS

Content management systems pose a special challenge for web development projects, in part because you may introduce a new software package and expect an existing IT infrastructure to take on its care and feeding. This can be a hard case to make. You'll need to show that your proposed platform will integrate well with any existing servers, uses programming languages that can be supported by existing staff, and is or can be made to be sufficiently secure. The platform choice that goes into this discussion can be an oddly difficult one, because designers, developers and system administrators all want different things from the system.

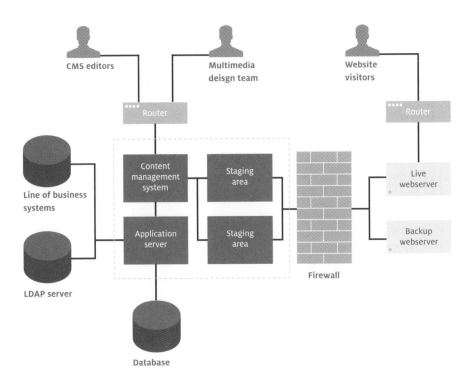

A content management system introduces some complexity into the IT environment, and you will need to keep in close contact with the owners of the various systems

The use of a CMS can also introduce another, subtle integration issue – the problem of saving state. Usually IT people are used to storing information in well-defined repositories, whether those be relational databases, document or record storage solutions, or non-relational transaction storage mechanisms.

Here are a few things to be aware of when you get going with the CMS part of your work.

Quick mock-ups using prebuilt templates can be misleading. All of the CMS vendors can show you installations that seem to be beautiful and flexible. But without taking a look under the hood, you don't really know how well you can make a platform work for your content and your project.

Create staging sites early. Just because the designers and web developers on the team will do most of the CMS selection, integration and customisation doesn't mean that you shouldn't treat the CMS as a real software project. Stage releases of the CMS platform to a production-like environment as soon as you can, to make sure you don't have bigger issues to deal with closer to launch.

Schedule releases from development to staging. Just as you would with other kinds of software environments, keeping discrete DTAP (development, testing, acceptance and production) environments will help you keep the quality up and avoid errors. To keep your content and designs working as expected, find a way to add your content and designs to a CMS instance where you can test consistently, then move on from there to each environment. Managing that deployment process is just as important in a CMS environment, and you'll probably have to do some tweaking to database dumps or shell scripts to get your content in and out cleanly.

Making a list

Reverse engineering a line of business application is difficult
More than one web design agency has been told that they'll be integrating some feature of the new website into an existing business system that does something useful for the organisation. Every such agency has been told that integration will be "no big deal" and that they, the client, will "give you all the help you need." More than one agency has walked cheerfully into this trap, figuring that it can't be so hard, especially with the client's IT department all ready and eager to help out.

It's not so easy, really. If you're lucky, the business application will have an API all ready to go and well documented. If that's the case, the work you'll have to do is merely difficult. For older systems, or more complicated ones, the work of just figuring out the operation of the business systems could take more time and budget than the rest of your website redesign project combined. It's even possible that you'll have to examine the operation of the business software the way an anthropologist learns a new language: carefully posing questions and recording the results, slowly, with minor variations until the basic syntax and grammar of the machine's language starts to make sense.

Complete input/output list
Assuming that you have a well-documented system to work with, you're going to need to figure out all the things you'll need to send to it from the website system. You might send data through the site's CMS, or it might be easier to write a standalone script or program against the site's database. You'll send data and queries, so figure out what that communication is going to look like.

- First off, what are the names and order of fields of information that are expected?
- For each field, how many characters do you get?

- How are characters to be encoded? If you send information that looks like normal text, you'll need to know what to do with line breaks, special characters like ampersands and quotes, and those curly quotation marks that are added by word processors.
- You need to know whether the information you send needs to be checked or validated in some way. Are there fields for which only one from a set list of values will be accepted?
- How about anything where you send multiple answers to a single question, like the names of ticked checkboxes on a form? How are those answers listed, and how are the bits of such a compound data field delimited?

Once you've figured that out for the input side, you'll need to make the same list for the outputs. Yes, with just as much detail. I wasn't kidding when I said that this could take you a while.

Error conditions

Of course, things don't always go to plan, even when you speak to robots in their own language. You need to work out the error conditions that the system will have to deal with, and for each type of error you'll need to know what happens. If you send information into a business system and it throws out an error, what do you do? Dump the data and apologise to the user? Make a note in a file and hope that a system administrator can piece it back together later on? Find a version of the system that's working better and send the data there?

And if there's an error of some kind when you retrieve data – what then? You could display the error code and message directly to the user, but that's usually not very helpful, and also makes your website look broken. You can try again in a few seconds, and hope that things have cleared up. You could politely ask the user to check a particular field to make sure that what gets sent is reasonable. For web services, be sure to have a fallback strategy. All sites fail sometimes.

If it isn't obvious enough yet, this is one part of the project where you need some spreadsheets and flowcharts: spreadsheets to keep track of fields, formats, messages and so forth; and flowcharts to figure out what to do when things go right, and what to do when things go wrong. It's good to have the client's IT guru by your side, of course, but for the sorts of things that web developers are often asked, you'll find that in many cases no one got around to writing a manual for it.

Checking it twice

Integration always seems fairly straightforward until it's time to write the code and get things going. You'll need a few things to get started, so be sure to work this out before you get in over your head.

You'll need a development instance to test against – this isn't negotiable. Using a production version of an integration system won't work: you won't be able to take it offline to test errors; you won't be able to feed false data back in; and you won't be able to run proper load tests. Use the acceptance or test environment, and make sure that what you develop against is a true copy of what you'll see in production.

You need access to the right people – this, too, is non-negotiable. Integration without the cooperation of IT and the business unit owners won't work, no matter how much the marketing director wants it to happen.

You can only estimate this work after you've seen the line of business or web service app. Integration can be quite straightforward, but you won't know until you try, and chances are it will certainly be harder to estimate than the web parts of your project.

Like all testing: get the typical case, and both edge cases (big and small data). Test all of these conditions, including the ones that feel unlikely.

It's easy to assume in testing that the service you communicate with will always be working and sending you data. Be sure that you check for the exceptions: when the service you're trying to reach is offline, or sends you garbage, or sends a malformed message, or the communications are interrupted.

Managing the business process

If you were brought in by the marketing or communications department to work on a website, it's possible that you haven't been introduced to some of the people you'll need to work with on any line of business system integration for the site. Get your highest level contact to introduce you, and make sure that the business unit has some time set aside to work with you. If you can, try to get a high-level stakeholder to tie the success of the business department, in part, to the outcome of integrating their system with the website. Having everyone with the same incentive is part of making the process work well.

Be aware, though, that the departments who control systems like customer relationship management, billing or accounting may not completely agree with you about the value of the website you intend to build. Yes, almost every organisation needs some some sort of web presence, but for line of business application managers, the website or web application may seem like a distant second behind their own technical development and maintenance requirements.

The trick here is to get people excited, and also blended into the team working daily on the website. Don't just invite the IT manager to the kick-off and then let them show up again in the middle of the build phase. If you're using some variant of an Agile process, fold the line of business system owner into your daily Scrum. Treat them as a stakeholder when you do interviews. Assign research and user testing and market research tasks. The more closely the various departments are involved, the smoother the integration process will be. You'll hear sooner about problems with your requirements, and you'll hear about workarounds before you know you need them. You'll tackle security and deployment challenges earlier in the project, and the functionality of your website will be richer. It all comes from a sense of engagement and shared goals. And creating a shared goal is about a lot more than writing a great project initiation document. Shared vision is developed through the day in, day out collaboration and working relationships that you build into your regular work.

One more note on integration: there are sometimes some terms and conditions that you may not think of. If you rely on a Google service that resolves an XML feed to download current exchange rates, you may find after proof of concept but during build that the service can only be called a few times before the service is throttled. The same goes with a billing or CRM system. API or web service calls that work fine for your early demo may fall over at higher volumes. Querying a transactional database fifty times per second to look up customer addresses may be fine, but then again it might put new load on a server that isn't designed for real-time queries. These sorts of problems can have architectural implications: you may have to create a caching tier, or proxy your requests, or download data in batch dumps rather than in real time. Any of these strategies might work, but it certainly helps to know where your data is going to live before you get too far into the build. A social network API may turn out to have limitations on commercial use that will affect the site you're building.

Of course, you should try to build the richest, most relevant and compelling web experience that you can, which means personalisation and deep integration into product delivery, customer service and digital asset management facilities. Just be sure that you're aware what you can do and what you can't. The way you'll know is to ask the people who work with these systems every day.

Managing change

Change management is a discipline in itself, and one worth studying if you start working with larger clients and organisations. Just as steering an ocean liner is harder than steering a small sailing boat, larger organisations can develop a massive inertia that works against any change of course. This isn't necessarily a bad thing, and you should try not to be frustrated: this inertia of forward motion allows for a predictability and steadiness of purpose that can create real value for a lot of real people. But you're making a new website, which will introduce a certain amount of change. Even a simple rewrite of an existing site will introduce changes to the organisation: the editorial workflow; the marketing of products and services; in relationships with customers and other businesses.

Change doesn't happen when you talk about a better way of doing something, and this can be frustrating. Here are a few more things that won't create change:

- Showing that a new technology is superior to the previous version.
- Drawing a chart that shows a more efficient way to structure an organisation.
- Demonstrating that an existing way of doing something is inefficient.
- Presenting the results of research that shows a shift in marketplace conditions.

These are intellectual arguments. They don't speak to the motivations of the people involved, even if perfectly reasoned, logical and objectively correct. Change requires that people believe there is a better way to do something, and then feel motivated enough to learn a new skill, technology or process, and then have the patience to work through the inevitable transition period when the new way is less efficient than the old way. That won't happen on the back of intellectual argument – real change requires getting at motivation.

When thinking about change management for your projects, your starting point is a complete business process analysis, at least for all the parts that your website will affect. Look at capabilities, attitudes, financial and HR processes that will be affected by what you're proposing. Provide incentives for your team to support change management. Don't just criticise the developers for adding elements without recording them. Create a framework in which approving and recording changes is simple for everyone.

Don't forget that a new website demands change from a lot of people in an organisation. Be sensitive to what people need and how they work, and leave enough time for new workflows or technologies to be absorbed and put into practice. Be prepared to support the organisation during the transitional period.

Agreeing a technical specification

Getting a good technical specification approved makes sense and will reduce risk, but it's tempting to spend time in the wrong areas. Specifically, it's tempting to spend a lot of time writing down obvious cues ("The user is presented with options for OK and Cancel. If the user selects OK, the operation is completed; if the user selects Cancel, the operation is terminated.") and not enough time writing down the actual hard parts.

Here are the things I've found to be most important on technical specification writing.

Write the specification around the edge cases, not the obvious, correct paths. "Retrieve a user's name and address from the database based on the userid being supplied" is straightforward. "Userid supplied is not found in the database" and "A database connection cannot be established" are edge cases. You'll learn more and write more robust code by focusing on the latter.

Involve the IT people who are closest to the technical system you're looking at, but recognise that they aren't always the people who are best at writing down what they know. Pair someone with a flair for words with the IT person, and you may get a great specification. Use interviews, collaborative boxes and arrows on a whiteboard – whatever works to extract the information you need.

Never treat the technical specification as done. As much as we tend to write catchphrases at the start of our documents saying things like, "This is a living document and will change over time", the incentive to keep a technical specification up to date decreases dramatically to the point where it simply won't happen. If you can automatically generate your documentation based on the code you're creating, that's probably best – look at the structure of Javadoc[2] or Ruby-Doc[3] for examples. Trying to write everything down at the start won't work – there's just no way that you can think of everything that you need, at least in the timescale of a typical web project.

Best of all, involve the IT systems people you need on a daily basis. Even if it seems that they won't have enough to do, getting this time commitment in advance will make so many things go more smoothly. And the technical specification will continue to grow along with the website, which is just the way you want it to work. Hoping to get a complete technical specification in advance of your web work is futile – much better to include the people you need to create the first draft, then keep making changes as your understanding of user journeys increases. As you prioritise or remove features from the website, the technical specification for integration will keep up.

[2] http://www.oracle.com/technetwork/java/javase/documentation/index-jsp-135444.html

[3] http://ruby-doc.org/

Speaking the language

There may be some vocabulary issues as you get into the nuts and bolts of communicating between different systems, and communicating with people who are used to different systems. Rather than talking past each other, it makes sense for everybody to identify patterns of integration – templates for how machines communicate that have been written down in a generic way. These patterns don't depend on the specific languages or systems involved, so can give you some common vocabulary.

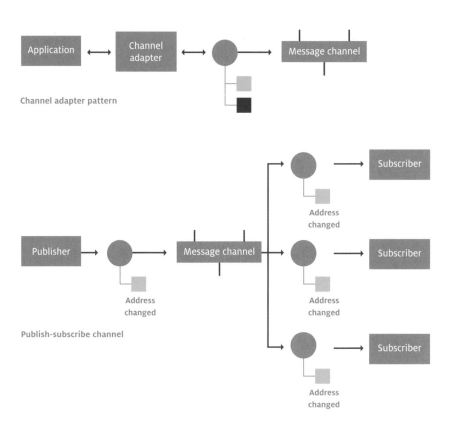

Two examples of messaging patterns, adapted from the book *Enterprise Integration Patterns* by Hohpe and Woolf

TOOLS FROM THIS CHAPTER

• Technical specification
• Integration pattern
• I/O list

FURTHER READING

Systems integration is a big area, and the field contains a lot of very smart people earning a good living by doing only this. Your requirements for a given web application are probably not as complicated as for some other integration projects, but it's just as important that you write a robust system and that you handle inputs and outputs between systems cleanly.

The books listed below describe the patterns of integration between systems, including some that may not seem obvious. The technologies of integration change fairly frequently, but if you develop a good working knowledge of synchronous and asynchronous integration patterns, you'll always know what you're talking about when you attack your next project. Speaking the same language as IT people is a big plus!

Enterprise Integration Patterns by Gregor Hohpe and Bobby Woolf (2004, Addison-Wesley). You'll find the pattern library at *http://www.eaipatterns.com*.

Design Patterns: Elements of Reusable Object-Oriented Software by Erich Gamma, Richard Helm, Ralph Johnson and John Vlissides (1994, Addison-Wesley).

TIME TO BUILD

"The longer a defect stays in process, the more expensive it is to fix."

— **Steve McConnell**[1]

What's here: Writing compliant, working code; Agile building from the inside out; and some notes on estimating.

Depending on your point of view, building the website can seem like the crux of the whole project, or an anticlimax after the excitement of visual design. Either way, it's an important phase to watch, especially as so much of the work will start to seem a bit abstract to non-technical people. Your skills as a two-way business-to-technical translator will certainly be needed. And while there have been lots of workshops and decisions up to this point, there are lots of decisions left. As a project manager you'll still have to protect your development team pretty closely from radical scope changes.

This chapter talks about getting the team geared up and the management systems in place to make a streamlined, fun and efficient process. It's not your job to do the building, but you will probably be the one to explain to both technical and non-technical stakeholders why a particular technique or technology gets picked. Anything that you can do that helps with the jargon will probably seem like a good idea.

Making websites takes care and concentration, and there really isn't such a thing as a typical website. (Or rather, there is, but it probably isn't what you want to build). Now that a perfectly good

---

[1] "An Ounce of Prevention" by Steve McConnell, IEEE Software, May/June 2001.

website can be made by deploying a prepackaged template on a blogging platform, creating an attractive web page with words and images and reasonable white space no longer quite has the magic that it had in the mid 1990s.

Organisations these days want to stand out: they want to provide a compelling user experience; they want to create an integrated experience online that supplements, enhances or replaces their offline brands. For all of these things, you have some coding to do. Whether it's adapting a WordPress theme, beginning with a CSS-based grid or hand-coding HTML and CSS from scratch, this is where what you do on the web most closely resembles server-side software development projects.

Agile development

Incorporating Agile and Scrum ideas

Agile is all the rage. Beginning with some early experiments in extreme programming and other radical ideas, large organisations, governments and small enterprises are all buying into Agile processes. While there are many Agile techniques that you can follow (and more than a few rituals of dubious utility), the essential nature of Agile is pretty easy to understand, and it's all about risk.

Writing code is risky, and writing complicated code is riskier. There was a time (and it's probably still true, depending on how you count it) when most software projects failed. Not just the underfunded ones, or the ones with inexperienced people, or the ones solving insanely difficult computer science problems in artificial intelligence or human language parsing. (Shows how old I am, I guess – we used to think that understanding human speech was one of those hard problems that would never be solved. Now I ask my phone if I'll need an umbrella in Stockholm next Wednesday and I get a perfectly germane and accurate answer.)

Complexity adds risk, and complexity tends to multiply by itself as it grows, quickly creating massive uncertainty in time estimates, costs, usability and even achieving the basic objectives of the project.

Such complexity wasn't a good match for the classic way of developing requirements. While pure waterfall methods have perhaps never been a great idea in the software world[2], the typical way to specify a software project used to be something like:

- Write down all the things that the software project needs to do (requirements).
- Write down exactly how the software is going to do those things (algorithms).
- Write down the information structures that would be needed to do those things (data model).
- Write down the information being passed between different parts of the system (messages).
- Write down all the configurations that the system can be in (states).
- Write down all the instructions that a user might pass to the system, and what the correct response should be (interface).
- Write down how you will test each of the user instructions, states, messages, data structures, algorithms and requirements.
- Start building a system to do all that stuff.

It was complex, difficult and (some would say) impossible. Trying to do that much analysis up front created a huge pressure on the actual writing of code. After all of that work and time invested, your system really had to work – or else! And when you're in the middle of trying to code to a truly complete specification, you really have to hope that all of the analysis and modelling done earlier in the process still applies to what the customer wants to see. With a process that took months or years before even beginning to build working code, the chances were fairly high

---

[2] The first application of the waterfall model in software development is generally considered to be set out in "Managing the Development of Large Software Systems", an article by Winston Royce appearing in "Proceedings of IEEE WESCON" (1970). Although Royce was critical of the idea that software could be specified completely in the absence of a prototype, the Royce paper was cited by subsequent US Department of Defence software standard documents as support for strict waterfall model software development.

that by the time you got around to making something work, the needs of your users would have moved on, or a competitor would have found a better solution, or there would be a new hardware platform offering new capabilities; or the further refinement of some infrastructure like processing power or network speed would mean that the design constraints that had been carefully analysed and compensated for were no longer issues – and something else was.

Projects ran these risks:

- Not delivering a system at all.
- Delivering something too broken to be retrievable.
- Writing code that was too slow to be realistic.
- Creating something that wasn't relevant to the problem at hand; in other words, solving the wrong problem.

These were expensive risks and expensive problems, and all of the negative outcomes above happened frequently.

So, to manage these risks, Agile takes some opposing approaches. Rather than specify everything and then build, Agile says that you start building as soon as you can, then make what you've built better and better until you've completely met the requirements. Rather than making lists of requirements, data structures and so forth, on roughly the same level of hierarchy, Agile says that you constantly review and sort the features (user stories) that you are going to tackle next. Rather than specifying in one phase and building in the next, Agile says that you specify-build-test, then do it again, and again. Rather than keeping the finished specification as the unchangeable factor (which often requires moving on your estimates for build time, build quality and build cost), Agile says that you define your timelines quite strictly, usually in month cycles and in day cycles, and then keep taking on a calculated amount of new scope (requirements) in each cycle. Rather than planning a complete schedule in advance for projects that sometimes take years, Agile says that you plan your next cycle (sprint), and don't really commit beyond that.

I'm simplifying, of course, but when explaining Agile processes to your team or your client these are the trade-offs that you'll talk about. The chance of shipping is now very high; the chance of delivering a useful product is now very high. The chance of delivering everything you expected to make, using exactly the resources you expected to use, and taking exactly the time that you expected to spend remains small, just as it always has... but now you have a much better chance of getting to a minimum viable product that meets your client's needs, even if you aren't able to get done quite what you expected to do.

Blending Agile with fixed price

This is all quite interesting in a theoretical way, and it does address the central transaction-cost problem exemplified in books like *The Mythical Man-Month*[3] and *Death March*[4]. After you try Agile processes for a while and learn their vocabulary and rituals (daily stand-up meetings, pair programming, Kanban boards, and so on), you may be ready to get going with a completely Agile approach to the build of your application. And then you run right into the reality of web work.

Like most client-vendor relationships, clients aren't particularly interested in paying you to be indefinite advisors and infinitely available, slowly-cycling Scrum teams. Clients want to know what the work is going to cost. From your point of view, this means knowing the number of hours that you can spend on the problem. So how do you do this if you commit to an Agile cycle?

My friend Greg Hoy has written a good article about the problem of using Agile within fixed-price contracts[5]. It's a good technique, but depends on a certain amount of trust already built up between the web builders and the client. If you are trusted to do the work, you can follow a process somewhat like this:

---

[3] *The Mythical Man-Month: Essays on Software Engineering* by Fred Brooks Brooks (1975, 1995, Addison-Wesley).

[4] *Death March: The Complete Software Developer's Guide to Surviving "Mission Impossible" Projects* by Edward Yourdon (2nd edition, 2003, Prentice Hall).

[5] http://www.alistapart.com/articles/agreements-equal-expectations/

- Make a statement of work (contract) that explains how you work, and gives several examples of what you might do within each phase of work. Don't commit in advance to things like the number of design iterations, the specifics of persona development and so forth.
- Indicate in the contract how many hours you expect to spend in each phase of work.
- Once you're engaged in the work, concentrate on doing the highest-value activities that you need, and create deliverables only if it is directly useful for the client and for you.
- This is where you can iterate in true Agile fashion. For most web projects, a weekly sprint is about right. Each week you'll demonstrate what you have achieved so far (perhaps only internally, but if possible with clients and with representatives of user communities), and you'll take on the requirements (user stories) that you hope to get done in the next sprint.
- Cycle as much as you can – each complete site prototype or build that you're able to put together at this point will help move you to a more stable system, and along the way you'll solve the environmental issues around code versioning and deployment that you would have to spend time on at some point anyway.
- If you spend more time than expected on a given area (perhaps because of inconsistent or hard to please feedback), notify the client when you reach 80% and then 100% of the allotted budget. If the client wants to keep iterating, that's fine, but you'll need a change request to handle payment for the extra hours you put in. If you mutually agree to stop the phase and move on to the next, that's fine, too.

Ultimately, the team might prefer working within a fixed-price (and possibly fixed-time) project – and the client will definitely prefer this. It's a constraint, sure, but good work is all about balancing constraints; undertaking a creative project when you know in advance how much energy you can put into each phase helps to balance the excitement of the engagement with the practicalities of delivering on time. Focuses the mind, as it were.

Getting started with Agile

If your team isn't used to building using Agile methodologies, here are a few things you can start with.

Get a Scrum coach

Having someone around who has been through the process before will be a lot more helpful than just reading books and websites. Let the coach do things like calculate team velocity and help you assign points to user stories.

Take a certified course

There are courses in Agile methodologies, some of which result in certifications. While there aren't a lot of these yet (and I've yet to see a client ask about your Agile certification), it can be helpful to make sure that everyone in your group uses the same words and has a sense of a common process. Training as a team can also be a good way of developing your collaborative skills as a group.

Pilot project first

If you're just starting out with Agile techniques, you probably don't want your first engagement to be with an important client, when you're on the clock and under pressure. Begin with a less stressful project that you'd like to work on internally, and use that to fine-tune the method that works for you.

Use Agile for business processes, not just software development

Don't forget that you can use Agile processes for things other than pure software development. You can use Agile to manage any business process, pretty much, though there are some specialised terms that make more sense in a business rather than software context. The nice thing about business Agile is that it can help you spend the right sort of time aligning what everyone is working on in a group. You might be surprised how often things like daily stand-up meetings can throw up issues that would otherwise wait much too long for resolution, but can be fixed quickly at the time.

Expect to spend some extra time up front as you learn the process
It's never obvious how to get into something new, and you should
leave some time to work things out. It can be tough to figure out
the jargon and daily rituals of building software with Agile, and
you'll spend some time worrying that you are writing down too
much or too little, and talking to team members too much or too
little. This is distracting, but the team will find a rhythm soon
enough – just leave a bit of extra time for this on your first few
Agile projects.

Small cycles are good
You need to get feedback as early as possible, because the later
the response, the more costly the fix. Small development cycles
will help.

Interdisciplinary teams are usually fast
Rather than move work around between departments and throw
work over the wall between activities, it's often a better idea to
identify and group your core people early on. Get a UX person, a
designer and your front-end and back-end coders together early in
the project and let them work together. They'll get to know
each other's work, and the varied concerns will help you to see
risks earlier.

Measure velocity as you go
Don't wait for the end of the project stage to look at how fast you
are getting things done. Measure weekly and even daily, see how
fast you burn through pages or features or bugs. Knowing your
speed will help you to estimate changes, and also make the hard
choices about effort earlier on.

Get buy-in before the work is locked
This seems obvious, but it's amazing how often projects get well
into a late phase of work before some key person sees the earlier
bits. Sometimes this works out fine, sometimes it doesn't. If there
is a person whose opinion could derail the project, make sure they

see the work before you move on. If that means holding up all
work until you can schedule the meeting, so be it. It's still better
than proceeding and having to undo large chunks later on, and
the late feedback will cause you problems with scheduling team
members to make the revisions.

Building from the inside out

So, that's some of how to do the work; what about the substance
of what you're building? This may seem a bit out of scope for a
project manager, but it's important that you have at least a basic
idea of how the website is being built. For one thing, you'll be
explaining to the client how things are being done. For another,
knowing the order and the sequence of events will help you
plan the team resourcing and choreograph presentations and
workshops along the way.

There are various schools of thought on the specifics of
building webpages, but most of the leading people who make
websites agree on some common principles. If your team wants
to break these guidelines, go right ahead; but the idea here is that
certain kinds of risk (mostly the risk of having to do unexpected
and unpaid revision and maintenance work) are reduced by
thinking along these lines.

Start with type and rhythm

It's always tempting to start with boxes on a page, and then to
fill them in with text. This isn't the best long-term way to think
about webpages, though. Pages on the web scroll, they shrink and
contract, they are displayed on a wide variety of screen resolutions
and sizes, they are printed, they are read – there is almost nothing
on a webpage that will stay where you put it if you start with the
idea of boxes that have to line up just so. Of course, there are grid
systems, there are lines and alignments, and these make up part
of what's beautiful about working online. But at the heart of your
pages will always be the content, the words and images that tell a

story or support an activity. That's what your audience is there to see – everything else just helps to find or describe what they're seeing.

Rather than starting with the big visual elements on the page (the masthead; the primary, secondary and utility navigation; the footer), begin the visual design and the page build with the fundamental unit of content. The fundamental content is different for different sites, of course – a magazine site might be about the article text, and a travel site might be about the booking detail. But start there. Figure out how much space and contrast you need to make the fundamental content unit easy to use and attractive in the page. Build the sidebars and footers and call-outs in relation to the fundamental content. Build navigation and mastheads based on the vertical and horizontal rhythm that you've already established within the page. You'll find that the page usually starts with the middle bits, then grows the surrounding window elements, then continues to harmoniously embrace the navigational and branding elements.

Of course, you're probably not building the website yourself, but it's quite possible that you'll be the one to explain to the client how the site is being built. When you develop workshops and presentations of what the team is building, you'll find it helpful to present ideas in roughly the order they were conceived, to show how things are coming together. If you started building the text elements, start by showing that, without all of the navigation and other bits on the page. Build up to the full picture, and the client will have a much better idea about how these things fit together.

Flashy stuff

Your clients will probably have questions about HTML5 and other web 2.0 or web 3.0 technology. While there isn't any such thing as web 3.0, this is the opportunity to have some serious talks about the purpose of the website. With all of the groundwork that you carefully laid in the early parts of the project, it will be clear that you considered audience, tone, style and content very carefully. During actual coding of pages, there may be a bit of a let-down when some elements seem less flashy than the client imagined.

There have always been flashy tricks on the web – ways to make things visually impressive that have nothing to do with the needs of your site's users. You will need to do some careful defence here, showing how the content and audience analyses have led to where you are, and how your designs and pages actually solve the real problem at hand.

Revised estimates

At some point, it's quite likely that something will go wrong with the build process. Someone will accept late feedback from a stakeholder, or a technical problem will prove too difficult, or there will be a problem with a data model. It's not the end of the world – you can pretty much count on at least one estimate being blown in a project. And there you are, looking at more remaining work than you expected, and a deadline that you're no longer confident about. So, what to do?

You only have two options: you can reduce the scope of the project to make up for the estimate shortfall; or you can add budget (and probably time) to allow for the extra work. This choice is considerably easier to make with the help of the client, the more senior the better. Show your client how both client and delivery teams contributed to the current time problem, and talk about the positive steps that you plan to take together in the future to fix things. Don't take all the blame yourself, but don't let yourself completely off the hook, either.

This schedule/cost summary sheet is adapted from Michael Angeles at *konigi.com*. It is based on averaging high & low estimates for each task

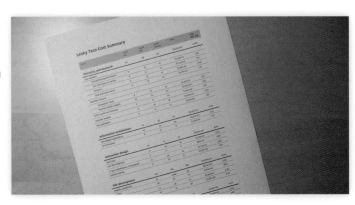

Being realistic

On keeping your build estimates reasonable:

- Remember that a functional prototype can feel like a step back in fidelity.
- Little decisions can have a big usability impact.
- Manage realistic internal issue logs.
- Face your stark choice: reduce scope or add budget.
- Keep track of to-go (time remaining) estimates.

You'll be tempted to blame the problem on client feedback, and it's quite likely that late feedback or a dilatory decision process was part of the problem. But some responsibility rests with the delivery team, too: someone on the team accepted late feedback, or didn't schedule a meeting in good time, or didn't bring a workshop session to a definitive close, or failed to properly document an agreement or decision.

It may be tempting at this point to add people, but this rarely works. Get a quick read from an expert, by all means, or ask your most intuitive and creative person to help you visualise your options for the project. But beyond getting some limited advice, adding new people to a project team will almost never result in getting back the time or the money that you need.

TOOLS FROM THIS CHAPTER

• Build estimate sheet
• Kanban board
• Velocity chart

FURTHER READING

You might enjoy a couple of good practical books about the fundamentals of managing software projects, such as *Code Complete*[6], and *The Pragmatic Programmer*[7]. Of course, there's always *The Mythical Man Month*[8], a book the author called the Bible of software engineering, because "everybody quotes it, some people read it, and a few people go by it."[9]

You've probably already heard of some of the best books about building good web pages: *Hardboiled Web Design*[10] is a new entry, alongside the popular *Designing with Web Standards*[11], *Handcrafted CSS*[12] and *HTML5 for web designers*[13].

You might also want to take a look at the Opera Web Standards Curriculum, developed by Chris Mills at *http://www.opera.com/developer/wsc/*.

During building, a couple of browser-based tools can help you get your web typography and layouts right: Typecast (*typecastapp.com*) and Gridset (*gridsetapp.com*).

---

[6] *Code Complete* by Steve McConnell (2004, Microsoft Press).

[7] *The Pragmatic Programmer: From Journeyman to Master* by Andrew Hunt (1999, Addison-Wesley Professional).

[8] *The Mythical Man-Month* by Frederick Phillips Brooks (1995, Addison-Wesley).

[9] "Quoted Often, Followed Rarely" by Daniel Roth (2005-12-12, CNN, *http://money.cnn.com/magazines/ fortune/fortune_ archive/2005/12/12/8363107/index.htm*).

[10] *Hardboiled Web Design* by Andy Clarke (2010, Five Simple Steps).

[11] *Designing With Web Standards* by Jeffrey Zeldman and Ethan Marcotte (3rd ed. 2009, New Riders).

[12] *Handcrafted CSS* by Dan Cederholm and Ethan Marcotte (2009, New Riders).

[13] *HTML5 for Web Designers* by Jeremy Keith (2010, A Book Apart).

TIME TO TEST

> *"If Ernest Hemingway, James Mitchener, Neil Simon, Frank Lloyd Wright, and Pablo Picasso could not get it right the first time, what makes you think that you will?"*
>
> **— Paul Heckel**[1]

What's here: Kinds of testing; writing good test cases; and a note on user testing.

Testing is an ongoing part of the project, and it's easy to underestimate the effort required. Many of the methods and mechanisms of modern prototype-driven web development are designed to minimise the difficulty and pain of certain kinds of testing, if only by bringing in the harder pieces early in the process.

Still, software testing is a discipline on its own. Between the user acceptance tests, the functional tests, the regression test, the unit tests, the performance tests, the security tests and the automated tests, you might think that doing good testing is something that will take you a dozen people and a dozen weeks to get right. "What happened to my budget?" you'll ask – and so will the client.

Testing a website doesn't take as much work as testing a new air traffic control system, of course, and is far cheaper. But it would be wrong to think that testing your work is just a question of showing it to some of the guys in the office before you push it live. Doing good web testing in a way that will reduce project risk and avoid the most damaging mistakes will take time and planning.

---

[1] *The Elements of Friendly Software Design* by Paul Heckel (1984, Warner Books).

Why do we test?

It may seem like an obvious question to ask, but there are some good reasons we should not only test our work, but involve both client and agency early on in the process.

Predict whether the project will deliver on objectives

The website that you're building isn't a self-contained goal in itself. The site you are building is a channel or platform to enable organisational objectives to be met, and the success or failure of the project depends on how comprehensively and how effectively you do so. A good sanity check is to take your initial project documents, communications brief and proposal, and look at the current state of the website impartially.

- Does the site do what you thought it would?
- Do the style and tone match up with what you were expecting?
- Will the right audiences find the site useful?
- Would your personas find what they need and complete their journeys?

That's the simplest kind of test, and in some ways the most important – you test the site directly against the business objectives. In general, that's all a test will do: tell you whether the site delivers the business objectives or not.

This sort of prediction is something to be kept in mind as you work through the site, but you'll also need a formal testing plan. The test should show that:

- Each page and feature on the site is working as it was specified to work.
- Each new feature or page doesn't break anything that was previously tested.

The plan should include the administrative, back-end parts of the website, as well – all of the CMS, for example. If there are special things you do with the database, scripts you run, and especially any integration with other business systems, these are things that will take some thought.

As a project manager, you should plan to be quite involved in testing the software. There are new people to talk to, relationships to manage and nerves to soothe. More importantly, there will be lots and lots of judgement calls. Is this a bug? Is this page doing what we said it should? Is this what we agreed? Is this design working? Did we agree to build that? The questions at this point can be subtle, and involve every aspect of the project documentation. You'll need to negotiate on a few points, concede a few others and always be ready to go calmly back to your workshop and notes to justify why a certain action was taken.

Focus on positives
You may be lucky enough to have a dedicated test manager to work with, either embedded in the web team or working with the client. Or you may work with someone like a content strategist or developer who doubles as the test lead. Try to bring in people who have as solid an understanding as possible of the customers of the business and the strategic goals for the website. This will bring you into contact with some new people on the client side, getting involved in the project somewhat late in the game. Avoid embarrassment, but also use the chance to develop positive relationships.

The testing phase can be a bit dicey politically, especially with some new people in the room – after all, you've put in a lot of time building this thing, and you aren't quite yet ready to deliver. The pressure will be on. But there are a few things that you can do to turn this into a positive phase for everyone.

Don't take it personally

The testing will inevitably point to issues that were known all
along, or even to choices made deliberately as a compromise
between competing priorities or design constraints. You have
to keep calm, acknowledge the feedback in a positive spirit and
reduce the list to what can be addressed, while gently reminding
everyone of decisions that were already made. This is where it's
particularly handy to fall back on all of those post-meeting recaps
that you posted along the way.

Use some new expertise

You'll have the chance to interact with some new people who
understand the goals and systems of your client's organisation
quite well. Use their knowledge, and the fresh eyes that come
with them. New testers haven't just been through a process of
understanding and then designing for your users, which might
mean they can represent your users best. They come to your site
fresh, without preconceptions, without knowing all of the drafts
that came before and were discarded, without knowing the pain
that's gone into some of your decisions. If you broaden your
testing to user representatives outside the organisation, you'll
learn even more, but be prepared for some misunderstandings
of what the new site is supposed to do and how it is organised.
Design decisions that weren't controversial at the time will baffle
some of your users, who don't come to the project with your high-
level understanding of purpose or a mental map of content to be
shared. Take their comments on board, and fix what you can.

Brief your testers well

It's tempting to be self-deprecating here: "Oh, we wanted to do
this thing, but the marketing guys wouldn't let us. This part never
did work right, it's a bit of a hack, but the users won't notice, and
it's better than what they have now." While a certain amount of
self-criticism may be OK and healthy within a web team, it needs
to be balanced by a feeling of accomplishment and pride in what's

been built. For someone new to the project, that sense of pride and shared accomplishment won't exist, so you may need to work hard to stay positive. It's a good habit to get into, though. Explain the features and design choices, connecting them to the user research you've done and the workshops you've held. Show how the user will be delighted by a particular path, and show how the new site fits into a daily workflow. Explaining what you've built within a goal-based context will get you better tests, a more committed team, and a lot less hassle and pressure for new or modified functionality.

Testing can seem never-ending

It's true – once you start finding bugs, it seems like they never stop. You start with twenty, then you have eighty; then you fix thirty, and find another fifty. I've worked on projects where the active bug count stayed above two hundred for almost the entire testing period – until it didn't. You must have confidence that the project will succeed, that you will work through this and get the bugs and questions down to a manageable level. Many will be interconnected, and there will be a number of things that you don't have the ability to fix, only to work around. That's OK. It's normal, and your project will succeed. Keep a steady and upbeat tone when you run these review meetings, explain carefully the causes and effects of defects to the management team, and you'll get it done. What managers want is to feel that you're making progress, that you have a handle on things, that your team has the skills to tackle what needs to be done. They'll deal with delays, with change requests, with cost overruns if they have to, as long as you maintain the level of trust by being in control.

Testing tends to generate new requirements

Even more than the visual design phase, testing is the part of the project where it's easiest to suddenly realise, "Oh, we picked the wrong approach – we should have done this!" The new idea may seem so completely obvious to everyone that it's inconceivable you would ship the site without it. You'll have to remind people that they're getting ahead of themselves. The time to go back and evaluate the success of particular screens, features and calls to action is after the site launches. You'll use instinct, sure, but also numbers and metrics to show what's working and what needs to be improved. Wanting to improve the site is a noble, worthy thing, and seeing everything together in its almost final glory may be the first and best opportunity to find new solutions to what seemed thorny problems. It's just too early. Write down what people find, and those suggestions will be the first to go into a Phase 2 of the project. Just before launch, stakeholders will get nervous and want to change things around, but this isn't the time to second-guess. This is the time to make everything work as smoothly as possible, and to adhere to the specification you've spent the duration of the project hammering out together.

Writing test cases

Writing good test cases is about playing devil's advocate – you want to come up with all the reasons that something might not work. As a project manager you have a pretty good high-level overview of all of the moving pieces, so you're probably in a good position to review test cases for completeness. Be sure to allow yourself some time for this, though. It can be time-consuming, and you might be surprised about the level of detail required.

Good tests will save you time and money, so it's a good idea to start on these as early as possible. The person who will be acting as test lead for the project must spend some scheduled time on the project during the requirements phase. They should be able to see from discussions of business systems, selected technologies and site structure roughly what's going to need to be tested. You can ask for a draft of the test plan well before the prototyping phase is finished.

There are completely test-driven development methodologies that call for writing the tests before you write the code for each user requirement. I've found that this works well for intensive software development projects, but less well for most content-focused web work. Still, if you want to try it, ask your test manager about automated testing frameworks that you should use. If you go down this route, the front-end and server-side developers will have to integrate these tools early on; there's probably not much point if you're retrofitting test code into an existing codebase.

There's some debate about how long you'll be on the hook for badly functioning software. Even if your contract specifies a limited warranty period, you should still expect clients to call you demanding fixes long after that period expires. How you handle that is up to you and your web group (the ideal case might be to develop a negotiated maintenance agreement of some sort, but this isn't always feasible). Just be aware that this may well occur – it's a good incentive to test as thoroughly as you can, as well as to reduce other kinds of technical risk. Your client will expect you to take remedial action to fix anything not working after the deployment, whether it's your fault or not, and whether or not you've already agreed something else in the contract.

Testing	What it is	How it's done
Usability	Poor usability is widespread and expensive. Usability testing is a way of addressing this.	Online tests, including audio recordings of thought processes (through *usertesting.com* or similar) are becoming quite popular as a way to give you a quick snapshot of user reactions to a design or process.
		Testing in person can be performed with an interviewer, a computer and some basic recording equipment. This gives you the chance for much more in-depth analysis of user needs and expectations, both met and thwarted.
		Focus groups can give you fuller understanding of problems, but can also lead to groupthink and difficulties taking realistic measurements of priority.

Testing	What it is	How it's done
Performance	Performance testing addresses perceived vs. actual performance, preferably with quantifiable metrics.	Usually performed with automated tools. Interpreting and showing results aren't always straightforward – you'll need someone with experience, not just the graphs created by tools. If in doubt, think about the change. Is this page getting faster or slower than last week?
Integration	Integration tests show moving parts working together, especially data being moved around. Integration tests are often skipped, because they're complicated to write and do well. But don't skip them.	Requires talking to people outside the web project – you have to keep them in the loop. You'll need an expert in the integrated system to show what an integration test script looks like. These tests are incomplete without the error conditions. Think about what happens when the other application can't be reached, when a customer number look-up doesn't return results, when there's a network problem in resolving a DNS name or sending a file. Take some time here – it's slow and detailed work, but necessary to avoid hard to find and expensive to fix bugs in the future.
User acceptance	A user acceptance test should provide a go/no-go decision about deploying the software.	Usually managed against a bug list. Launch is possible when the known bugs drop below a particular number. Bugs tend to be classified according to severity. It's helpful to graph the different severities over time to show the progress of the testing team. This testing may use client people, the web agency or be outsourced. The user acceptance testing scripts and bug reports should be clear enough that a relatively unskilled user would be able to reproduce the action or error. User acceptance testing promises to create a site that is accepted by users – this is something of a misnomer. You could receive bug reports about a website or software system working exactly as designed, but not how a particular user expects it to work. In this case you need to log potential features or changes for future work, while making it clear that you understand and appreciate the tester's concern.

TOOLS FROM THIS CHAPTER

- Test script
- Online user test

FURTHER READING

Beautiful Testing[2] is a collection of twenty-three essays about the process of integrating test processes into Agile software development. What I like about this book is the variety of fields represented – it's really nice to see some good non-web (and non-software) case studies presented in a readable form.

Some more highly readable advice on testing is to be found in *Agile Testing*[3], by Lisa Crispin and Janet Gregory. They get into making tests maximally effective, which I have always found to be a big problem – it's tempting to spend too much time on low-return activities.

---

[2] *Beautiful Testing* by Adam Goucher and Tim Riley (2009, O'Reilly Media).

[3] *Agile Testing* by Lisa Crispin and Janet Gregory (2008, Addison-Wesley Professional).

20 # INTERVIEW: *NIEK JANSMA*

Niek Jansma is an Agile coach and trainer at the ABN-AMRO Dialogues Technology Incubator, based in Amsterdam. He works with multiple Scrum teams providing Scrum workshops, organising certification training and coaching Agile teams for external customers.

Nick spoke to Breandán about working with an Agile methodology and how that influences all aspects of his project management duties.

First off, tell me just a bit about what you do day to day.

Sure. Day to day, work depends on what project I'm on, obviously. You could summarise it all as project management for IT projects. It's always based on Agile and Scrum. Sometimes I'm the Scrum Master, but most of the time I'm an Agile coach, which involves teaching companies how to do Scrum and making myself obsolete as soon as possible. Coaching is actually what I like to do most.

Right now, I'm a Scrum Master in a project, so I'm not doing any coaching. That's my day-to-day job: managing backlogs; letting product owners know what they have to do; doing stand-ups; advising the team; making the kanban boards; and stuff like that.'

Building with Agile

A lot of people are interested in Scrum and other kinds of Agile development, but it's not always clear how this method fits with a particular project. From your experience, is there a kind of project or company in which you've seen Agile working best?

---

[1] http://en.wikipedia.org/wiki/Kanban_board

First off, Agile could work for any project, but, obviously, there are projects that are a better fit for Scrum than others. The bottom line is: the more change in a project, the better Agile will fit that project. Logically, if you had a project with absolutely no change – and I've never seen one – you shouldn't use Agile. If you have a customer who has a completely detailed plan of exactly what they want at the beginning of the project, then try to convince them that this specific plan will not be what they want in one and a half years! Scrum adopts change and helps the customer to see what it is that they actually want.

Like you say, if a project is overspecified, there's very little room for making changes. It's less likely to work.

Yes. Even an overspecified project can still use Agile, but you'd need to advise the customer that there are going to be a lot of changes. The customer may be thinking, "Oh, I've got this very well-specified, so now they can just build it, and I won't have to be involved any more." But it's not like that. In Agile, the process is about really involving the customer by doing a demo every one or two weeks to see if you're still going in the right direction with the project.

Sounds like that is one of the keys to making Agile work: keep the customer involved in the process, no matter how well they define the project at the start. They need to be involved every day.

Yes. And try not to over-specify the work. Keep it vague. Only specify the next one or two sprints.

Fixed price, fixed delivery

Projects as a whole often have fixed budgets and fixed timetables. So how do you use an Agile approach within that fixed framework?

Fixed time and fixed budgets are not the problem. Scrum can work very well with fixed time and fixed budgets. The only problem is fixed scope. If the scope of the features is fixed, that is a problem because you cannot change your features to be able to fit everything within the other two – budget and time. To my customers I say, "On this date we can deliver for this amount of money. But we cannot tell you exactly what we're going to deliver." That's always a hard discussion, of course.

On a broad level, you can still tell the customers what they're going to get. It's the same as building a house. You can tell them that they're going to get a house with this many windows, this many doors, this many rooms, and a couple of things in it. But, at the start, you can't tell the exact way the house is going to be built. And along the way you'll see that this part is more important than that part, so you want to spend a little more on this and a little bit less on that. You discover those things while going through the project.

If we're going to talk about building a house, building requires that certain materials be on site at a certain time, and there are a lot of dependencies between different teams who are all doing the work. Does Agile help you manage dependencies as well?

Absolutely. You can still see the dependencies coming within an Agile project, if you have your high-level planning done. And over the next two sprints, you always plan the details, so the plan becomes even clearer. In this case, having everything on site, would be part of the definition of ready. In Agile, before the story can be put in the sprint, it has to adhere to the definition of ready: all the materials have to be there, so to speak. On a web project, the materials could be the designs, the HTML, an Excel file. Everybody also has to understand the story, and it has to be properly estimated.

Testing

When you're doing these estimates for the next sprint or two, how do you create estimates for the ready conditions, the preconditions, and all the testing on the other end, given that testing may show issues that must be worked on immediately? Does that throw off the whole thing?

> No, no. Including testing is one of the most important things. Actually, there is no other end, so the testing is always included. The tester is part of a multidisciplinary team. For instance, you have a couple of developers, a tester and a designer in the same room talking about how to estimate this feature or that requirement. They talk to each other, because a feature may be simple to develop but hard to test, or the other way around. Together they can make a complete estimation of everything including testing.

> A story on the backlog can only be finished if it's completely tested and accepted by the product owner. It's tested, and if it's not right when the tester tests it, it goes back to the to-do list.

Makes sense. Is testing more or less important when you have these short cycles?

> I would say that it's more important, because the shorter the cycles, the more often you test. And more features get tested, because of the integration tests. The tester should be really involved in the team. We usually have a dedicated tester on an Agile or Scrum team. You really need to calculate testing into the project. At every sprint, in theory, you could go live with what you've built, because it's been completely tested and accepted.

Minimum viable product and simplicity

Is there a danger in trying to build a minimum viable product set? Do you think that products end up not being as multifaceted as they should be, because of having to break them down into short sprints?

First off, I don't think that products can be simpler than they should be, because all products should be as simple as possible. I wholly believe in the lean start-up idea. I think Scrum advocates minimum viable product, because you build the simplest possible product first. Then, if the product owner accepts it, you build further on to that thing. I don't think we postpone complex items, because we also consider business value in Scrum. Some complex items have low business value, so of course those would be postponed, in favour of simpler items with higher business value. However, some complex items have very high business value. I don't think that Scrum makes things too simple; I think that Scrum makes things simpler. And that's good.

Integration

How does the Scrum method work when integrating with other complex systems, like databases, content management systems, software libraries, billing systems and accounting systems? What can a team do to handle these integrations cleanly?

I think integration in an Agile project is not different from integration in a traditional project, because integrations are always hard. You have to bring two different systems together. The way Scrum handles this task, when integrating, is by doing even shorter iterations than usual. We're actually doing something like that right now. It is such a big item that we cut it up into pieces that are as small as possible while still having business value. We do a really tiny piece first, just a couple of days' work. Then we put that in the demo. It's not going to be pretty, but we can show the product owner some data, review what we've done and check whether we're on the right track. The next sprint, we work further on the next piece.

There are more checks and balances in the integration with Scrum as well. Scrum projects are more transparent. You need to communicate with people working on all the different systems in an integration. Lack of communication could cause an impediment. You discover those problems earlier in a Scrum project. For instance, if a developer needs a file from the developer on the other side, but it hasn't been sent, the Scrum master needs to remove that impediment quickly. Call the developer, or whatever.

It's just more transparent. But there can be problems on the project management side of integration. If the other system is completely waterfall-based, and you're using Agile, it is a challenge to get your two release cycles in sync. You always need to remember that waterfall projects have releases with three-month cycles, for instance; whereas with Scrum you're releasing in two, three, four weeks.

Agile in an organisation

Do organisations that you advise often try to do Agile projects in one area, but not others? What do you do if you know that you're within an organisation that isn't fully committed to the Agile process?

What I advise is to get a clearly bounded independent project and do Scrum there first, so people see how it works. Get one Scrum team dedicated to this project and complete that project as a Scrum. The rest of the company will slowly adopt the method, because after the project is completed, the team is split up. It's like a cell – you start with the cell, then the cell splits up in two, then those cells split up and those cells split up… That's the best way to get Scrum in your whole company.

But if you have an Agile project with a lot of dependencies in a waterfall environment, that's always going to be a challenge.

In that situation, how do you make it work?

> *I wouldn't adapt the Agile process. I'd want the waterfall to get a little more Agile, but that can be really hard. One of the first things to do is to get higher management in to support your Agile process – that's really, really important. I've done a project here, a big Siebel² implementation, where the business department were open to Agile, but their IT department didn't want to do it. (This was the other way around from the attitudes I usually see in business and IT.) And IT didn't want to do an Agile project because they didn't see the advantage of transparency.*

> *If you introduce Scrum somewhere, it's sometimes going to hurt a little. Because it's so transparent, you notice where there are obsolete people or people slacking. You see a lot of things which can be a little bit painful. That could pose problems – especially in a political organisation.*

Planning and estimation

Do you have any examples of misunderstandings between people paying bills and people trying to do the work? Or the people doing project management and estimation?

> *Well, one of the first things I saw at Europeana, in introducing Agile and doing estimations, is that their original planning had absolutely no basis. Within Agile, the people doing the work estimate their own work and deadlines are more realistic. Of course, it's still estimation, but on average the planning is much better. One of the first things that you will see when introducing Agile is that the original planning estimates are really far off.*

---

² A customer relationship management product from Oracle.

You see estimation as something that's hard to do, at least in the long term?

Not always hard – starting the estimations is hard and so is explaining how to work with complexity points. But by sprint two or three, an Agile team gets on automatic pilot with their estimations. They get a feeling for the complexity. To help with that process, you can introduce relative complexity points. Ask, "How complex is this feature compared to that feature?" Maybe this is a three and that is a six – then the product owner knows this one is twice as big as that one. The product owner can prioritise accordingly. Estimations are not hard, and it actually makes a lot of sense for the team to do estimation by itself.

Benefits of Agile development

Sounds like that's one of the drivers that makes an Agile process something you'd want to use in a business environment.

Absolutely, yes. I understand that the business department may want something fixed before a certain date, but everybody wants realistic planning. And product owners can prioritise features better when they know that this feature is twice as big as that one and fifty times bigger than another one. Or that this other one is tiny but really important. They can make educated guesses based on that information.

Just to close, do you have any thoughts about the web or software industries that you think people should keep in mind, either on the side of making software or paying for software?

Make less distinction between business and IT. It's always bad communication that makes things go wrong, right? Do more together. That's one of the biggest advantages of Scrum – business and IT are in the same crew. Usually, IT says, "Business has no idea what we're talking about" and business says, "IT has no idea what we're talking about." So just talk to each other, then! That seems

*really straightforward, but usually people push the boat away. They say,
"Please do this. I don't want to see it any more, and I want you to deliver it on
the day I want it, the way I want it." They don't connect with the team. Just
talk to each other!*

That makes a lot of sense – we're supposed to be on the same side here.

*Exactly – we're all intelligent people. Business people and IT people, they're
different kinds of people, but they're both intelligent. Give IT people the
freedom to think of solutions that a business person might not have thought
of – and the other way around.*

**I think if we all did those things we would have much happier projects, with a lot
less stress.**

*I have to say, with a successful Scrum implementation, that is one of the
biggest feats that I try to accomplish. Get people working together more and
being happier – and usually that works! With a full Scrum, everybody feels as
if, finally, they are a team. Developers feel that they have more of a say in the
matter, and business people get the idea that they can change things. Usually
it's, "Oh, it's a change! Oh no! That's not in the contract." But now, with Scrum,
it's, "Oh, you have a change? Sure, we'll plan it in! We'll work together."*

Excellent. Anything else you'd like to add?

*I'm actually really happy to be a part of this book, because I like to spread the
word about Scrum. I'm working on my certification as a Scrum trainer. I'm still
working this way because I see the difference between traditional waterfall
project management and Agile project management. One of the biggest
differences is that people who work Agile are happier. Has to be something
about it!*

Even if it's just because of the rituals followed in Agile, it does give the idea of being a creative process. People relax a little bit more. Maybe they're not so self-conscious about their title, their role or who works for them?

> That's an important thing you're saying there – people relax a little more. On the one hand, you get more done with Agile. The pace is really, really fast. You usually hear people say, within a company, that suddenly it all goes faster. But on the other hand, people relax more. You get more productivity with more relaxed employees.

PART 5

Deployment and Evaluation

With the project nearing completion, you can see the light at the end of the tunnel. But there are a few more things to address before the site goes live. In this section, I discuss checklists, disaster planning, social marketing strategy, handover, goals, metrics, analytics, and converting your finished projects into sparkling case studies. I will also review a few tools and techniques for planning for the future after wrap-up is completed, including support contracts and team development.

PREPARING FOR LAUNCH

"Luck is what happens when preparation meets opportunity."

– **Seneca**

What's here: Flipping the switch to launch; some notes on checklists; practice making perfect; handing over the site; and launching to the public.

You're probably getting a bit tired at this point. You've worked hard, made some compromises, managed the issues. You've gotten to know everyone on the team much, much better than you ever thought possible for a professional engagement. You're almost ready to flip the switch.

But even with the designs done and dusted, the code built, the server environment ready and waiting, some massive mistakes have been made. And you'll want to make sure that you leave the project with all of the energy and enthusiasm and good thoughts that you had going in. You want to end on a creative high, not with an exhausted whimper.

So take stock, figure out what remains, do some practising, and you're almost there. And after that: yes, there is life after this project. Everyone will go on to the next, and there will be lessons learned and applied.

But now isn't the time to stop paying attention. This is the part when little moves and some practice can give you a celebrated public success. Building was fun, but there's more to going live than uploading files to an FTP server.

You must be careful here. The actual process of launching a website is a little harder than it used to be. There was a time when you just uploaded some files to an FTP server. And that may still be a part of it. But now there are templates to manage; third-party

API keys to update and test; analytics to hook up and verify; data to migrate (this is a big one); content to check; user accounts to configure; even media to notify and a launch event to plan.

You want this to go smoothly and, of course, if you've been doing your homework, there won't be any major problems. But projects have been known to linger at this ready to deploy stage for months before going live. And for all the time you hold a project open, it's sucking time and attention from your team, meaning that you're paying for the project out of your own pocket at this point. Your final invoice isn't going in, and you're paying people, and you probably can't recoup their time with any increase in the project scope or budget. Do you want to be the one raising an eleventh hour change request to the client because there's some silly technical reason keeping the site from going live, when you're not even really sure whose fault it is? Didn't think so.

So while you may be most of the way to a completed site, spend a bit of time now to make sure you have all the moving parts in place. It can be fast, it can be smooth, it can be exhilarating. Launch can be everything that you imagined back at the start of the project. And even better.

Checklists save lives

The hospital central line infection checklist

Hospitals have some really smart people working for them. They employ smart doctors, smart nurses, smart anaesthesiologists, smart operating theatre technicians, smart pharmacists. Even the guys who mop up spills are pretty well-trained in infectious disease control. But we all know that there are errors. Horrible, unaccountable errors. People go into hospital with normal, benign-sounding ailments and should come out, but don't. There should be no excuse. With that many well-trained, smart, conscientious professionals on staff, where's the room for all those errors?

It turns out, doctors and nurses and emergency medics get stressed, too. They get distracted. Sure, they know more than most about controlling infection. But infections still kill 17,000 patients a year in the US[1].

As reported in the British Medical Journal[2], doctors came in with a magic bullet of sorts, which after one year of use, reduced infections by 66% in Michigan hospitals. After three years, the rate was down 86%, with the median rate flatlined at zero. So had they introduced some new kind of great antibacterial drug, or an innovative filter for respiratory circuits? No, the change was procedural: they brought in checklists, and trained clinicians to follow them, even when the steps seemed obvious.

Clinicians initially objected, saying that they knew all about infection control, and they didn't need to waste time being walked through steps that they were taking anyway. But the checklists saved lives, and are still saving them. When the World Health Organisation introduced a checklist for surgeries, the death rate was cut in half, and complications reduced by 60%[3].

It seems obvious, and it can almost seem insulting to tell professionals to make checklists for important tasks. Most of the work you do on the web won't have the same direct impact on the health of your users, but the principle is just as important. If you want to be able to perform a process repeatably and well, make a checklist, and then follow it. Lots of times. And when you're doing something tricky (migrating a database, restoring a backup, making router or DNS changes as part of pushing a site live), you'll be very glad that you did.

[1] O'Reilly, Kevin B., 2010. Infection rates drop as Michigan hospitals turn to checklists. American Medical News, March 1, 2010. *http://www.ama-assn.org/amednews/2010/03/01/prsa0301.htm*

[2] Pronovost, P.J. et al., 2010. Sustaining reductions in catheter related bloodstream infections in Michigan intensive care units: observational study. BMJ, 340(feb04 1), pp.c309–c309.

[3] Haynes, A.B. et al., 2009. A Surgical Safety Checklist to Reduce Morbidity and Mortality in a Global Population. New England Journal of Medicine, 360(5), pp.491–499.

Where you might get some ideas

If you're really stuck for ideas, you can look to some established standards. Need a checklist for human-centred design practices? Look at ISO 9241-210:2010, which includes an eight-page checklist for just that. Look at the manual pages for your server software – chances are that it includes a series of steps for site deployment that maybe you never read.

Of course, any process can be repeated, even your own. All it takes to perform a professional task reliably and well is to write down how you do it, then follow those steps again. Really, that's it. Show your checklist to the client to get some feedback. Post it on your own blog and see if anyone has any better ideas or ways to save time. But at the end of the day, you'll want to work from a list. Not the sexiest tool in the drawer, but probably the most useful.

Practice makes perfect

People don't believe the checklist approach, and they don't believe that such an analytical approach is the most efficient way forward. But web development isn't all a black art. Not everything requires an auspicious alignment of stars, the incantation of a genius and the talismanic mounting of a project icon on the studio wall (though if these things help you to stay motivated, then do what you have to do).

What does work is practice. Boring, sure, but so are studies and scales on your musical instruments, and endless still life details on your sketchpad. Doing something many times makes you good at it, almost without trying. That's not completely true, of course; it's focused and mindful repeated attention that yields rewards. But for smart and motivated people, it's actually hard to do a job deliberately badly or with boredom. As a web-building team, if you repeat certain activities enough times, you'll generally get pretty good at them.

What if you deployed the site, did the database migration, updated the API keys, did everything required a month before you had to, even before the bugs in the page templates were fixed? What if you did it again the next day, and found a few things that you could automate with a script to handle the tricky bits? What if you did it again and automated even more. Eventually, don't you think that the actual launch would be smooth and error-free?

Sure, you could wait to the last minute, wait until the templates are finished and you've received client sign-off on every artefact. You could wait until all eyes are on you and the team to pull off a complete migration of data and content, instantaneously, at a time when everyone is anxiously waiting to see the results of months of their hard and creative efforts.

Why take the chance? Don't you think you'd rather get the deployment down pat, land it, cold, a month early? And then script and practise and repeat every day until it's almost literally a question of flipping a switch for the real deal? Well, that's how the pros do it. And no wonder. It makes everybody look good, especially the client. And wouldn't you rather be enjoying some fine hors d'oeuvres at the launch party than huddled over a command line terminal at 3am the morning after the official launch, on the phone to tech support and wishing you were anywhere else in the world?

Deployment scripts

The tricky bit about making these practised deployments work is to script as much as possible. There are many ways you can do this and a lot will depend on your technical environment. But make sure that you have something repeatable, and that the scripts themselves are part of the version control system that your project uses for source code.

Capistrano and other package managers

For Ruby applications, I've had good success with Capistrano[4], which lets you set up most of the critical bits of building, packaging and deploying your code to various environments: "cap deploy staging" and "cap deploy production" and you're done.

---

[4] http://capistranorb.com/

```
$ cap production deploy
  triggering start callbacks for `deploy'
* executing `deploy:set_nodes_from_remote_resource'
** Deploying to app01 (primary, db), app02, app03
```

Using the capistrano command, you can automatically execute a series of scripts to consistently deploy code to a target environment, whether a development, staging or production server

In the Java world, Ant[5] has long been the standard for building and deploying applications, and can be made extremely flexible. You can accomplish many of the same things with shell scripts (bash, or your flavour of choice). One way or another, treat the development of your deployment scripts the way you would any other code. Version the scripts, and look to bulletproof them as much as possible. When you get to the final deployment you'll have time to focus on champagne and press interviews.

Managing database versions

It's important that the databases you work with are part of the whole build process. You'll want to generate a script that can create your database from scratch, including setting up indexes and loading any required data files. Check the script into your version control system, and treat the migration of your database as you would the migration of code to a new version. Ruby has some great tools for managing database versions consistently and automating the migrations between one version and the next; take a look for similar tools for your platform.

Regression testing

One of the more frequent mistakes I've seen is when a team moving towards launch, flushed with excitement and ready to rock, fixes some trivial thing and introduces an error in some other part of the website or system. Everyone celebrates the quick-witted

---

[5] http://ant.apache.org/

bug fix, and the system gets promoted to production with the newly introduced bug. You fix the handling of time zones on your blog entries and suddenly the system stops retrieving up-to-date customer account information. Or you fix the CSS for a drop-down menu that's dropping right off the screen on mobile, and you introduce a problem with the spacing of menus. This sort of thing is easy to fix if you're looking for it. As you get closer to launch, keep running your regression tests, and remember that no bug is completely trivial.

Disaster planning

As any romantic comedy will tell you, things generally don't go to plan. Just as space mission launches used to superstitiously assume one glitch per mission, you'll certainly have something go wrong with the project on the way out of the door.

It's always been hard to plan for disasters, as seen in this 1919 image of a hardware store fire caused by a broken water main. Image courtesy Seattle Municipal Archives, www.seattle.gov/CityArchives/. CC BY 2.0

Sometimes it will be something subtle and easily seen and corrected. Sometimes your data centre will get hit by lightning and your routers will melt (this happened recently close to where I live). The comedic or tragic consequence of the disaster will depend entirely on your attitude towards risk and your ability to do proper disaster planning. A plan is great – but not much use when compared with some actual practice sessions.

Simulated failover

If you have a plan for one service or server to failover instantly to another, great! Now unplug one server from the wall while it's running your database and see what happens. If you don't do real, physical tests of your disaster scenarios, you don't know what's going to happen.

Redundancy

This tends to be a budget question, which is why it's never a good idea to promise full redundancy unless you really have some high-quality infrastructure to work with. Two web servers available to serve your app? Sure. How about redundant network routers? Redundant cables? Redundant power supplies to the server? What about redundant power supplies to the server room? What about when a digger slices through the cable that feeds ones and zeros to your data centre? (This actually happens a lot.) Plan for what you can, and be ready to get a replacement copy of your site up again quickly using a new set of network and hardware providers, if you need to. The better your deployment scripts, the better you can recover from failures.

Measuring uptime

You'll probably want to keep track of the success of your servers in staying alive, but think about measuring the staff behind them, too. How long does it take to answer a support email? How long to respond to a tweet from an annoyed customer? How many people recommend your site to someone else? Measuring and even publicising your uptime success in these areas might help the team to focus on what matters most to your users. There's a lot more to perceived site performance than page load times.

Handover

When the time comes to turn over all of your hard work to the people who will be running the shiny new website, you might be tired. You might be inclined to downplay the handover event, or even feel vaguely embarrassed about all of the lovely features that didn't make the cut. Don't! A handover event can be a pretty joyous occasion, and it also happens to be the best time to set up your agency or web group for a chance at the next interesting project.

Who needs to be there

Invite the department heads. Invite the CEO. Invite the head of marketing and the person from corporate communications who was sceptical about your project from the beginning. This is the time to get important people in the room and show how you solved the problems with the current website, while creating some exciting new possibilities for the organisation over the next few years. Make a nice presentation and share some colour handouts.

Creating a sustainable codebase

Of course, the details of the handover will have been figured out long before. Your code, design assets and scripts will all be checked into the version control system used by the people who'll be maintaining your system. You'll not only have written good instructions, but the new website owners will have been actually pushing the button for the last few deployment dress rehearsals. They'll have practised making a change like fixing a bug, and checked in the new code for the plug-in, template or application module, repackaged and redeployed using the scripts you wrote.

Packaging design assets

At this point there will probably be design assets, documents, specifications and conversations all over the place. You'll find a lot in Basecamp (or the project management system you use); there will be quite a few stashed on a network share that your team uses; probably a few things in Dropbox; and more than one critical Photoshop, Axure or Fireworks file on the hard drive of one of the web team. Take a day or two to find and extract everything and make it into a nice deliverable. Provide a table of contents and a cover. Print everything out on a colour printer and copy it to a CD with a label. This may seem like extraneous activity, but believe me, this sort of thing makes a huge difference to the client or stakeholder taking over the website. These sorts of touches, even when unasked for, go a long way to setting up future work and maintaining goodwill.

Launch activities

When it's time to flip the switch, you have a couple of decisions to make.

Content checks

Before turning things on, you should take a quick look through the site to see if there's anything missing. Do you have a blog or news section? If you do, make sure there are some posts in there! Is there a section for staff photos and biographies? Fill it up! Are there any sections at all for which the content hasn't arrived, and you have empty space or placeholder text up there? Now's the time to turn off those pages or sections. It's OK. Content is late, people forget, departments delay getting you their stuff, and it's fine. Turn off what you don't need, and make a note for the folks inheriting the site. They'll get the content and make those pages live soon enough; it will be good practice for them, and will reinforce their sense of ownership of the site. It's fine to release without all of the pages that you planned, but empty or placeholders won't do you or your users any favours.

Soft launch versus big bang

You can decide to do everything at once, or you can do a soft launch, where you switch things on privately and don't make a big deal about the new website until a bit of time has passed and you're sure you don't have any major bugs. Lots of people are taking the soft launch approach these days – there doesn't seem to be much of a hit on public perception or brand issues just because the site has been live for a few days.

You're going to end up with at least a bit of a soft launch no matter what you do: with websites, the variances in updates of DNS records will tend to mean that your website will take between an hour and a day to be seen by most people, assuming that you're replacing another website at the same address. Unless you're doing something fairly complicated with internal load balancers and DNS resolvers, you'll probably want to let this update window pass before you start to do any real publicity about your new site. On the flip side, you'll want to make sure you make DNS changes a day or two before you have something public planned – there's nothing worse than distributing the press release and having journalists call you, rather confused, because they see the old version of the website. For this reason, as well as for general sanity, you should release most code the night before it goes live and do some quick checks.

Celebrating publicly

You may be tired, but a new website represents some great work by you and the team. Put some thought into celebrating the new achievement.

Plan a launch event

You can have a party with just you and the team, but it would be beneficial to invite some key people from the client organisation. Better yet, do something in public: make an audio podcast or video webcast of the launch event, and either stream it live or put it up on the new site. Ask someone influential from the industry sector to show up and say nice things about the website. When I launched a traditional Irish music website a few years ago, I managed to get some well-known Irish singers to perform at an event in the National Museum of Ireland, and the Irish prime minister showed up to make a speech and talk about the website. The team building the site had a great time, and the public attention validated everyone's hard work.

Getting media attention

It can be hard to get press coverage of a new website – after all, every organisation has one, and a new one doesn't seem like such a big deal. Remember, though, that your hard work has created a new service for the public, perhaps informational, perhaps social or maybe related to advocacy on an important issue. If you can explain the benefits to the public of this new service, you can probably get journalists to write about what you've accomplished. If the mainstream media aren't interested, move on to bloggers and smaller outlets. Then you can send links to slightly larger blogs or online magazines, and then send that coverage up to the bigger news outlets. Once a lot of other people are talking about your site, it won't be so hard to get the sort of exposure that you want – just take it in stages. Go back to your newspaper of the future exercise from the kick-off meeting. Think about whether some of those publications might want to cover your new site and its features.

Gathering testimonials and reviews

You'll talk about the project on your own website and via social channels, so get some testimonials ready. Maybe give some key people in the industry an early look at the site and get their feedback. You can give access to some bloggers who cover your industry and get their reviews, so that by the time launch activities roll around you're ready with the case studies, testimonials and reviews that you need to really tell the story.

TOOLS FROM THIS CHAPTER

- Launch plan
- Deployment script
- Handover and go-live checklist
- Uptime chart

FURTHER READING

As a manager, you should probably be familiar with the book, *Continuous Delivery*[6]. Thinking about your website delivery as a process rather than as an event will help you to see things coming and avoid risk. There is nothing more frustrating than being at the end of a project, at the end of the money, and being *almost* ready to go. With good continuous planning and testing, you'll be OK.

The O'Reilly "carp book", *Building Scalable Web Sites*[7] was written by the very smart Cal Henderson of Flickr. Cal covers a lot of what you might need to handle deployment issues, mostly by getting you to think about scalability issues as a development problem, rather than pushing all scalability issues over to the system administrators.

This starts getting into the area of DevOps, a popular concept these days, stressing the collaboration between software development and IT operations. Not a bad idea, and getting web developers used to this amount of responsibility should strengthen their skills. For a good introduction, try another O'Reilly book, *Web Operations*[8].

---

[6] *Continuous Delivery* by Jez Humble and David Farley (2010, Addison-Wesley Professional).

[7] *Building Scalable Web Sites* by Cal Henderson (2006, O'Reilly Media).

[8] *Web Operations* by John Allspaw and Jesse Robbins (2010, O'Reilly Media).

Social strategy

*"Twenty years ago no one could have imagined the effects
the internet would have – entire relationships flourish,
friendships prosper[...] there's a vast new intimacy and
accidental poetry[...] not to mention the weirdest porn."*

– J. G. Ballard[1]

What's here: Defining social media; establishing a community; building brands; and
getting permission.

Making connections

Requests for proposals often include sections about social media.
You've probably noticed that a lot of mass media advertisements
on billboards and bus stops are listing Facebook addresses rather
than company or product webpage addresses. For hundreds of
millions of people, the social web really is the web. With all of
the hype about social media it can be hard to take a common
sense approach.

While you're hired to build a website, your job probably
won't stop there. Your group are the experts on social media,
whether you think of yourselves that way or not. Your client will
look to you to find new ways to connect their offline and online
presences, including social media. You're the one with the luxury
to look at the client's business goals and make judgements about
how they could and should be using the web.

This chapter isn't about whether to include a Facebook Like
button on your pages. You can if you want, though you might find
that people are more strongly motivated to follow your website's
calls to action if you don't give them such an easy way to engage.
Extending the reach of your new website, and thereby meeting the

---

[1] Interview in The Guardian, 22 June 2004, *http://books.guardian.co.uk/departments/sciencefiction/
story/0,6000,1245664,00.html*

business success factors you developed early in the process, does take some kind of marketing effort. These days, that includes a social media campaign.

What are social media?

Social media are just online communities. You know about Facebook and Twitter, probably, but QZone, Tencent Weibo and Sina Weibo (China), Habbo (Finland), VK (Russia) and Badoo (UK) are also virtual communities with more than 100 million users. Those of us raised before the age of Zuckerberg might idly remember MySpace, or even – gasp! – Friendster, Usenet or CompuServe. From the earliest days of bulletin board systems (BBSes), users have been eager to chat with one another, create profiles and topics of interest, and comment on their activities, hobbies and collections of friends. The networks get built one user at a time, and usually through a personal invitation or connection.

Why would you bother?

The information represented in the social graph – the web of connections between people, interests and preferences, as represented in the associations of social networks – is enormously valuable to marketers. Naturally, these mass audiences are attractive to companies building their brands. Social platforms can create new touchpoints with a brand, new places where the brand can form a part of a daily workflow for a potential customer or partner. Most organisations and brands are doing some form of social media marketing now.

There are some easily measurable benefits of such connections. Having permission to connect to a social account allows you to better track your users, which is a reason why you see a lot more Facebook links on billboards these days. Social platforms can even seem like free promotion. Once a user clicks or follows through that one link, they enter your webspace, and you have some overt and some subtle ways available to talk about your product or service. But there is a cost: once you start communicating using channels usually reserved for other people, you have to behave like a person. You're free to express a personality, which is great – but if you don't come across as genuine and likeable, you'll provoke negative emotions like irritation, annoyance or even hate.

Getting permission

Getting permission from a person to send them information is the key part of social networking. Unless you understand how that permission is obtained, and what it is that you're implicitly promising, you should be very careful about the channels that you make available.

From the mass market to the personal connection

Think about the process of taking out a magazine ad. You pay money to a publisher to print information about your product, interleaved with content that is valuable or interesting to the reader. In this model, you get a second or two to grab attention. You hope that your ad will catch a reader's eye while they're trying to read something interesting. You want to spur on a particular action right then or later, or perhaps just reinforce some quality of your brand so that when the reader is in about to buy something at the supermarket, they will think positively about the product you're selling. You don't need the reader's permission to run an ad – within some limits you're free to say whatever you like in any publication read by your target demographic. In this advertising model, you're generating brand impressions in the hope that somewhere a brain cell gets burned with a positive idea about your product.

There's nothing wrong with that. That's the model not only of magazines, but also of newspapers and broadcast television. It's also the business model of Google and the other online ad networks: show your message to a lot of people and hope to make a good impression, paying the owner of the medium for the privilege. There's no commitment on either side; your advertising target is anonymous, and the game is about numbers: how many eyeballs, how many conversions. It's a model that has worked since the rise of mass communications, and remains profitable and measurable. You can get real results buying space near the things your audience actually want to see, because people are easily distracted and will often unintentionally see what you want them to. It's a perfectly legitimate model, but it's not the way social media marketing works.

Person-to-person
The first long-distance social network was probably the postal service. Once you met a person with whom you wanted to share ideas, you learned where they lived, and then sent them letters or postcards. Your correspondent responded in the same way. The telephone network functions this way, too, but is a bit more intrusive: meet someone interesting, ask for their telephone number. If they give it to you, they're giving you permission to call them, even if that means interrupting what they were already doing. One person at a time, you accumulate addresses and telephone numbers of people willing for you to communicate with them about topics of mutual personal or commercial interest.

Once these networks were built, though, businesses quickly saw the potential for both technologies. The ability to transmit your printed communications directly into someone's home or business meant advertising circulars, catalogues and direct mail. Telecommunications lines directly into offices and homes meant broadcast faxes and telemarketing. Networks created with the idea of connecting people were hijacked by mass marketers with predictable results: printed circulars became resented and labelled junk mail. Telemarketing and blast-faxing became extremely unpopular, leading to regulation and do-not-call lists and telephone preference services. If you do your social media marketing on the telemarketing model, you will be just as resented and disliked. And if your brand is just another name for your reputation, as Seth Godin says[2], your brand will sink rapidly.

---

[2] http://sethgodin.typepad.com/

Setting up a Facebook account may be free, but that doesn't mean you can do social marketing for no cost: the cost is in building trust and permission relationships. Social web channels are not broadcast media, because the social web is about building up familiarity in an entirely different way.

Real relationships

Social media marketing builds brand familiarity through relationships, not repetition. Mass marketing may use blunt repetition to build awareness, but social marketing is about adding value to a relationship by plugging into a trusted network. It's too easy to see people as cynical or unengaged, or simply able to tune out commercial messages. While it may be true that people are developing a more finely tuned radar for selling, the problem isn't that people are hearing less. If that were the case, your best strategy would be to shout louder, and to do more shouting in more places. Instead, people are becoming more discriminating about who they trust and why. People will accept developing a trusted relationship by means of electronic media – they just won't accept phoniness.

This is where telemarketing went wrong. Telephone lines wired directly into people's homes meant that businesses could call at dinner time, and abuse of that privilege led to a call for a revocation of that right. But people didn't reject the idea of using the telephone to connect with companies – on the contrary. Free customer service lines were and are extremely popular. People don't mind reaching out to a company, as long as the people can set the boundaries of the relationship. The same goes for email, and even more for social networks. Once you've asked for someone's social media handle, you have the equivalent of their telephone number. This gives you the ability to reach out directly, whenever you want. But reaching indiscriminately isn't what builds a brand. If you get permission and let people control the relationship, you can be a trusted friend on the other end of the line, not an annoying salesperson.

Being authentic

The biggest thing about the shift from repetition to relationships: you have an enormous chance to be consistently interesting, valued and sought after.

It's a rare thing, but we know a good advertisement when we see one because it's striking or beautiful or interesting. A good ad can actually be entrancing: something with so many ideas that we want to hang on to it for a moment. We sometimes forget that the ad is about a product or a service. We also recognise the opposite: cheap or mediocre marketing, instantly recognisable as mere flash. Poor marketing conversations are artificially exciting, or loud, or noticeable. It doesn't enchant us, it just captures our attention for a moment – we can't even see anything else for a short moment because our attention is seized by a neon sunburst. But that impression doesn't stay with us, except for a lingering sense of annoyance.

Good social media marketing can actually be engaging, in a way that stays with you. It takes time, because you have to keep it up to date. It requires the sort of judgement and sensitivity that comes when you use real, genuine people to manage the account day in and day out, without automatic replies. If you provide information that's thoughtful on some level, people will reach out to you. When you telephone someone because you like them and want to converse, you expect the response to be just as personal and thoughtful. That's the real hook: you have to be interesting or useful or thoughtful in some way, so that people will approach you because you seem worthwhile. And you reward that contact with your own time and interest. Honestly, doing this right takes much more time and money and upkeep than most organisations are inclined to put into it.

You might still crash. Even if you do everything right – start your campaign early, post consistently interesting dialogue, avoid mass bombardment – you'll still crash if you present material that's simply loud rather than resonant. You have to say things that people will think about after they've logged off. It has to be material that you would tell your friends about, without sounding like a jerk.

That can be the hardest thing: when you're wrapped up in the project of building something, it's hard to think about anything else. To you, it's interesting, which is why you're in the business. Other people need to hear about the complex ideas that you've been living with. Other people need to see the interest of your project, not just why it exists. It's hard to put up exciting or compelling content week after week. But if you do, that's what transforms a good social media campaign into an excellent, phenomenal one. You need people to miss what you have to say if you weren't there to say it. That's what works.

Timing

Because of the time involved in building authentic relationships, don't expect to develop a social media campaign (for you or your client) quickly. While it's true that you can only link to a website once it exists, you have plenty of time to start planning the campaign early in the process. In the mass media world you might get away with taking out a big billboard and magazine push in the weeks before a product launch and expect to see a good number of purchases. But there's a better way. Just as Microsoft or Apple build excitement around a launch, you can start teasing potential users of your new product early on.

If you were publicising a new film, you wouldn't release the poster the day before the movie is out in theatres. Instead, you'd line up actors to do promotion tours, invite critics in for early screenings, give screener copies to awards reviewers, all in an effort to build excitement. You'd like some key influencers to pay attention; you want to build a connection between filmmakers and audiences; you want to humanise the production process and make the launch feel like a natural extension of a long-running conversation. In the movie business you'd be using the press as an intermediary in the conversation – when you're running a social media campaign you'll be creating these conversations organically and directly.

Give it some time. Show the inner workings of the process, and reveal the results of your user research. Create a private beta for a new application, and then a public beta, and then a real release. Throughout it all, your social media voice will become more and more associated with you, the person and the team. The human values that you demonstrate in your side of the public conversation will carry through into the values that your users associate with your new product.

Measuring your social results

You can check how you're doing with various tools, but analytics are only part of the story. If you want to realistically assess your social media presence, you'll need to compare yourself with similar organisations and products, recognising that any company is at a disadvantage when it comes to being authentically human. Set realistic goals when you start the social campaign – that will give you a benchmark for checking your progress. Check your conversions, and if a social channel isn't working, consider abandoning it; it's far better to put effort into other areas of your project than to spend time maintaining an ineffective channel. By most measures, it's harder for an organisation to do a good job with social media than almost any traditional mass marketing strategy. It's really not for everyone. But if you pull it off, you can create demand for your thoughts and products that translates into a fanatical customer loyalty.

TOOLS FROM THIS CHAPTER

• Social marketing plan
• Marketing strategy
• Market segment analysis

FURTHER READING

If you don't believe the number of social media networks, take a look at *http://en.wikipedia. org/wiki/List_of_virtual_communities_with_more_than_100_million_users*. Surprising, at least for those of us in Western Europe and the US!

If you're interested in marketing at all, you should read Seth Godin's blog at *http:// sethgodin.typepad.com/*. Seth talks about brand being equivalent to reputation, and he can tell you more about permission-based marketing than almost anyone else out there.

Read what the Intercom folks say about getting and keeping customers – their blog is at *http://blog.intercom.io/*. They have some great things to say. (I like the software they make, too!)

Please, please stay away from sketchy books about social media. There are lots – it's insane. Just figure out who you trust, and listen to them.

MEASUREMENT

"'Forty-two,' said Deep Thought, with infinite majesty and calm."

– Douglas Adams[1]

What's here: Establishing baselines for your website; finding ways to analyse financial performance; formal post-launch testing; and measuring results using site analytics.

Baselines and metrics

The success of a site goes beyond just existing – but someone has to find and demonstrate what that success means. This may be the job of the client's marketing person or department, but often this search for value is the responsibility of the web team. When you get close to launching a new website, it's not easy to find the time for baselines and metrics. Lack of time leads to shortcuts, and a shortcut for measuring websites is to measure only page views, or tweets, or unique visitors. It will take time to leap beyond the obvious and the facile, but once you do you'll have a better understanding of why you built the site, and you'll know what the next version needs to look like.

Websites tell stories. Sometimes they serve as the foundation for a community of interest. Sometimes they're tools for lobbying or galleries for inspiration. And sometimes they change the world. If you want to know whether your project is done, truly ready for deployment, go back to your excited notes from the beginning of the project. Go back to your stakeholder interviews and to your first workshop. Figure out how to measure whether your site stacks up, and then get the instrumentation in place. Be prepared to meet some, but not all, of your goals on the first try. But be ready to measure, with optimism and with honesty.

---

[1] *The Hitchhiker's Guide to the Galaxy* by Douglas Adams (1979, Pan Books)

Remember the business case?

Asking about the success of a project is just a question of re-examining the reasons for the project. If the original pain-points and problems were solved, you win, no matter how many or how few visitors you get. If your stakeholder criteria weren't met, then the website doesn't yet do what it needs to do.

Matching stakeholder goals to site performance

When you asked your stakeholders what they needed from the project, you heard a variety of opinions. To use just one classification scheme, you probably heard about success factors that were related directly to customer needs, to financial goals, to internal process enhancement, or to learning and development as a team. It is reasonably straightforward to measure financial goals: did you sell enough widgets using the site? Did the cost of order fulfilment go down as anticipated? Customer needs are a little harder. Did you deliver a new channel for customer service that is faster or richer than the competing techniques? Did you find a way to disseminate information in a new way or make something transparent to customers that was formerly opaque? Process goals get harder still, in part because websites sometimes introduce new wrinkles into service and product delivery, and usually end up requiring more care and feeding than anticipated. Team development goals are easiest to ignore and hardest to measure, but sometimes have the biggest pay-offs in the long term.

Team goals

Team development benefits can accrue to a lot of people who didn't even work on the website build. For instance, someone probably learned enough about writing for the web that they can keep some text up to date. Someone else might have learned about creating effective imagery to tell a story quickly and visually. Someone on the web team explored the next release of a content management system, found a new technique for faceted navigation or automated another step of the deployment process.

Project stakeholders learned how to be rapid and decisive when prioritising features. Managers of back-end systems learned how to secure a line of business system while allowing for internal access through the abstraction of an application programming interface.

These kinds of team success come slowly, and cumulatively, and often too subtly to be noticed. But they come, and multiply successful future effectiveness. The collective memory of a client organisation or a web team is a valuable thing, and by overlooking these kinds of success, you're missing one of the best parts of doing a complicated project with smart people.

Financial goals: justifying the project

The financial goals will always be important to stakeholders, and rightly so. However well-designed, most websites are functional in the way that graphic design is functional. Design has many reasons for existing (including financial ones), but generally you pay skilled professionals to apply their skills in your cause because you believe that they will deliver a positive return on your investment. But this doesn't exclusively mean sales. The website for a political party, for example, might sell T-shirts and key rings, but the value of the website isn't measured only in online orders for mementos.

A political site might be trying to build a brand, enlist volunteers, raise awareness of a cause, or simply win an election. None of those outcomes will be directly measured by counting money, but that doesn't mean that the website isn't cost-effective. Remember that the political party has a number of channels available: it can print posters, or buy television advertisements, or hold events. The website is another channel, and should be measured using the question: is this website the most efficient way to deliver significant value to me? Or put another way: is the money that I'm investing in this website generating more value than the same money invested in a different channel? If success means votes, then the equation is votes delivered per euro or pound or dollar spent. Effectiveness means the votes per dollar for the website against the votes per dollar for a poster.

Most campaigns (political or not) will employ a mixed strategy, in that the people being reached can best be targeted through a mix of online and offline activities. The website won't be the whole story, but it has to hold its own when compared to the other channels available, or else it's not worth the investment. So while a website isn't necessarily expected to turn a profit directly in order to be successful, it is perfectly reasonable to compare the value performance of a website to the other channels on offer.

A website is an expensive undertaking, especially a site being custom-built by a team of highly skilled professionals. The skills don't come cheap, nor should they. A well-made site will deliver value for far longer, be easier to maintain, be more adaptable to future needs and serve as a more flexible container for future content. And because you generally get what you pay for, a more expensive website will deliver more value over time, in part because you buy more thinking time from more smart people who will reflect more deeply about an organisational challenge and deliver a more appropriate and tailored solution. You probably won't know in advance exactly how the numbers will work out, though, in this as in so many other fields, it is often a false economy to simply buy the cheapest option on the table.

Formal testing
There's a formal way of measuring website success: testing. If you've written down your user requirements accurately enough, you can measure fairly easily whether you meet those targets through a regular and repeated system of regression and unit tests. This may not tell the whole story, of course. Regression tests can tell you things about process by showing that transactions complete smoothly. They can also tell you about customer success factors if you've accurately captured user workflows and expectations in your requirements definitions. But tests carried out entirely within the context of a single system won't be able to tell you much about success factors relating to money or team development. For those, your analysis will need to look further afield.

Just to remind you:

- Regression tests prove that you haven't broken anything. You should accumulate more and more of these over time.
- User acceptance tests tell you whether you're meeting your stakeholder success criteria. User acceptance tests are valid only if they are run against the original set of requirements, with no scope creep allowed.
- Keeping bug lists and drawing them down shows that you are fixing problems that could have a negative effect on your users or processes. While software doesn't always ship bug-free, shipping with known flaws probably means that you'll pay more in customer service and maintenance hours than you would have in development hours. Quality almost always pays for itself, and earlier is cheaper than later.

Thinking about analytics

Google Analytics: the easy answer
You probably already use Google Analytics[2], which has become a staple of the industry, but there are a few other tools that you might want to take a look at.

A/B comparisons
You might want to think about a service that lets you compare different versions of a design or piece of content and tells you which is performing better. The preference test function of Verify[3] lets you test two designs against each other to see which is more likely to attract your users.

---

[2] http://www.google.com/analytics/learn/index.html

[3] http://verifyapp.com

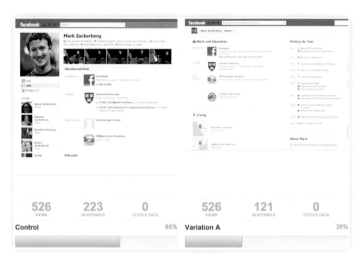

Using a simple online A/B (preference) test, such as this one from VerifyApp.com, you can quickly learn which variation of a design better matches user needs or preferences. Image courtesy of ZURB (zurb.com)

Heatmaps

Sometimes it's helpful to see where people are clicking or selecting within a page. While Google Analytics can tell you about URL popularity, you might learn more by looking at a visual representation of clicks overlaid on your design. This can show you quickly whether your calls to action are working the way you expect.

Image courtesy of Crazy Egg - *crazyegg.com*

Clickstream

Google Analytics isn't yet very good at telling you about user journeys through your website. Sometimes what you really want to know is the path that people take, how many times they go back to retrace their steps, how many pages deep they get, and similar clickstream information. This data can probably be extrapolated from your web server logs, but is difficult to analyse and display without a dedicated tool. If you're measuring the success of your webpage against the expected user routes that you defined early in the project, this sort of tool can give you a sense of whether you're succeeding.

Clickstream analysis goes beyond content popularity or unique visits to tell you how each visitor behaved. By breaking down individual sessions, clickstream analytics can tell you exactly what your visitors did, in what order. Image source *OpenTracker.net*

Eye tracking

If you're in full usability testing mode and can afford it, you can ask people to use your site and see what part of the page they look at by measuring where there pupils go. This kind of test is expensive (mostly because the equipment is costly), but will tell you whether you're drawing attention in the way you expect.

Image of a Tobii Eye Tracker courtesy of Tobii Technology AB, released under a Creative Commons license at *www.tobii.com*

Setting up funnels and goals

Assuming that you are using Google Analytics or something similar as a general-purpose tool for your new website, you should be aware that you'll learn a lot more if you spend some time thinking about the setup. Consider a metric like time on page. Long times on a given page may mean that visitors are engrossed in what they see, but may also mean that they're searching fruitlessly for a link. High bounce rates may mean that visitors aren't interested, but may also indicate that your users quickly find what they need and then go away, satisfied. Without some more specific information, you just don't know.

On the other hand, if you think about the goals that your users should achieve on your website, you can set up ways to measure this. E-commerce is probably the easy case, and is always used as an example: you want people to buy things, buying things requires a specific sequence of pages, so you measure how far people get through the sequence – this is perfectly reasonable. But even for non-financial goals, it helps to think about what you want your users to achieve on the website. You might want them to follow multiple pages of a story; you might want them to use some element of your web application's interface; you might want them to type something into a search box and then follow a link from the results page. These are all objectives that can be defined as part of particular funnels and goals and measured by your analytics tool. Go back (again) to your stakeholder success criteria and map the desired outcomes to sequences of pages that would meet these needs. Then configure your analytics properly, and suddenly you can graph a particular kind of success over time. Yay!

Real-time site monitoring

Something else to measure: what's happening on your site in real time. If you don't have a pretty good idea about the requests per minute and the visitor traffic on a typical day, it will be harder to know what progress will look like. But beyond the performance and security monitoring that you're doing, there are some real-time metrics that have more to do with customer satisfaction.

There are a couple of services that allow you to embed real-time customer response channels into your website. Seeing what your users are doing might help you to intervene at just the right moment:

- Maybe you want to see when someone gets to your pricing page and then hesitates. You can use this to trigger a chat session with the visitor, offering to help make a good decision.
- You could see if a lot of people experience security permission problems. If so, perhaps there's something wrong with your registration or login code, or perhaps documents requiring login are being linked to from a public area of the site.
- Of course, there are security concerns for which a real-time view is very helpful. Lots of requests for suspicious administration scripts or database configuration tools installed by default on many web servers? That's something that you'll probably want to know about as it happens, rather than later.

Are page views relevant any more?
In the early days of the web, page views were an excellent metric. If you knew how many times your server had processed a request for a particular HTML file, you knew more or less how popular your site was, how it compared to other sites, and whether you were getting more or less audience share over time. The nature of the web has changed, though, and our page view metric hasn't quite kept up.

With dynamic and asynchronous technologies like Ajax, page views no longer have much to do with your site interactions. For many web applications, the user will stay at a single URL for much of their experience. With browsers prefetching pages and prefollowing links, server-side measurements of page views don't even necessarily reflect user intent, but perhaps just that some links appear earlier than others on a popular page.

Unique visitors and time spent on site have become much more popular metrics. By filtering IP addresses and by using client-side browser cookies, it's possible to get a good sense of who is visiting you, from where, and for how long. These numbers, along with the new versus returning metric have become much more important in the modern web. There are various reasons why even these measurements aren't always accurate, however. Most users these days have cookies turned on, but not all. Some browser makers are getting more aggressive about their default security settings, so you may find that the session cookie or JavaScript routine that you were relying on doesn't work so well any more. Users behind certain kinds of corporate firewalls may all appear to be the same person. Mobile devices may misreport all sorts of things about themselves in order to facilitate their own rendering strategy. So take the stats with a grain of salt, and measure people rather than pages.

Measuring business impact

To match the analytics and measurement strategy to your expected business goals, you'll need a baseline. Most web projects these days are refreshes and rewrites rather than brand new experiences, but even when replacing an existing website it may be hard to come up with good numbers that reflect fair comparisons.

It's certainly fun to watch page view numbers climb rapidly. To get a sense of business impact, though, will take a bit of patience. Get all the analytics that you can from the old site, by all means. Equip the old site with the same analytics tools that you'll use after the transition, tune the funnels and targets as much as you can, then compare after launch. However, by changing the visitor's experience of the information or service you're presenting, you're also changing their behaviour, so don't take the before and after numbers too much to heart.

Maybe your new site creates a stronger emotional connection with people and offers a better customer service experience. The long-term effect might be to increase loyalty for subsequent engagements or purchases, or to boost the word-of-mouth publicity that you get. Those very positive metrics may not show up in your sales numbers quickly, though. Building an online brand, like any form of mass communication, can take time and you might learn more from a customer survey than from your early analytics results. Write down the problem that you're trying to solve with your new website, and figure out how you'll know if you're successful. Don't worry too much about raw traffic unless that's closely related to the business goal that you have in mind. If you measure the right things and give the new site time to settle in, you'll learn what you need to know.

By the way, this sort of extended follow-up is a perfectly good reason to call clients after a few months to ask how things are going. After all, it's your reputation out there as well, and it's reasonable for you to want to know whether the website is performing as hoped. Showing this sort of extended concern is part of why clients will come back to you for their next project. Whether or not you have a service contract, there are good reasons for keeping up with the performance of the sites that you've put out there in the world.

Making a measurement plan

When you're putting together a strategy to measure the results of the new website, think about these ideas:

- Get a baseline early on. If you know what you're starting with, you can show what impact you're able to have.
- Determine genuine social connections. Move beyond page views and visits to judge the effect of the website on the more lasting relationships between people and organisations. This will probably require more qualitative research, like surveys.
- Match website conversions to financial impact. This may seem obvious, but include not only direct on-site purchases or subscriptions, but also online-influenced sales or leads. A lot of what you want to see may not be in the online transaction system itself.
- Quantify leads and sales. Your online leads are valuable, just as they would be offline. Include the value of potential leads and contacts when you're measuring your online impact.
- Check back in a few months. Start at launch, but realise that websites take a while to settle in and reach regular audience levels.
- Measure publicity. Keep a file of mass media mentions of your site. Look through your website's referrer logs to pick up on mentions by blogs and social media. It's true that you've been paid for the work and moved on, but these are the numbers that you need both for case studies and for pitching future projects.
- Set up a Google Alert to make sure that you hear about new mentions of the website. You might catch some customer service or satisfaction issues just through knowing what people are saying about you.

It's great to know about market share and satisfaction, and it's great to be able to measure things. Some of the tools that you need are free and easy to use; others are not. For some of these marketing insights you'll need to go down the route of a traditional market or brand survey, which can be expensive. Unless your project includes this sort of market analysis, it may be beyond your budget. But learning how to measure online success and being able to relate that to the online tools and metrics that you're already familiar with could represent a useful added value service for your web group. You're the ones documenting a lot of the initial success factors – maybe you can play a strong role in seeing how well the project does in meeting them.

TOOLS FROM THIS CHAPTER

- Measurement plan
- Google Analytics
- A/B test
- Stakeholder requirements

FURTHER READING

If you'd like to learn Google Analytics without too much SEO strategy getting in the way, try the O'Reilly book, *Google Analytics*[4]. A second edition of the book will be published in early 2013.

If you'd like to get a visual sense of where people click on your site, the CrazyEgg heatmaps might give you some good insight: *http://www.crazyegg.com/overview2*. I've sometimes been surprised how some major page elements with lots of contrast are completely ignored by visitors.

There's a good Smashing Magazine article that you might enjoy about A/B testing: *http://www.smashingmagazine.com/2010/06/24/the-ultimate-guide-to-a-b-testing/*

For the mildly-obsessed, you can think about a multivariant version of A/B testing, with automated selection of the best-scoring variants: *http://stevehanov.ca/blog/index.php?id=132*. There's more than one way to do this, of course.

And please don't read silly books about SEO. There is such a thing, and there are SEO experts out there, but there are also a lot of charlatans and fools in that particular business.

---

[4] *Google Analytics* by Justin Cutroni (2nd edition, 2013, O'Reilly Media).

So, did we win?

"My definition of success is doing what you love."
– Tony Hawk[1]

What's here: Lessons learned and projects closed; reflections on finishing projects; and finding energy in closure.

Looking back over your project and seeing accurately what worked and what didn't is just as important as looking forward to a new project and making accurate predictions. Now the project is done, you can synthesise some of the bits of what you've learned from each phase to use as a checklist for the next. But first: take a bow, get some rest, and write up what you accomplished with this project.

First, take a bow
One of your success factors is your team! Everyone involved with the project has continued to learn, and there have probably been some unexpected moments of genius along the way, so it's a good idea to recognise the people who made it happen. Even in the event of a complete catastrophe, and a website that will never see the light of day, the research, design and development work that you did will be an important input for the next project. There's always something worth celebrating.

Launch is anticlimactic for everyone unless you're already thinking about the next challenge. Switching a website on, when you've been staring at versions of it for months can seem like a bit of a let-down – it's quite hard to see it as fresh, new and substantially different from what came before. Keep this in mind, and don't be afraid to take the compliments from people seeing your work for the first time.

---

[1] Tony Hawk, skateboard pro. Interviewed by Gary Cohn for Entrepreneur Magazine (October 2009).

Find a way to reward the team and soothe frazzled nerves. It's inevitable that a few things aren't going to go quite as expected, and there are usually some conflicts around requirements or compromises. But the battles are never as big to the outside world; major disagreements can (somewhat shockingly) read more like matters of differing personal style. Take some time to reintroduce people who have disagreed. Spend a bit of money going out to celebrate, or picking a fun outing. The fact that you recognise people's contributions matters a lot more than the scale of the money you spend.

Mend the bruised egos. There may be a few around the place, and that might even include your own. We put a lot of ourselves into work that we do to be seen by others; sometimes the others in our audience show us a thing or two that we didn't expect. It's OK – time to move on and do useful things in another context. Some old-fashioned team building and group socialising can go a long way here.

Be honest

Once the project is complete and paid for, it can be tempting to sit back and tell yourself stories about the experience. You're the hero in these stories – the project often seems rather mythical, and your role starts to creep up in importance. But you should take a moment and look for some honesty about what you and the team have done really well, and what you could do differently.

The easiest lie is the one you tell yourself

We all tell small fibs to ourselves. But at the end of the project, thinking about the next round of work, you really have the chance to be truly honest. You've already been paid for the gig – what's holding you back from the complete, unvarnished version of what actually happened?

To avoid misguided thinking, you should try some of the following techniques.

Write about your project as if you were an outside observer. Take the part of the client, take the part of a friend of yours – look from the outside in and examine what actually happened on the project. What was promised, and what was delivered? Did the schedule really go the way the project proposal thought that it would?

Look at your internal measures of busyness, the time cards or Basecamp time reports or whatever else you use to track your own time. Add up the hours you spent, across the whole team. Compare this to the effort that you estimated in the proposal, and perhaps refined as you worked on the requirements. Did you spend more time than you expected? How about the overhead – your time as someone concerned with project management, the time of your partners or creative directors or business development people?

If you put it all together, did you get a number of hours that you can live with for future projects? It may be that your biggest projects make you the most money, but also have the lowest margins. All told, sometimes big projects can actually lose money for your group. Make sure you know what actually happened.

The next project will be better

If you find that you spent more time than you thought (most projects are like that), don't worry too much. You got through the project, you delivered results, the client is more or less happy. Doesn't sound like a stunningly high bar to get over, does it? But remember that most technical projects fail altogether, never really delivering the expected benefits. If you delivered the website that you expected, you should be happy with how things turned out. If you negotiated along the way, if you developed reasonable requirements, if you were able to push back when you were asked for changes that would be completely out of scope: you've probably reached the end of the project in pretty good shape.

However, that doesn't mean that you can't do better.

For the next proposal you work on, be sure to come back to those numbers that you just put together. How much time did you wear your project manager hat? How much time did your boss get involved? How much time did your system administrator end up putting in to get the domain sorted, the environment set up and the database tuned? How much time did the creative director spend fiddling with interior page layouts, even after the design direction was officially signed off?

You need to get a good number for each of those people, and then think about whether that number is likely to scale with the size of the project. Except for the overheads of running an office and so forth, a lot of your staff costs are going to be proportional to the size of the projects that you take on; bigger projects are more complex to begin with, and you're more likely to keep fussing with things (and refining them much too late) when you're dealing with an important client.

Don't forget to be honest about the positives

No matter how your project went, though, there will certainly be some positives that you'll want to recognise! Think about the planning phases of the gig:

1. Was your estimate close?
2. Did you understand the brief well?
3. Were you and the client both excited to be doing the work?

And in the execution:

4. Did you work well with the client, perhaps surprising you both with the ideas that were developed as a result?
5. Were you happy that you had the chance to find creative solutions to design problems?
6. Did you and the client both learn something new about the problem areas, and perhaps even find a simple and elegant way to approach audiences?

Even if the project took too long (many do), or cost too much money (often borne by the agency, in a typical fixed-price bid model), you might well still have delivered a website that will be profitable for both you and the client. Think about this one a bit, because it might be one of the best chances to learn: did you make back your staff and overhead costs for the project, including a reasonable margin? Is the client likely to recoup the value of their investment in the project using whatever metrics are appropriate? Remember that this could be expressed in goodwill, market attitude, customer satisfaction, or (and this is often overlooked) in reduced internal customer service costs. Maybe the value to the client is simply that staff can spend their time on higher-value activities, leaving much of the day-to-day information dissemination, ordering or customer service to the website.

If you and the client have made a project that neither of you could have made alone, and if the project was profitable for both parties, you have a successful product. No matter how many hassles or minor blow-ups there were along the way. Time to celebrate!

Case studies

It's hard to overestimate the importance of good case studies. You've got the finished website, true, and you've got sketches, screenshots, communications and documents from along the way. Much as you might want to simply point to the finished URL, you could miss a fascinating opportunity if you don't take the time to write a proper case study.

Somewhere in there is a story, a story that you want to tell. A web project is a long and complicated thing – so your documentation is too big to be understood at a glance. The finished site has a personality of sorts, but a coy one that doesn't reveal its backstory, even on close inspection. What you need is something in between: a way to explain, to distill, to convince even. The website that you've delivered is at best a mute witness to the end of that story. You'll thank yourself later for getting this right.

Case studies tend to include a standard set of elements: a description of the problems being solved; a few salient details about the process you used to solve them; and a couple of details about the design and functionality that solved the problem. If your website was reviewed positively or won awards, you could mention those. It's a good idea to gather some quotes about your website, from the client stakeholders certainly, but also from people on the website team who know the details of the solution, and can relate the details to the big picture of client needs. Showing the evolution of your thinking can be a very nice touch – it's fascinating to insiders and outsiders alike to see the way a design, particularly a graphic design, improves iteratively, moving closer and closer to the finished product.

OUR RESPONSIBILITIES:
User Experience
Design System

AWARDS:
People's Voice Award in the "Best Navigation/ Structure" category for the 15th Annual Webby Awards

"Best In Class" award in the retail category of the 2010 Interactive Media Awards.

ZAPPOS.COM HIRED HAPPY COG to partner with its tremendous internal UX, design, and development teams to help Zappos.com find its voice. Zappos had the enviable "problem" of expanding at ludicrous speed and outgrowing its digital experience. Zappos' cheeky voice and fanatical dedication to customer service were missing from the resulting e-commerce experience and were the cornerstones of Happy Cog's redesign. Happy Cog articulated this graphic design, UX, and copywriting thinking through a modular design system.

Zappos
POWERED*by*SERVICE™

Visit the Site

> We are pretty keen on viewing design as a verb, not a noun here. We never finish designs, we never "redesign," we evolve. Business needs are always changing, economies change, customer needs change—hence how we tackle these issues need to evolve."

— Jaimee Newberry,
Former Sr. UX and Product Manager
Zappos.com

A good case study not only shows off your design, but also highlights the skills you brought to bear. To really be effective, find a way to give your clients a voice as well. Image courtesy Happy Cog Studios, LLC – *work.happycog.com/zappos*

Case studies are a standard sales tool, certainly, but bear in mind that they are also a teaching tool. Other studios, independent developers, designers and other clients will read what you write about the problem and how you solved it. It's important that these case studies be honest. If you went in an unproductive direction for a while before straightening out into what became the obvious solution all along, it's OK to say so, and no one will blame you for not having magic precognition skills. If your initial sketches were way off, or if you started using a technology stack that turned out to be inappropriate for the problem at hand, it's fine to talk about it. Others will want to know what it was about this challenge and this client that led you toward a particular graphic design style or a specific content management system. It's OK to admit your bias as a team, too. Knowing a certain platform inside out is a perfectly sound reason for selecting it for the gig, and starting with what you know speaks well of your ability to manage risk.

The teaching potential of a good case study isn't all one-way, either. To sit down and write a good account of your project in a systematic way will help your thinking as well, and help you recall what worked and what didn't, things you'll need to write a good project review.

Wrapping up

A formal, closed wrap-up meeting is important. It keeps everyone from thinking about the open loops and half-done stuff that could have be done better. Whether you see it now or not, wrapping up this project formally will give you a great boost of energy and confidence when you approach the next gig. Project reviews can feel more like project post-mortems – something has to die for them to occur at all. And a perfunctory list of congratulations followed by a four-hour whingeing session won't result in a balanced message. Prepare carefully, and you'll have a springboard for future business. Bring the wrong attitude and you'll deflate whatever enthusiasm came from the launch of the new website.

Here are a few things to keep in mind for the session.

Planning

- Plan for a post-launch follow-up meeting, and get it in everyone's calendars long before the actual launch date. There shouldn't be any sense that this meeting was called in response to either positive or negative news.
- Involving all of the project stakeholders for the wrap-up will let you learn about some kinds of success that you weren't even aware you had to measure. Don't leave anyone out, whether because of rank or functional role: everyone should have a voice.
- If you keep a worksheet to contain lessons learned with you during the project, you won't have to do as much soul-searching or hold frantic diary negotiations at the end.
- The new site owner needs to prepare for this meeting as well – it shouldn't be just the design and build teams. They should bring new numbers, if they have them, and refresh everyone's memories about the original business goals.

Topics

- Look at how technology, market or user research assumptions shifted during the project. You can't expect things to be the same at the end as they were while you were working on a proposal.
- Use the risk register that you created early on. Look at each risk – did it happen? What was the impact? What could you have done about it?
- You should bring the project management basics with you: hours; money; deliverables; milestones; deviances from the plan. You shouldn't harp on about these numbers and dates, but they're part of the evaluation process.
- In part, team members are evaluating one another, as well. Don't be afraid to say what you found when working with the other organisations involved – but it goes both ways! Be sure to give credit to everyone on the client side: the site wouldn't exist without them.

- For both you and the client, writing down what seems obvious at the time will be of great help later. Even when helpful tricks or management snafus seem obvious at the time, if you don't write them down, the next team will definitely have to discover them anew.

Negatives
- There will certainly be some problem areas. Where there's a gap in expected success metrics, think about a constructive solution.
- Be creative about how to avoid the problems or hassles that you found.
- Don't forget to include things that worked, but were stressful. Stress brings its own consequences, and it doesn't pay to take it for granted.

Positives
- Talking about success is definitely warranted! Lessons learned include things you should do again, in the same way, because they worked brilliantly.
- Positioning for new work doesn't have to be obvious, but it can be part of the project review. A very natural follow-on from a project might, in fact, be a new project.
- You'll have to constantly nudge the conversation back to the agreed success factors. It will be obvious at this point why certain compromises were made, and it will be tempting to evaluate the website against a set of standards that were never agreed. Stick to what you documented and you'll be fine.

One more thing: take care to preserve a complete version of the new website – things change pretty quickly on the web. Keep a completely clickable set of pages somewhere, along with static forms like PDFs. Include small-screen device screenshots and renderings, too – you're not just designing for the desktop any more. Having a full set of screens from your new site will save a lot of bother later on when things have incrementally shifted well past the graphic design and content that you remember from day one.

TOOLS FROM THIS CHAPTER

- Case study
- Project wrap-up meeting
- Site archive

FURTHER READING

Designers like Dan Mall (*http://www.danielmall.com/work/crayola/*) and shops like Mule Design (*http://muledesign.com/portfolio/evening-edition/*) know that it's important to highlight case studies. Case studies can be brief and still give a good idea of what's going on.

NOW WHAT?

"The best way to predict the future is to invent it."

— **Alan Kay**[1]

What's here: Client relationships; offering support contracts; and other directions for your web group.

Seeing the future

You just finished a project – congratulations! But there are more projects yet to come, and finishing this one will make the next easier to start. At the same time, the end of a project is probably a good time to stop and take stock; see what you're doing well as a group and what you'd like to do better next time. You might want to think about how you'll do more work with this client, or maybe how you'd like to become better-known in the industry. Maybe you should finally get around to figuring out your agency blog or think about some speaking engagements.

Whatever you decide to do, there's no time for complacency. Without billable work and deadlines, you can probably find a few hours to invest in your own processes and capabilities – investments that can pay off down the road.

The future of this client relationship

First, though, look at the project you just finished, and think about whether there might be any natural follow-up. Look at your Phase 2 log, the things that you knocked out of scope during the early stages. You could write that up into a brief – knowing the challenges better, you could do a good job of setting up what the

---

[1] Alan Kay. Stanford Engineering, Volume 1, Number 1, Autumn 1989, pg 1-6. http://www.smalltalk.org/alankay.html

next project should look like. Even if there isn't immediate budget for getting on with a new website, now is when you have the business domain fresh in your mind. The brief that you provide at this point might be returned to you later as a request for proposal. Or perhaps your expertise will simply be noted, or you might get a new referral, by far the best and most lucrative sales channel.

As you prepare for the final project wrap-up and evaluation meeting (which should already be in the project budget), you might also spend a session brainstorming about potential new projects for the same client or group of stakeholders. These projects might be extensions to the new website you just built, or they might be new directions suggested by your user research. New platforms are always a possibility – perhaps a project taking unique advantage of a mobile device platform. For this brainstorm, bring your early research presentation, and the mood boards that were created during the design phase of the project. Imagine taking the same information and serving a new audience segment, or perhaps finding a new value proposition for an existing channel. Be creative, and run the session the way you would any client workshop, with creativity and flair.

If you want to really impress your current client, you might come back to the business again with fresh eyes, perhaps doing another competitive review. Or review your new site using the same sort of criteria that you used to look at the old site. Think about the strengths and weaknesses, the content gaps, the voice, the expected audience and their needs. How do you measure up? If you're feeling particularly brave you could even ask an external usability or research group to come in and reassess the new site. You can be confident that all of the good thinking you've put in will push the bar higher.

These activities are partly about sales, in that you want to be first in line for new work. But they're also about focusing the team on what worked and what didn't. Seeing the roads not taken alongside the direction you chose to go can be eye-opening. While I'm sure you made the best decisions you could with the information at hand, you inevitably come out of a project knowing so much more about the people involved, about that sector of the industry, about what is possible. You should expect to learn from these projects, so plan the learning opportunities along with the building activities.

Support contracts

A quick note about support contracts. Some web groups push hard to get them signed, knowing that things break and wanting to have the best chance of developing the website in a controlled fashion. Support contracts are a nice, steady source of income or budget for your group – not an easy thing in the consultancy-based world of making websites. Some client groups will be interested in a support contract, and I've known some who will even make the availability of support a requirement before selecting a web design vendor. If you want this to be part of your methodology, try to get it agreed early on, though. It's pretty awkward to go back to a client near the end of an engagement and try to get a contract signed. It can look like you're just wringing more money out of the engagement, and can also make it appear that you don't trust the quality of the website you plan to deliver.

There are some pros and cons to be aware of.

Reasons to offer a support contract

- Support contracts are a regular and predictable source of income, which can help to balance the financial risk of hour-based billing for projects.
- Each contract will continue your relationship with a client, increasing the chance for follow-on business.
- A support period can be an easier time to hand over responsibilities and offer training – less hectic than the run-up to the website launch date.

Reasons not to offer a support contract

- You can devote your team's full resources to each new opportunity as it arises. This could let you keep your core team smaller and more efficient.
- You have more flexibility in planning holidays, conferences and other time away from the office.
- Not having a support contract might result in cleaner code, since you know you won't have a chance to fix things later. Things that don't work correctly will probably be removed completely from the codebase, rather than left for further development when there's time.

Either way, watch out for an implied indefinite warranty. This is a topic of some debate in the web world: not everyone thinks through what's implied by your warranty, or lack of one. You want to stand behind your work and leave the relationship on a positive note, but you don't want to commit to an indefinite and unpredictable resource drain. Most people I know now include a limited warranty in their statement of work – something quite short. This gets you off the hook legally, but can sour the relationship if anything goes wrong. The only real way that I know to mitigate this risk is to test thoroughly during development and before launch. The fewer bugs you leave and the better you document your requirements, the easier it is to leave the project in good shape.

Agency and team development

Beyond the current project, though, there are many others, just waiting to be built. It's part of your job to prepare your team to take on the next set of challenges.

Pro bono work

Working for nothing may go a bit against the grain, but it offers more than just good karma. Doing some pro bono work tends to be exciting for your teammates, who like to feel that they're giving something back. You'll become more embedded in the community where you work, which is good for recruiting talent, and also good for hearing about new leads. Pro bono projects are a good chance to structure some deliberate learning into your work, either by stretching your skills or by trying out some technology or design experiments that you wouldn't be as comfortable with if you were on the clock in the usual way. And, of course, the karma thing.

Writing and speaking

It can be tempting to focus all of your energies on building websites. After all, that's what you and your team are good at, and what you're paid for. You've developed some great skills, and there's nothing quite as rewarding as getting the best new solution out the door.

But don't forget that you and your team need to do some self-development, as well. You need other people to know about you and what you do; you need to know what others are doing; and you need to keep your skills sharp. In the long term, growing as a studio, freelancer or in-house design team will happen only if you are an active member of your web design and development community.

Investing some time in your own writing and speaking is not only good promotion for your agency but also improves your practical design skills. Take a look at Jessica Ivin's post[2] for a few good resources on public speaking.

Conferences can foster relationships

Conferences are probably the most obvious way to reach out, and there are certainly plenty of conferences to choose from! Conferences on everything from typography, design, coding, marketing and social media abound, in almost every country

[2] http://cognition.happycog.com/article/so-why-should-I-speak-publicly

where there are web people. SXSW[3] is best known as a way to meet up with venture capitalists. An Event Apart[4] is a popular place to learn from some of the best leading-edge professionals in the industry. And Future of Web Apps[5] and similar events will give your knowledge a great boost on web development technologies.

But be careful. Conferences are loads of fun (the buzz will stay with you for a while), but they're quite expensive in terms of time and money. Registration isn't the only cost – there are also travel and accommodation expenses to consider. Also, for the duration of travelling and the conference, you're not billing clients for work. If you try to do a project from a conference hotel room, you're wasting time and money trying to do too much. Before you register, think about how you'd answer the following questions:

- What are my goals for the conference? Are they generating sales leads, learning a technique, learning more about the market? Each goal needs to be something tangible and measurable.
- What do I expect to learn from this conference? More than just current industry trends, are there technologies that you're curious about, like mobile app development or the latest CMS? Are there fundamentals that you should revisit, whether related to typography, communications or content strategy?
- How will I apply what I've learned to my daily work? Will methodologies change? Requirements templates be updated? Development tasks reordered? Certain tasks be done faster?

Once you've figured out what you expect from the conference and how to measure your results, go have a great time! You'll have the chance to wave the flag for your team, firm or self and rub shoulders with some great people solving similar problems. Just be sure that you can measure what you get out of the experience on the other end.

---

[3] http://sxsw.com/

[4] http://aneventapart.com/

[5] http://futureofwebapps.com/

Sponsor book clubs and local events

Is there a design-related book club in your area? Want to start one? Getting involved with book clubs and other events can help boost your reputation while teaching you and the team a surprising amount. Being known as a local sponsor of web-related events might make your name come to mind the next time a client is thinking about a project or another firm is looking for some help on a gig.

It doesn't cost much to do this sort of thing – a book club will take a bit of beer and pizza, some organising time and a space to meet. You can offer your studio or workplace, find a café or book another neutral venue. Getting things going and keeping attendees motivated will take a small time commitment. Do a bit of local promotion – create some business or promotional cards for the book club and leave them at popular cafés, which are often frequented by web freelancers. You just need a few tweets before everyone knows what's on and what to expect.

Create a really good corporate social responsibility plan

While it can seem self-centred and pious, a corporate social responsibility (CSR) plan can pay dividends in greater billings, if only because of the free media and publicity that comes out of such a programme. You don't need me to tell you that it's also the right thing to do – as reasonably well-remunerated people we have an obligation to help out our fellow humans and our world.

A CSR plan isn't just a charity contribution tin in the lunchroom. Are there charitable and not-for-profit organisations in your area which need design and web services, but can't afford them? Think about whether community colleges need help setting up an interaction design programme. Imagine if your organisation's skills in designing and implementing web and social media campaigns could be put to use directly helping an organisation that you'd be proud to support. Chances are, there will be far more of these opportunities and ideas than can be acted upon by one design agency. Pick just one or two, and get to work improving your part of the world. You'll be happy you did: your team will develop new skills and your agency will get some very welcome positive attention. While it will certainly make good business sense for you to get involved, you have the chance to be a positive force in people's lives at the same time. What's not to like?

Write blogs and books
You and your team have spent a lot of time honing your skills, transforming from a group of talented people into a professional services organisation. You might want to share with your colleagues some of what you know and what works for you, even what you wish had gone differently. Doing some writing will do some very real and very good things for your organisation.

- You'll improve your skill at communicating with an audience, which is among the most important capabilities for your job.
- You'll gain a reputation as thinkers in the industry and among your peers.
- Your personality and brand values will be expressed through what you write. Clients and partners will see this, and over time you'll develop a better fit between your team and the clients you choose to take on.
- Most people formulate thoughts and ideas much better when writing them down. Going through a process of structuring and expressing your ideas will help you to define your own processes, polish your skills and actually help you to deliver your projects better.

A company blog is a pretty trivial thing to set up and it makes perfect sense for most agencies to have one. Beyond just designing a blog section of your website, though, don't forget to put some time into planning who'll do the writing, what topics you want to cover and whom you're trying to reach with your writing. Just like any other content strategy exercise, you need to know why and how often you're writing in order to get good results. Once you do, you might be surprised at how much more widely known you become and how much more friendly clients seem when they contact you for work.

Looking back

Time between projects is a great opportunity to take a good look at the tools you use daily and experiment with improvements. Don't get obsessed about this – finding and playing with tools to enhance productivity can be a bit of an addiction! But it's worthwhile taking a look with a few people and seeing if there are some quick improvements you might make now or play with for later.

Project plans

You might outline these formally through planning software and documents, or more fluidly through online project-tracking tools and presentations. Do the plans that you draw up communicate a realistic view of where you are and what's to come? Ideally your project planning should make clear where dependent activities fit together, without going into a counter-productive level of detail.

Meetings

These can be incredibly productive or a complete waste of time, and most of the differences come in having the right people and the right preparation. Do you treat your meetings as real decision-making opportunities, or do you fall into the trap of regular meetings that are held simply because they are regular meetings? Do you assume that your client meetings will be boring, while your internal meetings are full of life? If so, re-examine those assumptions – your client stakeholders are just as willing to engage creatively, if you give them a chance.

Estimation worksheets

Were you way over or way under? If so, look again at some of those spreadsheets or other tools that you use. You can even put in a fudge factor to automatically account for the amount that your estimates were off.

Deployments and scripts

These have a way of being a bit cobbled together, so be sure to document and examine what it is you do to move code and assets between environments, run backups and perform monitoring. This might be a good area to play with some new technologies – there are always newer and better ways of solving these problems.

Communication channels

Does your project communication work well? Does everyone know what they need to know, and access the information they need? Whether it's an online tool like Basecamp or a very sophisticated document library application, make sure that your tools are complex enough to support your communication needs, and no more so. Ask your client stakeholders whether they found themselves in the loop to the right extent, or were left wondering, or were bombarded with more information than they could process. Knowing this will help you calibrate the tools you use.

Keep track of what you learn. If you are becoming sophisticated enough to need management software for your design assets, look at setting some up. If you had trouble keeping your source code in sync, make sure that your code repository is both powerful enough for the branching and merging you need and understood well by everyone on the team. Every group is going to need some sort of long-term asset storage, just to keep handy the pieces that are used to build each project. Make sure that your archive is redundant and there for the long term – you have no idea when you will need to pull something out of the files.

Partnerships

As you grow in experience and (perhaps) size, you can start looking at other sorts of partnerships and directions. For example, you could start bringing in contractors to help you with specific areas like graphic design, experience design, content design or development. This will expand your capacity to take on work, but involves a couple of risks. First, you won't necessarily learn what you need to as a team. Secondly, you can end up in a difficult position when it comes to support and warranty fixes. On the other hand, of course, these relationships are flexible and give you a good way of scouting talent before you invite people to join you full-time.

You might think about forming some alliances within the business and technology sector. If you're focused mostly on building websites, you might want to find a group particularly good at brand and identity development; you might want to partner with a firm with facilities and contacts for user testing or research; you might develop a preferred hosting provider for the websites you build. Any of these relationships can strengthen your value as a web group in a flexible way. The trick is to develop close working relationships with these external players. The better you are able to work together, the easier it will be to align the strengths of each group in a non-competitive way. At that point you can offer the full spectrum of services, ranging from business and digital strategy through to implementation and then hosting and support.

Products

You could go into product development, focusing your group on either a part- or full-time basis. Building software products and applications is a logical next step for a lot of consulting web agencies, and it could give you a chance to bring the skills that you've developed working for clients to something that you can build for yourself. There's even a chance to scratch your own itch by building services that you wished you'd had access to when you were building websites for clients.

A danger here is that you can spend enormous resources on these projects without developing firm market intelligence about how your product will be received. It's a chance to turn sporadic, hourly revenue into a steady stream of licence money, which is great. Understand that it's risky, though, just as it would be for any internet start-up. I personally have enjoyed working for start-ups, but it's good to recognise the risks. When you transition from client services to products, you won't have the time pressure of either a client contract or the expectations of a group of investors. Without this time pressure you can be inclined to spend years iterating ideas before you start shipping anything. Not a terrible thing, but your chances of success seem to be highest when you can ship something and then improve it, rather than waiting until you get the perfect feature set.

Services

You could go into services beyond making websites, if you like. There are some good natural alignments, like application and site hosting. These days, there are some good jobs to be had brokering the various cloud services available for computation and storage. Internet marketing is a good fit, since you probably have spent a lot of time thinking about the various flavours of search optimisation. Creating a software service such as a proprietary content management system might work (though if you do, please have a better reason than that not being able to figure out how to configure Drupal).

Services can bring in good revenue, but require a complete shift in how you market yourself, how you acquire clients and how you recruit your team. You'll need some sales people good at making connections within corporate IT, which isn't easy. Hosting is a low-margin game these days, and you'd be competing with some big players in your sector. Internet marketing and social media consulting are solid businesses, but there are a lot of unscrupulous outfits in these sectors and you'd have to work hard to differentiate yourselves. I don't want to discourage you, but remember that moving into service provision means that you'll need to start committing a lot of time and money every month, whether you're bringing in the revenue or not.

Wrap-up

You don't have to expand in any of these directions. If conference speaking seems like a distraction for you right now, don't do it. If you're tempted to bring in contractors or form partnerships but aren't sure enough about the financials, skip it. If you value the flexibility (and closure) of starting and stopping discrete products, don't go into ongoing services. If you want to run projects by bringing together dream teams of the best freelancers in your area, then disbanding at the end of the gig, that's fine. So is gradually growing a small business of permanent staff into a bigger business, and building that into an organisation that can take care of practically any business, IT or web challenge in your area of specialisation.

In short: find what's true to you, and what you believe. Be authentic and real in your dealings with your team, your clients and your stakeholders. Learn constantly from your own work and find mentors to push up your game. Make friends in your community. Build respect and trust by dealing honestly with your neighbours. Be sensitive to what your teammates need to feel successful, and think about what you need to feel satisfied at the end of each day. More than any five-year plan, your best direction is the one that satisfies those values, every day. The business and the projects will be built around that core, and the rest will take care of itself.

Now go out there and build something that you're proud of!

TOOLS FROM THIS CHAPTER

• Corporate social responsibility plan
• Support contract
• Project tracking tools

FURTHER READING

I recommend reading *Insites: The Book*[6]. It isn't about case studies per se, but is a series of interviews with some masters of making websites. Take a look at what these folks are proud of making. And then think about how to make your project something you can look back on in the same way.

[6] http://shop.viewportindustries.com/products/insites-the-book

Index

An 'i' or 'n' following a page number indicates that the topic is mentioned only in an illustration or footnote.